President's Messages
&
Flyer-Side Chats

A collection of messages
by Lewis F. Kornfeld
addressed to employees and customers
of Radio Shack

"Homo sum: humani nil
A me alienum puto."

I am a man and nothing that touches
Humanity is foreign to me."

Quoted from Terence by Cicero . . .
Exemplified by Lewis F. Kornfeld

Lewis F. Kornfeld

LEWIS F. KORNFELD was a prominent businessman and benefactor of the arts, whose 97 years spanned a multifaceted life as *Radio Shack* Corp. president, journalist, U.S. Marine Corps captain, business book author, novelist, poet, accomplished pianist and fervent supporter of the arts.

After graduating from the University of Denver, where he served as editor of the paper and first literary magazine, he became a reporter for the *Rocky Mountain News* in Denver. His journalism career was interrupted by World War II, during which he served - mostly in the South Pacific in aviation communications - as an officer in the U.S. Marine Corps, retiring as a captain in 1946.

In 1948, Mr. Kornfeld went to work for a one-store Boston electronics company named *Radio Shack*, where his work focused on merchandising and advertising. By 1955, he was instrumental in launching its entry into the import-export business in the Far East, as well as several dozen company-owned manufacturing profit centers and the company's in-house ad agency.

After Fort Worth businessman Charles Tandy purchased *Radio Shack* in 1963, Mr. Kornfeld was appointed president and moved to Fort Worth from Boston in 1970. He was nationally known for getting *Radio Shack* uniquely into both the personal computer retailing and manufacturing business as early competitors of IBM, Apple and Commodore with the company's nationwide best-selling *TRS-80*.

The first of the eight books he authored, entitled *"To Catch a Mouse Make a Noise Like a Cheese,"* was likely the first tome written entirely on a PC-- then called a microcomputer -- and was based on the *TRS-80*. Published in 1983 by Prentice-Hall, it sold over 100,000 copies.

Mr. Kornfeld served as *Radio Shack Corp*. president until 1981 and was a board member until 2003.

He was honored in 1981 by Boston University with an honorary doctorate degree (LHD). He was also given the distinguished Professional Achievement Award by the University of Denver. With his love of music and art, he served on many local cultural boards, including the Arts Council, Fort Worth Symphony, Chamber Music Society, which he co-founded, Amon Carter Museum, Fort Worth Opera and the Van Cliburn Foundation piano competition, of which he was for eight years its vice chairman.

An avid tennis player his entire life, he continued his weekly tennis games through the last year of his life and took up golf in his 70s, which he also continued until most recently. He will be greatly missed.

In 1943, he married the late Ethel Hardy of Fernley, Nev., who died in 1990. In 1992, he married Rose Ann Pearson Hobbs, a native of Fort Worth. He is also survived by his sons and their wives, Nicholas and Lee Kornfeld, and Hardy and Xin Kornfeld; grandsons and their wives, Nicholas and Masi, and Jay and Nancy; great-granddaughter, Katie, and another on the way; Ann and John McReynolds, Tyler, Marsland, Kirk and Kaitlin and by Vance, Jonathon and Josh Hobbs. He was also survived by his brother, John Kornfeld; and sister-in-law, Celia Kornfeld, wife of his late brother, Robert Kornfeld.

Published in Star-Telegram from Aug. 13 to Aug. 14, 2013

CONTENTS

147   Part II   Flyer-Side Chats   April 1974 – July 1981

INTRODUCTION
August 2015 – Heart and Soul
by Richard Hollander

AS I SIT HERE PREPARING MYSELF to write about my friend Lew Kornfeld, I have Ella Fitzgerald in the background, singing *Heart and Soul,* that classic love song by Hoagy Carmichael and Frank Loesser. I know that Lew would want me to give credit to all three of these artists because he always gave credit to others. He was just that way. Lewis F. Kornfeld was the Heart and Soul of *Radio Shack* (he would also want me to remind you that it was two words, as we often spoke about that).

Lewis F. Kornfeld was President of *Radio Shack* when I came to work for the company in 1972. He had been with *Radio Shack* since there were only two stores and stayed President until there were 8,000 stores. He would tell you that he was an advertising man and a merchant. He just loved merchandise, especially interesting merchandise. He loved watches, just loved them. Any time you bought a new watch you would get grilled on all of the features of the watch. You had to take it off so he could examine the watch. At the time, I suspect he was thinking about how he could sell the watch (not that particular one, but lots of that one). He was looking for the unique feature that would make that watch exclusive. Exclusive was good, and that unique feature was what you talked about, that your competitors did not.

Lew was much more than the President of *Radio Shack* and the Vice Chairman of *Tandy Corporation*. He was our heart and soul. And he was also our voice. Lew set the tone for our advertising, but he set the tone for more than just that. As you read this book, a collection of his *Flyer-Side Chats* and *Messages from the President*, you can just hear the tone Lew set for our company.

Lew made us fall in love with *Radio Shack*. I still covet the watch Lew gave me as he made me a member of his President's Club. In this book you will see how Lew wove the magic that helped build *Radio Shack* into the biggest consumer electronics store in the world. His ability to spin a phrase, create a brand, and put us in just the right place in the consumer's mind were his special talents.

For the last several years I worked at *Tandy Corporation*, I had the pleasure of officing next door to Lew. We went to lunch together at *Tu Hai* several times a week. Lew ordered number 12 and Dave Beckerman ordered number 2, but sometimes number 12. I would order various items, always to be examined by Lew and Dave to see what was new. The two of them had over 100 years at *Radio Shack* and *Tandy Corporation*. I can't tell you what an education I got over these lunches, and much of that education is also packed into this book. We would look at ads, and Lew and Dave would show me how to make them better. Lew was always a teacher, but you will see that for yourself, in this book as well.

I asked Lew about his time growing up in Boston. It was fascinating. He went to High School with Mike Wallace from *CBS' 60 Minutes.* They were on the tennis team together. (Lew continued to play until the very end of his life.) He told me that both he and Mike were candidates to become captain of the school's tennis team. Lew, always the giver, thought that he should vote for Mike because he did not think that he should vote for himself. Mike, apparently did not feel that way. Mike won the election by one vote. They both lived long, productive lives.

So to paraphrase Mr. Loesser:

But now I see, what one embrace can do
Look at me, it's got me loving you
Madly,
That care and wit you showed
Held all my Heart and soul.

*　　*　　*

Part I

President's Messages

July 1970 -- May 1981

JULY 1970
Well Hello, Dere!

HOW DO YOU ANSWER THE TELEPHONE in your store or office? Oddly enough; it does make a difference.

One of our best Franchise Store owners in Pennsylvania thought it important enough to send me a cassette recording of his thoughts on the matter. And they were so good we added a few notions of our own and emerged with a formula for all of us to use.

The real slob will answer his phone very explicitly; he'll say "Yeah?" A better man might say -- "Hello, *Allied Radio Shack*."

I can't do much for the real slob, but I really think I can help the better man because he has already done part of the job. He has identified his Company. Fine. But the caller already knew he was calling us!

What we recommend is quite simply: *"Good morning (or afternoon or evening), Allied Radio Shack – Mr. You, speaking, may I help you*." And at the end of the call: *"Thanks for calling Allied Radio Shack."*

People like to know to whom they are speaking. People like to be helped and thanked. And incidentally, people HATE to have the answer-er ask: "Who's calling? That instantly implies potential selection at your end. If you're so important you have to accept some calls and postpone others, then I've got news for you: *you're more important than our Chairman!* You read me correctly: Mr. Tandy accepts ALL call from anyone, anywhere, without identification of the caller. Try him sometime.

People also like to have their call answered on the first or the second ring. It shows them their call isn't an interruption or an aggravation.

And there is one more thing people like. They like to use the telephone. So how about it, Old Buddy – get with our new standard phone call answering technique and show me you too are a believe!

AUGUST 1970
The "Allied" Spirit

FOR ALL OF US OLD RADIO SHACK HANDS, I want to welcome the team then many new employees we've retained from the former *Allied Radio Corporation* staff.

Some of them have moved to our new headquarters in Fort Worth. Some are remaining in Chicago and other ex-Allied locations. All of them are great or we wouldn't have selected them to stay with the combined companies.

I met a number of them when I spent a few weeks at Allied in Chicago in May and June. And I was particularly impressed by the *"Allied" Spirit* they displayed in a variety of ways, defending *Allied's* thinking and *Allied's* merchandise even – I might add – when it wasn't under attack by confrontation with new thinking and new merchandise!

There was one buyer who, when his own (*Allied's*) art department suggested he imitate some of *Radio Shack's* advertising copy techniques, rejected the notion flatly, adding a written note to the effect that *"Allied is Number One, followed by Lafayette, and then by Radio Shack, and if Shack is Number Three I don't want to copy third-rate advertising"*. The quote is almost verbatim!

Somehow, the guy hadn't discovered that *Radio Shack* was actually Number One and *Allied* actually Number Three in consumer electronics

But – no matter. *That man was playing to win.* And nobody had told him that he wasn't winning. And that's what I mean by the *"Allied Spirit."* And that kind of man is a man for me.

In point of fact, *Allied* WAS winning, but in a way not big enough for today's market and money conditions, in a way not big enough to beat back competition. Yet even third place gets you a medal in the Olympics, if you think about it.

While welcoming the winners from *Allied* and giving them a well-deserved chance to reach for the gold medal at last, we remind them – and ourselves – of one thing important to all of us.

If the advertising or merchandising or procedures of Number Three – or even Number Thirty Three – can teach us ANYTHING, don't be proud. Be taught!

SEPTEMBER 1970
The "Selling" Season

RETAILERS OFTEN REFER TO THE PERIOD of September through December as the "selling season" because – sure enough – sales go up. But of course they're as wrong as rain.

The *"selling season"* is a 365-day affair. Sales go up from September through December because there are more buyers around. The number of SELLERS remains constant and horrifyingly low. Most of the *"sellers"* are really ORDER-TAKERS and order-taking – in my book – is the world's second oldest profession.

To SELL means to convert a looker into a buyer, to build each sale up to its maximum potential. When we give away flashlights we have to SELL the batteries. When we offer a product with an empty headphone or tape deck jack we have to SELL the products that fit the empty jack.

SELLING IS REMINDING . . . that our extension telephones use jacks, plugs, extension wire, amplifiers; that an extra pair of stereo speakers can be added to hi-fi receivers; that outdoor FM antennas give improved reception over the line-cord antennas included with most FM receivers and radios; that tape recorders use tape and accessories and that better-than-furnished mikes will improve recordings; and on and on and on. SALESmen don't expect customers to remember!

Reminding also means showing prospects things they don't even know about . . . things like home protection devices, wireless intercoms, hands-free walkie-talkies, mobile CB communications, test tapes and demo records, the good sense of changing over to a diamond needle, the new longer and thinner magnetic tapes, the fun and utility and economy of *Science Fair* and *Knight-kits*, the new lower price in a marked item; and on and on.

Order takers – like blind Milton, the poet – simply "stand and wait." They never sell. They don't remind. They never build a customer following. They wonder why their "sales" are soft, their paychecks thin. What a waste of time and manpower!

I have just moved to Texas and I am greatly impressed by the amount of SELLING done down here. From the popcorn girl at *Leonard's* to the presidents of the big banks, everyone I've met has ASKED FOR AN ORDER and suggested what should be bought in the way of goods and services. Ain't nobody heah waitin' for the *"selling season"* to open on September the first!

OCTOBER 1970
In Memoriam: Goodbye, Bob

A MAN MOST OF YOU NEVER MET. His name was "Bob" Lewis. He was coming to visit us here for the first time in November. And you might have met him then. He was *Radio Shack's* chief engineer from 1946 to 1964, and *A & A's* director of merchandising and engineering since last November. He passed away in Tokyo in August.

Bob was a man you could emulate and never look back, as they say in Texas. A better, more practical audio communications engineer had never come down the pike, but he didn't go to college and he didn't have an engineering degree. Engineers at places like *Scott, Fisher, Bogen, Electro-Voice* and *Harmon-Kardon* held him in very high esteem. Because quality recognizes quality and titles (and degrees) don't mean a thing when the chips are down.

Bob was a man who came to work early and left late. Because he liked what he was doing. He didn't know any other way of living. And he didn't complain about others not pulling an equal load for equal pay; the mark of a professional.

I met Bob in 1947 when I went to *Radio Shack* in Boston to buy a hi-fi system. He was the best hi-fi salesman I've ever met. He didn't tell me how dumb I was, how smart he was; he didn't twist my arm. But quietly, gently, he steered me from $400 to $700 by comparing sound and explaining the difference – which I couldn't hear until he told me how to listen.

He personally built us the country's first hi-fi listening room, called the *Audio Comparator*, and copied the world around. Visitors and customers included Arthur Fiedler, Morton Gould, and E. Power Biggs. And Bob sold them all.

He built the first FM receiver ever produced in Japan. It was a *Realistic* product. It was also sold in Japan under the *Trio* name and it put *Trio* into the hi-fi business. *Trio* is now known in this country as *Kenwood*.

He designed the *Realistic Electrostat-3* tweeter (still used in our *Electrostat-2A* system) which was a check-rated best buy in *Consumers Research* magazine, the first such award ever given to a company specializing in electronics retailing.

Our company is distinguished by its people and their contributions. Readers of this testament will do as well or better in the years ahead than Bob did in the years behind. And some will go. But none will get a better or fonder "Goodbye" from his fellows than this man who gave and gave until suddenly there wasn't any more.

NOVEMBER 1970
How Do You Day "No" to a Pro?

THE OLD-FASHIONED DIFFERENCE between a Pro and an Amateur was money. But that was in sports, wasn't it? In business the Amateur gets paid. So the difference boils down to the fact that in business the Pro gets paid better.

How come? Who pays him better? Both answers are easy. The business Pro sells smarter. And he gives himself a "raise" on each sale by selling UP.

Let's take an example: three radio/phono systems that all do the same thing. (A) *Modulaire system with changer, No 12-1471, $129.95.* (B) *Stereo Concertmaster system with changer, No. 12-694 with No. 42-2935 (GROUP No. 42-2965), $187.45.* (C) *STA-36 system with changer, No.34-1002, $239.95.* All are stereo FM-AM with speakers and changer, all good products, no extras or add-ons. Average price spread $55.00.

Each of these systems is a family investment that gives many years of pleasure. They may be the only hi-fi system the buyer will ever purchase. Why should he be a logical step-up to a better system?

Here are 6 EASY AND PROFESSIONAL REASONS.
1. Bigger speakers equal bigger sound, better bass.
2. More watts of power at lower distortion.
3. More sound controls, meters, inputs, outputs.
4. Better FM sensitivity and stereo separation.
5. Better cartridge and auto-turntable motor.
6. Better appearance and feel, heavier weight.

The Pro starts out by assuming that the customer can see and hear a difference. He makes sure of it by selecting good FM and a good record to demonstrate. He doesn't sell by "knocking" any of the systems because each is obviously satisfactory as a value.

He starts by selling the value. And by observing that $55 extra is infinitesimal over the life of the system. And by putting himself in the buyer's shoes – the buyer who wants to make the smartest purchase; smart for his dollar and smart for his family's benefit. By selling up from good radio to better hi-fi – each the same number of components, the Pro has made more money for himself and done his customer a legitimate service.

FIFTY PERCENT of the time the Pro will make the sale at $187.45 by showing the three systems. TWENTY-FIVE PERCENT of the time he'll end up at $239.95 or better when the "advertised" system was $129.95 – because "we haven't got space to advertise everything we sell."

Finally, after the sale, the Pro will demonstrate a headphone with the newly sold system and recommend the immediate or future addition of a tape deck.

And the Amateur? Well he's getting paid to play. So he goes home at 6 o'clock. And does . . . just that! Customers have said "no" to him all day. But how do you say "no" to a Pro?

DECEMBER 1970
Lucky 13

A RECENT TANDY CORPORATION PROSPECTUS told me something I didn't know until today: "The Company has approximately 13,000 full-time employees . . ."

What a lucky number! A thousand more than 12,000. Ten thousand more than 3,000. Who said 13 wasn't a winner.

At this time of the year in particular when, among other things, one is apt to be counting one's blessings, it's worth examining some of the good fortune you and I have in being members of *Tandy*'s select group of 13,000 people.

- We are with a Company whose growth pattern is impressive in any group of American businesses.

- Our Company is not in activities affected by any of the really major problems of our time, thus job security is exceptional.

- Expansion-cum-Profits makes *Tandy Corporation* an unusually good employer as it offers work and advancement opportunities in every state of the union and abroad.

- Those of us who have seen and acted on the benefits of our Savings Plan are capitalizing upon a most generous and unusual system for creating an estate, yet another reason for liking your Company

- Success, security, opportunity, heart, room at the top and the top always getting bigger – these are some of the quite obvious reasons why *Tandy Corporation* is a good place to be in today's world.

But "obvious reasons" aren't always the reasons people talk about, just as "13" doesn't always seem lucky to those who let superstition affect their reasoning!
I hope, in a sort of corny way, I've given you a new slant on 13 in all combinations including 13,000. Think about it, and have a very pleasant Holiday season while you do.

JANUARY 1971
Matter of Philosophy

SOME "PRIVATE LABEL" VENDORS take a chassis made by Manufacturer "X" and change the external appearance. Then they put their brand on the best and call it their own. This is the easy way to get into the "private label" business, and it's also the reason so many look-alikes are on the market.

The whole thing is a matter of philosophy. Our philosophy at *Allied Radio Shack* is entirely different from the above example.

We design most of our equipment from scratch. An idea, a look, a price point, special features, repair-ability, longevity, maximum value for the consumer's dollar, and our desire to excel the best brands around.

All of our loudspeakers, our stereo receivers, our monitor receivers, our shortwave receivers, our CB equipment, and many other products fall into this *Allied Radio Shack* pattern of genuine originality. This gives our people in our stores a real edge on their competition . . . stuff that isn't a quick copy with a face change.

Occasionally our efforts get recognized by critics writing for nationally circulated magazines like *Stereo Hi-Fi Review* and *Consumes Research*. In recent months they recognized our *Allied 395* stereo receiver and our *Realistic* 2-channel wireless intercom as check-rated best buys among others similarly rated; our *Realistic Optimus-1* speaker and a *Realistic* FM-AM radio were rated above many of their peers; our *Realistic SCT-3* cassette deck was also rated worthy of "best buy accolades."

Naturally we don't manufacture to please periodicals. But we do like to strut a bit when the publicity is favorable and free. And we are particularly proud to see our basic merchandising philosophy rewarded for holding back the tide of mediocrity and letting some "loving care" come through.

If business was just Buying and Selling, if Creativity were just an empty phrase dreamed up- by admen, we'd be hard pressed to squeeze out yet another maker and breaker of records.

Got a good, original product ideal go keep our philosophy alive and well? I'm waiting to hear from you. Have checkbook. Will pay!

FEBRUARY 1971
In Memoriam: Alfred R. *Tandy*

ON FEBRUARY THE 15TH, Alfred R. Tandy of Tulsa, Oklahoma, passed away. He was the brother of our Chairman. He was a director of our Corporation. And he was the Chairman of his own concern, *Tandy* Industries.

To everyone who knew him, including this writer, he was just plain "Bill". Except . . . he wasn't plain in any way, shape, or manner!

Bill Tandy had a tremendous joie de vivre, a *Tandy*-sized ambition, a distinctive style, a will to live as distinctive as his will to win. One suspects he went out the way he came in: First Class.

The leather men around *Allied Radio Shack* and, more specifically, around *Tandy* Corporation, remember him as a real sportsman of the old school, the kind that knows where the game is and how to get it.

You just have to like that kind of man. And we did.

You just have to admire the entrepreneur who goes to another state, takes an ailing business, and turns it into something that makes buildings, money, and news. Such a man was Bill Tandy. And he won't be forgotten.

MARCH 1971
Think Shrink!

"WHO STEALS MY PURSE, STEALS TRASH," said William Shakespeare about 150 years ago, continuing on to explain how much more serious it was to steal one's "good name." Clearly the Bard was not thinking about businesses and their problems.

Our "good name" is not up for grabs. But it's one of our very few unpurloinable assets. Every other thing around the shop has an instant cash value and, despite Shakespeare's theory, is NOT trash!

Who steals from us does so from a very large group of people – starting with every one of us who owns stock either outright or vi the Savings plan. A stockholder is an OWNER.

There are two categories of folks who steal from us. Shoplifters. And employees. The former outnumber the latter, But the latter out-steal the former in terms of dollars. We catch a lot of them. We prosecute, and still they come.

I would also like to dispel another ancient notion – that it takes a thief to catch a thief. Quite the contrary. It takes a person who cares, who has a sense of outrage, who knows how to act upon the differences between wrong and right.

Any Officer of this Company is authorized to pay $100 to any employee furnishing information leading to the apprehension of a thief. This is not an informers rewired. It is a *protector's* reward.

I am told the best way to spot a thief is to see someone who consistently fails to follow established rules of procedure in paper work, cash handling, goods handling, and housekeeping.

What happens when something is stolen from our business is very simple. It produces a number smaller that it should have been. When a big number get smaller, it shrinks.

Think shrink!

APRIL 1971
Four Channel Sound?

BY NOW MOST OF YOU MUST HAVE READ something about audio's latest wonder child; four-channel or quad sound. It's just slightly Orwellian in that a part of its premise is "More is Better," a dangerous premise indeed.

Everything we've listened to adds up to just one thing. I can say without fear of contradiction: "More is Different;" With two more speakers, more gadgetry, and maybe two more amplifiers, you get a sound that is not only different, but probably saleable as well. Please note I didn't say "better" or "worse". Frankly, nobody knows as yet.

Allied Radio Shack will have this product to demonstrate and sell in July at the latest. It will NOT obsolete our present equipment. It is NOT as essential to music lovers as stereo became when it replaced mono. There will be many misleading claims made for quad sound but these will NOT be made by us.

There's no quad program material on the market at this time in significant quantity, thus the first quad stuff will be additive: two more speaker and a little black box. The sound will seem more omnidirectional, less directional, far from hi-fi's original aim of duplicating the concert hall – just possibly a step in the wrong direction!

We will publish for our managers a brief progress report and explanation of quadraphonics to keep them informed. They'll need it.

Four-channel sound and four-speaker sound effects are an opened Pandora's Box for every contemporary artist in the music business. Mixing, de-mixing, phasing, matrixing; this is the language of Audio 1971.

MAY 1971
The Name *is* the Game

THERE'S NOTHING LIKE A PLAY ON WORDS to start a guy thinking. For example, the biggest assert we have is the name of our customer. They say, technically, a customer name is worth $2 to $4 each on a cost-to-get basis. I agree. But some of our store people think the name getting is a game – not very serious – something someone in the front office dreamed up to aggravate them.

So they send in sales slips without names, or with funny names, like Mickey Mouse, or with made up names like Slim Chances or with names right out of the phone book.

Now if you know a guy or gal with a bad habit like that, please give him the word. If you're the creative wit, shape up! We spend about $600,000 per annum on the collection and computerization of customer names and they have to be letter perfect.

The sales yield from a mailing to customers (as against newspaper circulation or occupant mailing) is better than 8 to 1. That's why we treasure our customer list; that's why we have to keep it growing.

Be it on a sales slip or a mail order blank, we must get that customer's name every time. Printed neatly, legibly, and completely.

We've sent out an easel card to explain to the customer that this is required; please put the card by the register. Point to it when a customer says, "Oh no, not that again."

Actually, the whole game *is* something someone in the front office dreamed up. And this game – believe me – is a key reason why we continue to lead them all by a country mile. And the next comedian who sends up the name Rat Fink . . . had better start walking.

JUNE 1971
Progress Report

ITEM: JUSTICE DEPARTMENT "PRAYS" that we divest ourselves of "all interest in and control of *Allied Radio* and its assets." *Comment:* The outcome being unknown at this writing. I can say only that the net effect of a divestment (as these things are called) would be quite minor and not nearly so exciting as the various rumors blowing this way and that. But I will keep you up to date and my faith in the democratic process has not yet been shaken.

Item: What about four-channel stereo? *Comment:* In case you haven't looked, we're selling it today, and it's TRUE quadrasonic sound equipment – requiring 4 amplifiers. The gadget being sold by certain other folks for $29.95 or thereabouts, is actually a 4-channel sound simulator – takes regular stereo and gives and takes a little to each of 4 speakers. For confusion (and profits) we will market a simulator ourselves in about 6 weeks.

Item: Are we going to expand at the same rate? *Comment:* no we're going to double it! We have planned for 500 new stores to be opened between now and 6/30/72, or about 1½ stores per every working day. This must be a record of some sort?

Item: Do we plan to issue an annual catalog as usual? *Comment:* not merely because we don't like to do anything "as usual," we are going to issue two annual catalogs about a month apart. In August: a brand new Accessory Catalog – all the kits, pieces and parts. In September: a brand new 4-color catalog featuring equipment only. With big mailings plus store handouts on each book, we should go into autumn with a harvest of sales.

Item: What's this about "joint venture" and is it different from "franchising?" *Comment:* whereas the franchisee is an owner, a joint venture is a sort of partnership of ours. The big difference is that the latter does not have to invest nearly so much in his business. As you know, I hope – any employee is eligible for either program, regardless of sex, race, color, age, religion, size, IQ or blood group. You'll notice I did not say anything about cash or credit!

AUGUST 1971
The Millennium!

BY THE OPENING OF OUR 1000TH STORE, *Allied Radio Shack* has achieved the "impossible dream," a feat equal to the 4-minute mile, the 18-foot pole vault, 61 home runs. Or even . . . permanent peace. It's that much of a thing to all of us who were around when the number was 1, then 4, then 9, and then – Charles *Tandy*! When Mr. Tandy took over *Radio Shack* in 1963, we were the weakest 90-pound weaklings in the annals of the electronics business – an industry famous for weaklings.

He said, "I am going to open 100 stores." Later he said "I am going to open 300 stores. Still later, our computer coughed gently and printed out its theory; 1400 stores." We have since determined that our sights should be set considerably higher. In fact, by this time next year, I can predict we will have passed the number suggested by our computer. Mr. Tandy said as we opened our 10th store, "When we get there, everyone else will say they could have done it too." But he didn't believe it. And we didn't.

To "get there" you have to have a plan. The plan has to be acted upon. Setbacks have to be ignored. Conceptual changes must be eaten back. The idea of failure must become impossible.

The plan is 8 years old. It was and is a very simple program: first ion size, first in profits, one business – consumer electronics which sell in volume, and a manageable number of product mostly or entirely marketed under our own brand. The best plans usually are simple. Polaroid: cameras. Ford: cars, Texaco: fuel. And to execute the plan: good people in a good atmosphere for productivity.

In thinking about the distance we have come, I can't help but feel that the 1000th store in our *Allied Radio Shack* system – dated July 1, 1971 – will be the proudest milestone our Corporation will ever cross, even as it moves on to greater deeds and bigger numbers.

OCTOBER 1971
Dirty *Young* Men?

NOW THAT WE'RE ADVERTISING in the nation's most conspicuous magazines and on television in an exciting new test program, expect to be visited in your store by a whole new group of first-time prospects.

The added cost of enticing these folks into our 1100 shops is $1,000,000 and this is peanuts compared to the full price of such advertising if it is successful.

What will they see–these newcomers? Professionals in exciting, spotless premises? Or amateurs in disaster areas?

This is a fair question. We have too many places littered with hand-scribbled signs; messy windows, dusty merchandise; cannibalized equipment; and the general litter of forms, cartons, trash, and buts that typifies the *Radio Shack Nobody Loves*.

This is my *2nd Annual Shape Up Or Ship Out* editorial, written for slobs only. If it doesn't attack you, feel praised.

We're spending that extra advertising megabuck not merely to attract new buyers, but also to double your bonus. They're coming in tomorrow! So don't just stand there. Do something clean . . . today!

DECEMBER 1971
Thank You, Commander Whaley . . .
Wherever You are

SOMEWHERE AT SEA on the U.S.S. Vesuvius (AE15) – the Executive officer, Lt. Commander O.R. Whaley, U.S.N., has a pleasant November thought, and he sits down and writes a letter.

"Allow me to note and pass on to you're the fine performance of two of your products . . ." (Sir, I note and reply that this is the most refreshing opening of the Holiday Season in memory).

He continues; "Prior to deployment to the South China Sea, . . . this command purchased five *TR-99C Walkie-Talkies* . . . from your store. Even though subjected to extremely hard service (banging around in boats, sea and salt exposure), they have performed flawlessly. It is estimated all transceivers have in excess of 500 hours operating time . . . utilized as a command circuit from the commanding officer to his lifeboat officers or other officers . . . throughout the ship while conducting operations.

Surely, for such a brief (three paragraph) letter, Commander Whaley has done enough to make our 5150 employees rejoice! But no. Not quite. He turns a final felicitous phrase: "once again, a note of superb performance from a satisfied customer."

The complaints and occasional pettiness of 1971 fade away entirely. This is a splendid and fitting finale to our greatest year at *Radio Shack*.

The excessive consumerism and red tape of 1971 fade away entirely in the certain knowledge that our Designing, Engineering, Buying and Selling functions have come together so handsomely in behalf of our country. And that our country, in the person of the "exec" on AE15, took the time and had the desire to say "well done" . . . to all of us.

I am indebted to Commander Whaley for this year's Christmas card from me to you. This is it!

FEBRUARY 1972
In Memoriam: Lewis Shows

BY THE TIME YOU READ THIS it will be somewhat ancient history, and history has a way of quickly covering its wounds with the bandage of forgetfulness – I am not yet in the mood to let that happen.

In the fog of Tuesday morning, January 18, 1972, the *Tandy* Corporation jet went down in a remote Texas town killing all nine passengers and crew, among them our very fine Vice President, Lewis Shows, and his vibrant and devoted wife. They were on company business. This is quite comparable to dying in the line of duty. They boarded the plane around 7 a.m., an hour when most employees were not yet thinking of going to work for our stockholders.

Most of us in the *Radio Shack* management have used the plane for company business and a fine device it is for getting in and out of off-the-track places with a minimum of energy wasted on travel. I'd recommend getting another such plane immediately. I'd fly in it tomorrow, but perhaps never again with such confidence, and certainly never again with such satisfaction.

"Lew" Shows had a great past with *Tandy* and an even greater future with *Tandy* – up to that awful morning. When our chairman asked him to move from his easier job at Tex-Tan to a tougher one at corporate headquarters, including moving from Yoakum to Fort Worth and possibly at a reduction in income, he went. Period.

No doubt there are many other men in our group who would do the same. And then again, I happen to know there are some who wouldn't. *Tandy* will look a long time before they find the measure of this man.

Rest in peace. Lewis.

APRIL 1972
Too Much Consumerism

MY COMPLAINT MAIL THESE DAYS is replete with letters from customers which are but carbon copies of letters they sent to various and sundry personages, including R. M. Nixon, Virginia Knauer, the IRS, the D.A., Consumers Union, Ralph Nader, the BBB, a random senator or governor, and sometimes Jim and sometimes Charles. I feel lucky to be included at all.

Such is the temper of the times that some consumers seem to enjoy "squealing" more than they enjoy consuming.

My answers to these correspondents are invariably testy, full of grumblings about mail pollution and assertions to the effect that I can solve their problems more smoothly in private confrontation. But alas, without consumers we are, to put it succinctly, dead. And so the letters and copies get written and sent, and the postman staggers under his load of vintage '72 junk mail.

Will we end up, as a nation and as a people, as complainers in quadruplicate, as tellers of little tales, totally dependent upon the State to prosecute our least allegation and count every aspirin in our bottles? Perish the thought. Or – perish us!

Those of you who meet the public daily under our mighty standard can do your part to keep consumerism below epidemic levels by doing a few things smarter. Don't let customers get to the boiling point. Do have a little more heart. Use your brains instead of your muscle. Remember, when they write me AND Virginia Knauer, I go very mushy indeed and you lose anyway.

Treat customers the way you'd treat a guest in your own home. I'm convinced a glad smile and a clean towel will do it every time. If there's a splice in our splice-free tape; send me the reel and give 'em a new one. Don't say it can't happen. Virginia and I know better.

JUNE 1972
"Attsa Fine"

NO GOOD ITALIAN WOULD SPELL GIORGIO "Georgia: any more than he would spell Ristorante with an "e" where the "I" is supposed to be. Nevertheless, in Palm Springs, California, there is a good Italian who commits both of these orthographical heresies with large-scale deliberation. Why?

Secondarily, because he knows that wiseacres like me have a compulsion to tell him the error of his ways. Primarily, because Georgio is a showman. Now pull your chair a little closer whilst I direct a moral at our Store Managers and Salesmen.

Every day at Georgio's (sic) Restorante (sic) is as busy as a *Radio Shack* store on opening day. The traffic is fantastic. Therefore, one would assume Georgio is hidden away in an office somewhere in the depths of the Restorante pushing papers or clipping coupons. Wrong assumption. Georgio is at the front door, the back door, the bar, talking to diners at their tables, skipping back to work the register.

Why does an owner in his sixties work so hard when he has so many helpers and so much business and success is guaranteed even when he's absent? Because he instinctively knows success is not automatic and that helpers let down when the boss is out of sight. And because he obviously loves his work. These qualities shine like a beacon at Georgio's. Or at any *Radio Shack* in the country bossed by a man with success in his genres.

Every customer gets a copy of Georgio's witty menu and a small bottle of wine when he leaves. Remember this is a person who has already paid up and no longer needs to be treated like a king, or so you'd think. When I got my menu and wine, I suddenly thought about our Battery Card. A gift that leaves you with a "good taste in your mouth" AFTER the sale is made and for a single purpose: to get you to come back!

That, of course, is what business is all about; and when it happens, in Georgio's own inimitable words, "Attsa Fine."

AUGUST 1972
Electing, the "*Radio Shack* Way"

THIS INTERCOM ISSUE IS DEDICATED TO all the fine men who have just been nominated and elected to bigger jobs within our Company. Congratulations to each and every one of them!

I am particularly proud that it is *Radio Shack's* way to promote from within our ranks. This is in direct opposition to the habit of many large businesses of going "outside" for talent. "Outside" simply means: nobody inside was judged able to cut the mustard.

We have reached our point in growth and time without consultants and head-hunters and body snatchers and somehow we've managed to finish another record-breaking year. Our promotion-from-within syndrome should encourage any *Radio Shack* employee to think big and aspire to high places. We've only just begun promoting from within!

On the same subject but in a different vein: to G.R. "Bill" Nugent, my best wishes for continued success at *Tandy*'s GHQ. *Radio Shack*'s success is very largely due to the work and wisdom of this man. And I'm sure I'm not alone when I say he's the finest guy I've ever worked with and he will, indeed, be missed at *Radio Shack*,. Drop him a note at T/C if you agree.

His replacement, another winner from within, is Bennett Hunter. He got the job because his region (Central) turned in the best overall numbers and opened the most stores. Not only once, but consistently over a two-year period. He didn't even need a primary race or a delegate fight to get nominated and elected! But, come to think it, by George, he did miss out on giving an acceptance speech at 3 o'clock in the morning!

SEPTEMBER 1972
The $3,500,000 Caper

I HAVE RECENTLY RETURNED from addressing all of the 1500 *Radio Shack* Managers and assisting in the distribution of $3,500,000 in Manager bonuses earned during the past fiscal year which ended June 30. It was a real pleasure to see you. It was an even greater pleasure to be with you when the fruits of your labor were harvested!

As I said at our many meetings: it was YOUR money And YOUR day, and *Radio Shack* is not a charitable organization which hands out largesse in exchange for a warm feeling of brotherhood.

One hates to sound trite and hard-boiled, yet it bears repeating that warm feelings and cold feelings tend to part company at the Bottom Line. As *Tandy* stockholders, which the most and wisest of you now are, you know what I mean!

The really invigorating thing about the bonus gatherings was the revelation that we have so many five-figure earners in the under-30 age group. I wonder if you realize how much older we of our generation were before we broke through $10,000? *Radio Shack* is a truly "young" company! Only a handful of us are over 50. And there are no "friends and relatives" blocking anybody's progress to the top.

Your Management is continuing a very simple old *Tandy* tradition in its thinking, to wit — Store Managers are the greatest asset we have, Everybody Else is overhead.

If you Dear Reader, are not a Store Manager, the above isn't intended to mean we don't cherish you. It merely reflects the obvious. The person who actually sells our product to the public is the one upon whom our collective livelihood depends on a day-to-day basis.

In summary, the whole ballgame is largely in the hands of the under-50 gang who make up most of our Managers. At first the awareness of this alarmed me. But then I remembered the $3,5000,000 they just received. I think we're quite safe. Dick and George, so long as our society remains capitalist!

NOVEMBER 1972
Point after Touchdown

IN YOUR BEHALF, RADIO SHACK IS ONCE AGAIN going to the Boob Tube in search of customers. *This year it's to the tune of over $1,000,000.*

The Boob Tube, in case you don't know, is the moniker of that large cathode ray tube in your living room upon which pictures of the real and make-believe world flicker and bounce.

It's not true that only boobs watch the Boob Tube. But a lot of boobs do watch it, and some of them may be reading this epistle – and one of them may be writing it – if the following applies.

We can waste that megabuck in a flash if you don't know what we're advertising. If you're not ready for new faces, if you're running an amateur Radio Shack, if you don't look sharp as those new razor blades, if you don't sell product and service and image!

I want you to know our ads are first quality with Rod Sterling and William Shatner as narrators. They are every bit as professional as Sears, Gillette, Schlitz, Firestone and Polaroid, and were custom-filmed in Hollywood and Dallas. They were backed by quantity purchasing by us.

And we're in the big leagues of television – believe me – with the masters of the medium. Between October 15 and December 23, there are 47 such spots on NBC and CBS football – on network TV! Network means every single station in the country, every town an hamlet, not just local stuff like most folks use.

In parallel with this, in 27 major market where we do over half of our sales, there are 2300 spots in prime and fringe time, all featuring the same four films we're using on football.

And there, BUSTER, is our million bucks!

You don't win on the Boob Tube with money. Class and persuasion are all you've got. When you fail to make the point after, you usually lose the game. In TV, the touchdown is easy. All it takes is being there.

The payoff is the point after, like I said in Paragraph Four. If you don't get this point—and make it every day—our investment will be wasted, and TV will be scratched as a sales-maker for you (along with some of our nearest dearest friends).

DECEMBER 1972
1972: An Exciting Year

RADIO SHACK HAS TWO SORTS OF YEARS. A "fiscal year" which starts July 1 and Ends June 30. And a "calendar year" which starts January 1 and ends December 31. Since both 1972's were excellent, I'll just bump them together and itemize some accomplishments.

- *Radio Shack* opened *438 stores* during the year, only one of which was a Franchise store.

- *Radio Shack*, by the opening of a store in Oahu, Hawaii, finally achieved its modest goal of a *store in each of our 50 states.*

- *Radio Shack* expanded its rapidly growing *Manufacturing Division* by the addition of a tape plant; a communications antenna plant; a second wire factory; an electronics factory in Masan, South Korea; and we're adding 104,000 Sq. Ft, to our tape plant to house all Fort Worth 7th Street and Foch Street manufacturing.

- *Radio Shack* sales are now running at an annualized rate of about $240 million, which is to say better than *10 times the entire corporate sales of fiscal 1963.*

- *Radio Shack* and its subsidiaries now employ some 7000 people.

How can such things be when *Radio Shack* is in a highly competitive business and operating under historically tight government regulations and a time of global monetary unrest?

The answer is deceptively simple. *We have a plan for profitable growth* that does not rely upon outside brands and "me-too-ism." *And we have a plan for the growth of our people* that does not rely upon traditional concepts of job evaluation.

A good business-plan and a good-people plan have made *Radio Shack* a giant in consumer electronics. And 1972 has proved beyond dispute that we can, together, achieve any dream we dare to dream. So have a *Merry Christmas,* and a proud one, too. As for 1973 . . . to be colloquial: *you ain't seen nuthin yet!*

FEBRUARY 1973
Doing Our Own Things

A LOT OF FOLKS WITHIN THE COMPANY and, therefore, around the country are laboring under what is commonly called a misapprehension, That's a big ugly word for not "getting the word," but it means the same as "ignorance" and ignorance – no beauty either – is what we're always trying to have less of in this imperfect but only world.

The misapprehension centers around the theory that *Radio Shack* merchandise is the same as other people's merchandise except that it has our name on it. *The easiest answer to this myth is 'Taint so. And that's because "Taint so".*

For certain, many equipments look alike. There are just so many places and ways to attach knobs, dials, and so on. But our *'Taint so* goes for knobs, dials, and so on, and also the stuff inside – motors, circuits, power supplies, shafts, gears, PC board, jacks, plugs, UL label, the whole so called schmeer.

Every speaker system, hi-fi receiver, CB transceiver, scanner, walkie-talkie, and most of our radios, and most of our tape equipment, is engineered by our engineer plus (sometimes) engineers at the factory. Every item is externally designed by us in conjunction with an industrial design company that only works for one other electronics outlet.

Our bill for designs, prototypes, tools, dies and molds turns into astronomical figures. If we bought "off the shelf" as may do we could easily save $500,000 a year. But *Radio Shack can't afford the savings!* Because we alone are doing our own thing in consumer electronics, we have to look and be different – it's at the very heart of our success and our business philosophy.

The following items are made in factories *owned and operated by us* and thus obviously exclusive: all intercoms, all antennas, all recording tapes (except 8-track, and that soon), over half our walkie-talkies, some radios, some hi-fi equipment, most Science Fair and some *Archerkit* products, panel meters, audio cables, test equipment, tubes (branding, boxing, plating), most of our wire, and many other miscellaneous items.

Our communication product and speaker systems are made in factories whose output is 50% to 90% ours alone and, to make another point, each of our hi-fi equipments begins with an idea and a drawing – *not with something off somebody's shelf.*

Enough said? No, not quite. *Tell somebody*

MARCH 1973
The Roller Coaster

THE REASON SO MANY OF US WATCH OUR STOCK in the daily newspaper report on Wall Street is that so many of us are stockholders. A stockholder is a Concerned Person. All other persons (non-stockholders) are merely Grandstand Quarterbacks.

If you are not a stockholder, Sir and Madam, the question may be asked of you: are you really a Concerned Person? There may be better ways of demonstrating concern than owning 1, 10, 100 or any number of *Tandy* Corp. (TAN) shares, but I can't think of any today. "Concern" means something like "interest" but more like "betting on the increasing success of yourself in your job."

If you're not turned on to the extent of a $30-$50 bet on yourself and us, remember that other bet you're making today – the once-in-a-lifetime TIME of your life you use up each day you work at *Radio Shack*. I submit that either you're a stockholder or you put an incredibly low value on your time.

As for us shareholders and newspaper watchers, we do find the day to day changes in share value dazzling to say the least. One recent downside move was credited by "The Street" to *Lafayette's* (A competitor) alleged sales or earnings weakness! Another came on the heels of our excellent 2nd quarter and 6-month sales and earnings report! Such are the vagaries of the New York Stock Exchange, the biggest roller-coaster of all time.

A share of stock is the only authentic ticket for a ride on the roller-coaster. I hope I have indicated why – aside from mere profits or losses – it's time to consider taking yourself for a ride.

APRIL 1973
Join *Radio Shack* and See the ---- World!

THAT ANCIENT SLOGAN OF THE U.S. NAVY has a new meaning for all of us today, what with *Radio Shack*'s ambitious plan for overseas sales. Who knows, we may even take an old English maxim too – remember the one about the sun never setting on the British Empire?

At this moment, a significant advance force of 5 of our top Vice Presidents is in Brussels, Belgium, where the first *Radio Shack* overseas warehouse may be located. We have not sent amateurs to get us situated in the Common Market. Because the problems are numerous, complex, and novel.

So far, I can report that we do not know all the variations in "our game" required to master this job of marketing. But we do know the size of the playing field. And it is impressive. Statistic: the countries of West Germany, United Kingdom, France, and Benelux (Belgium, Netherlands, Luxembourg) together have a population of 190-200 million. Just about the size of the US market. In an infinitely more compacted space. Add to this: another 125 million for the other nations of free Europe and you have a market about 50% BIGGER than ours, and 15 TIMES bigger than Canada!

Radio Shack does not have a Messianic complex but we do have an irresistible urge to be the biggest thing in the world in consumer electronics. We are in the best position of any company to achieve this goal;. We have made (and corrected!) the most mistakes. We have the best team, the most know-how, the most coordinated plan for merchandising and operating. And we have shown our stockholders that we know how to do these things profitable.

Best of all – as the Europeans may discover – we have learned how to make successful businessmen out of the men we find on the scene. We will NOT export a lot of Americans, just a chosen few who can teach and develop people. In short, *Radio Shack* is on the threshold of becoming a "multinational" company.

To those who have been initially selected for overseas duty and accepted the challenge – our most sincere thanks and best wishes. It took guts. It takes optimism.

For those who may be learning about this for the first time: nowhere from Afghanistan to Zambia may be considered beyond the limits of our dream. Where do you see yourself? What can you bring to the table?

MAY 1973
How to Build a $250,000,000 Business

JUST IN CASE SOME OF MY READERS are under the impression that a Tandy or a Kornfeld can run *Radio Shack* with pushbuttons, whips, carrots, or money, I have done a bit of new-math for your consideration.

Also, on this 10th Birthday under the *Tandy* banner, I feel sufficiently generous to give away gratis to our competitors the Innermost secret of our success.

The new math is an inventory of our people. The Innermost Secret of our success is our people inventory. And this is all (well practically) it takes to build a quarter-billion-dollar business.

Store System	4903
Store Supervisors	139
Warehousing	563
Manufacturing (USA)	926
Americans Overseas	12
Franchise-ASC Program	50
Repair and Parts Program	309
Accounting	180
Management & Advertising	121
TOTAL	7203

Omitted from this grand total of 7203 people are all the nobles of the Corporate Court and all the Samurai who are waging our good fight in the Far East, for which a thousand pardons – and please, no memos.

The number is already big enough. And it figures to $34,700 in sales per person. Thus you know how much we have to sell to our customers to keep our people inventory at its resent remarkable level.

My message is fast dwindling to its close because I have an uncanny feeling that our Chairman – having been left off the list of 7203 plus having a Vince Lombardi grasp of fundamental numbers – will be on the pipe soon to tell me that $34,700 sales-per-capita is NOT ENOUGH SALES. Or too much capita!

And this, also, to be honest, is how you build a $250-million business.

JUNE 1973
Fiscal '73 – Our Best Ever!

JUNE 30 MARKS THE END OF OUR FISCAL YEAR. Thanks to all of you it was a whopper: biggest in old store gains, new store gains, profits, everything.

No strikes on the docks and minimal government interference helped, as did "consumer confidence" – a mysterious element referred to by pundits when the going is either very good or bad. We used the Martin Luther King method. We had a dream. And it came true. Good business like good gospel helps everyone.

Yet this, alas, was not the reading on Wall Street, a place to which I prophetically referred in my March (1973) letter as "the biggest roller coaster of all time." As readers know, the coaster went down in direct proportion to the way our results went up. I suggest that this is a good time to buy *Tandy* stock, particularly for those who like to buy low. I remind myself that roller coasters do not operate in only one direction. And that I have paid for by ability to reminisce. But profited on my ability to dream!

In another earlier letter to you I praised our Store Managers and said that all the rest of us were "overhead." A few readers objected and some couldn't believe that I would include myself in that category. The semantics are simple. All of us who do not directly sell a product to the customer are "overhead" and that certainly includes your correspondent. "Overhead" is no insult, merely a category on a business statement.

Among the excitements of Fiscal '73 was a vast realignment of *Radio Shack* regions involving numerous promotions in the "overhead" group of regional and district management. All promotions were from within, none came from the outside – neither from outside business nor the CIA nor the committee to re-elect anyone. For once I happily note that all our politics is internal!

At this writing prospects for Fiscal '74, which begins on July 1, 1973, look shiny bright. Our store opening program continues. Our Korean factory has passed the 400,000 unit mark in manufactured items. Our Fort Worth factories are humming. Our industry position is secure, also our jobs. Whatever the post-Watergate energy-short world has to offer, we are ready to capitalize upon our determination and upon our plan to excel.

JULY 1973
What Inflation Means to You

UNTIL THE JUNE PRICE FREEZE, "for a maximum of 60 days" (to quote Mr. Nixon) things were costing you more everywhere you went: butcher, baker, candlestick maker, carpenter, vintner, banker, car dealer. This spiral is likely to continue to the end of time. The thing that concerns you most is the rate of climb, not the climb itself.

Our business has not escaped inflation and the President's hasty Band-Aid cannot long prevent it from affecting our customers as well.

But as I look back on 25 years of consumer electronics progress, our industry has a remarkable record of being able to stem the tide of inflation (at retail) with the new technology and better productivity. At the same time we have brought our customers better, safer, and more versatile equipment. Our system also provides for competitiveness, which by its nature prevents runaway pricing.

In short, even at prices reflecting today's currency revaluations and the need and/or greed of parts manufacturers, consumer electronic items are a bargain relative to other things – such as wine, neckties, services and so on. You should meet your customers and prospects with this knowledge.

If you compare radios and tape recorders with these of 5 or 10 years ago it will be obvious to you that we are offering more for less. Our product looks better, feels better, lasts longer. The same cannot be said, I think, for automobiles and Hershey bars, to name a few recognizable items which have given up quite a bit to achieve acceptable price points.

Because of various political and economic factors, our Canadian and other good friends around the world pay more than you do for the same or similar equipment. In communist countries these things are either unavailable or subject to interminable waiting periods.

Sometimes we don't realize how well off we are compared to the rest of the world. Take a minute today to remember this. And then you'll face our really modest price changes with credible optimism.

AUGUST 1973
It's That Time Again

AUGUST AT RADIO SHACK IS SYNONYMOUS with the disbursements of the annual – as and if earned – bonus to Store Managers. This is done at a series of large meetings all across the country which I attend unless prevented by scheduling.

What I say to our many hundreds of "winners" is quite simple. It's THEIR day. It's THEIR opportunity in which they've made good. It's NOT a gift, Not an AWARD, BUT A SUM earned ACCORDING TO OUR PLAN AND THEIR EXECUTION.

The dollars distributed on Bonus Day run into the many millions and, believe me, we are delighted to pass out these checks; their size is in direct proportion to our total success.

To many, probably to most of the "winners" the amount is the single largest sum of cash they have ever received at any one time. That's what makes it so exciting. Instead of little bits dribbling out all through the year, there's one large BITE whose use (or misuse) can truly affect one's current history if not one's lifetime.

A man walks a little straighter if he has opportunities of this sort presented to him. A man can make meaningful choices, decisions, adjustments, investments; particularly if he has been able to get by on a lot less than his total earnings, for then the bonus will not have so many calls on it that it is diminished to the size of "just another' check.

Bonus Day gets to the basic heart of the matter at *Radio Shack*; the celebration of hard work faithfully performed in a manner worthy of man's time. I'm very glad indeed, to report It's That Time Again!

SEPTEMBER 1973
At This Point in Time

WATERGATE WATCHERS – and surely you must be one of them – have heard a number of pat phrases or verbal clichés which have been a source of wonderment to the TV and radio press. They include: At This Point in Time (meaning *then*), In Respect To (meaning; *concerning,* or *about),* In That Time Frame (meaning: approximately *then*).

The source of these verbal delicacies is not, as the press suspects, modern Washington, D.C. My memory serves me quite well in this area; it tells me they come from the scientist engineer fraternity of the 1950's and must have actually originated in colleges and universities at an even earlier date. But the 1950's and 60's saw the emergence of professor type from the research lab and lecture hall into the highest reaches of government and the defense community. I knew many of them in Boston and liked them despite their linguistic refinements

Another Watergate phenomenon is the poor grammar or pronunciation used by fellows who went to places like Yale. A standard feature: *Febuary* instead of *FebRuary*. A close second; frequent use of the verb "to be" with a pronoun in the objective case. These trifles can be very annoying to one who has lived within the guidelines for over 50 years. Fortunately, the months of June and March seemed to dominate the proceedings and I was not forced to hear *Febuary* during the time frame of every discrete witness. Note: in respect to 'discrete," that's another of those words.

And now at this point in time I am forced (by my perception of my office) to make all this stuff relevant to *Radio Shack* despite that, to the best of my memory, I cannot precisely recollect why I started talking about it.

Perhaps out of the sad shambles of honesty, decency, dignity and high office, you can perceive a message, a moral, or a reason?

Didn't somebody say "not by his words shall you know him, but by his deeds"? I never look up quotations and haven't seen a Bartlett in 27 years.

OCTOBER 1973
Europe: A Progress Report

ONE OF THE MOST EXCITING THINGS YOUR COMPANY is doing is goi ng overseas to do business. Retail business. I have just been there for a quick visit to our so-called "Brussels Sprouts" and can say for a certainty that they are getting the job done.

Our first store opened with a bang, also with a brief catalog. – in Flemish! Flemish is also Dutch with minor variations, so the same catalog will be useful when we go into Holland. And this will be soon.

The many of you who know Messers. Gregson, O'Brien, Bernabei, and Shirley, might drop them a line from time to time just to let them know they're not forgotten. The address is: *Tandy* International Electronics, Parc Industriel de Sauveniere, 5800 Gembloux, Belgium.

The reasons we are using the name *Tandy* instead of *Radio Shack* include: ease of pronunciation, bigger shorter signs, and corporate desire.

The store looks just like any other fairly large *Radio Shack*. It's on a busy highway near Antwerp, about 18 miles north of Brussels, set back in a sort of shopping strip that hasn't quite jelled and none of the buildings are connected except ours (to Pier 1 store).

The warehouse, except for being in farm country, looks like any other warehouse of modest size except that when I saw it, it was absolutely empty of merchandise. And like any other warehouse it will get – and stay – fuller than it should be before long.

The Belgian customers look and spend like any of our customers. They are as delighted with a free 5-cell flashlight as regular USA people. For this we may say Praise Allah because it's the regular types that have made us Number One to stay, not the philes and phobes that wish we were something else.

It's getting so the sun may really never set on *Tandy*'s empire. And that's good news, job security, and bigger opportunities for every one of us! Maybe even (please!) higher stock prices?

NOVEMBER 1973
Doing It "Our Way"

THE INTERCOM HAS BEGUN, at my suggestion, running a series of articles on company-owned manufacturing. I hope that at the conclusion of the series we can distribute a bound version of the series. It will make convincing reading for any customer and impressive sales material for any salesman.

We are now in the manufacturing business in a big way. In our last fiscal year ending June 30, 1973, the record stood like this: USA production FOB factory -- $23,588,000; Far East production FOB factory -- $13,926,639. For a grand total of $37,514,639. The figure for this new year will probably top $50,000,000.

Be amazed. This is $10,000,000 more than Radio Shack's SALES for all of fiscal 1968. And remember: manufacturing sales figures differ from retail figures in that the former exclude retail gross margin dollars!

Head count in our factories is above the 2000 mark. That's a lot of jobs. Each is dependent upon *Radio Shack's* ability to sell what they make.

Aside from mere profits at the factory level, here are some of the things we hope to benefit from by doing it "our way": (1) consistent quality, (2) consistent availability, (3) consistent ability to match building-growth with selling-growth, (4) exclusivity of products, and hopefully, (5) new, original products, not now in our line.

To get where we're going, a lot of value is attached to exclusivity and original products. These are difficult to achieve when someone else is the producer.

And then I think a lot can be said for the sheer pride involved. You stand a little taller; you sell a bit more confidently, when *Made by Radio Shack* goes on the package!

DECEMBER 1973
You Gotta Believe

FROM AL BOULIANNE IN STORE 2141 (Carlisle, Pa.) comes the notion that the above slogan contains messages for me and you. I agree. But in my own peculiar way. Because I am allergic to corn-ey (but not Korn-ey!) slogans. So here are my messages.

You gotta believe – that all those folks who think Christmas is too commercial are killjoys. I've enjoyed 56 of these experiences and I'm looking forward to Christmas again this year with all my old enthusiasm. Including the ads, the parties, the 4 purple neckties, the Rudolphs, the busted budget, the togetherness, the hedonism, the whole green-and-red scene. And yes (Virginia) there is a Santa Claus. The little sins committed in his name just don't compare to the big ones committed the rest of the year.

You gotta believe – your management wishes you a Very Merry Christmas even if we couldn't keep you (Managers) in CB and make crystals fast enough. We're never out of stock when it comes to good thoughts about you, including people who aren't Managers and even people who tell managers how to manage.!

You gotta believe – that ours is "certainly an intriguing business" says "*Financial World*" magazine on page 232. They go on to admit: "One might even say that this is Horatio Alger country, Small items bring in big sales and earnings." Merry Yule to the money magazines; they're getting smarter periodically. Yes Charlie, that's a pun.

You gotta believe – that there's an energy crisis. I'm already pooped from writing Xmas cards. Please don't criticize Xmas or I'll shorten it to X.

You gotta believe – in *Nation's Business* (magazine) when they say 82% of the customers who don't come back (to your store) do it because of salesmen's indifference and unadjusted service complaints. Open this package before Christmas, Al, because it's not too late to love a customer.

You gotta believe – in the strength of the system, the American way, the *Tandy* method, home, Mother, the buck, the integrated circuit, everything that has brought us to the top of what Bennet calls the Pile and what I think must be world's first (or third) oldest profession. What I gotta believe, Lords and Ladies, is Christmas is heavily involved.

JANUARY 1974
Benefits from the Energy Shortage?

BEING A BORN OPTIMIST, my first inclination at the sound of bad news is to see if any good can come out of it. I do find a wry bit of cheer from the energy crisis which, at press time, was wrapping the country in a thin blanket of darkness and gloom and impacting on other important sectors of the economy.

First: *Radio Shack* is an entertainment company and entertainment is certainly what the people of a dim and chilly world will be looking for in 1974.

Second: *Radio Shack's* product is affordable, unfrivolous, not a conspicuous waster of precious resources nor a despoiler of the ecology: it can be offered and sold without apologies.

Third: the number and variety of *Radio Shack's* locations are such that distant driving (in possibly gas-rationed cars) is unnecessary; we do not rise or fall on the success of a few giant roadside malls.

Fourth: if cars and air conditioners are actually hurt in sales this does not necessarily affect *Radio Shack* since (a) we do not sell cars or air conditioners, and (b) there will be more money in budgets for home entertainment.

Fifth: if you look at the back of any *Radio Shack* AC-operated product you will see – expressed in watts – the AC current required to run the equipment we well. You'll observe that most items run a watts-draw of LESS than that required to illuminate a 25W light bulb!

Sixth: we're in a hopefully-temporary shortage: paper, plastics, metals, petro-chemicals, and parts. This usually leads to customers being happy to get approximately what they want and happy to pay the price.

WARNING; all of the above sales aids which, as they say of medicine, will be effective if used as directed.

My New Year's message to all of you engaged in retail sales is to make effective uses of the above Six Benefits by letting your prospects and customers know that *Radio Shack* is, more than ever, "the right place to buy right" for 1974. Make every inquiry a sale! Don't worry about delays and shortages – capitalize on the many good things still available to you. Recognize that we are doing everything in our power to retain our supremacy in this business that has made so many good things happen for so many people for fifty years!

FEBRUARY 1974
What's in a Name

WHEN I JOINED RADIO SHACK IN 1948, the first dumb thing I did was to hate our name (*Radio Shack*) and aspire to change it. Now over a half-billion dollars in sales later, it our most unique and precious asset!

Do you agree? – or would you prefer *Ampex, Memorex, Masterworks, RCA, Philco, Farnsworth, Freed-Eisman, Philharmonic, Symphonic* or maybe just plain *Sony*? Chances are, now that the latter has come to mean something, you'd pick *Sony*, a name that didn't exist before any of the good clean, honorable wars; almost meaningless.

A name is what it stands for; a name is what you do with it, not the way it reads. George Eastman would have done as well with *Kadok*. Want to bet?

So all those well-meaning folks who think *Realistic* ought to be Rhapsodic or even Hyperthalic ought to stop to consider what *Realistic* has done that most of the 'good' names haven't – sell more and better equipment that most of the 'good' names haven't – sell more and better equipment over a period of 20 consecutive years.

While on the subject of *Kadok* (which is *Kodak* spelled backwards in case you missed the point), there are $10 K*adoks* and *Kadoks* at over $200. There are 25¢ *Kadok* publications and some very costly ones, some for amateurs and some for pro's. It hasn't set *Kadok* back one millimeter – just ask *Bell & Howell*. Thus I can't buy the notion that a $6 *Realistic* radio's existence threatens the success of a $600 *Realistic* audio receiver.

If you're looking for a reason for not selling more $600 *Realistic* receivers; I'll give you a name worthy of a real, hard, earnest, serious condition.

YOU!

MARCH 1974
The Things People Say

PEOPLE -- SOME OF THEM OUR OWN PEOPLE – often ask me how *Radio Shack* plans to answer the "problem" of new or aroused competition. They tell me about a new *K-Mart*, a new *Kennedy & Cohen*, a new *Lafayette*, a new hi-fi discount center that has just opened up in one of "our" markets. Or did I know *Panasonic* and *Morse* are on TV? Or what do we do if *Farfax* gets a top rating in *Consumers Research?*

When I want to be just a little cruel I remind them that they were the ones who used to send me the White Front ads from Los Angeles and a panic button. Now White Front appears to be fading rapidly. They were the same folks who showed me how far Lafayette was out front in a 4-channel stereo but forgot to note their slide in profitability as a per cent of sales. I'm not an expert on White Front or Lafayette and, in fact, I wish both of them well. I'm talking to the people who asked me what WE'RE gonna do about people who appear to threaten our market position.

When I don't want to be cruel, when I just want to be my rational abnormal self, my answer is slightly different.

I say: *"Nothing."*

"Nothing"? they say, with the startled look of a horse approached from the rear.

And then I go through my regular routine of questions that can only be answered one way. Can we stop *Pacific Stereo* from opening stores? Can we do anything about *Schmustom Shtereo* cutting *Pioneer* prices in the *Star-Telegram*? Can we stop *Thriftdrug* from selling batteries for a nickel? Answer. No. All we can do is read their copy and wonder about their balance sheet.

And on thing more: we can watch our sales reports and statements. 'Tis terribly trite, old Bucko, but it's what WE can do – not what THEY do – that counts.

While we're not oblivious to what THEY do, it's not our mission in life to react. We're actors, not reactors. If sales stink in Hoopla, Alabama, don't tell me *Sears* just opened a mall and took away all our marbles.

In fact: don't tell me anything about *Sears* at all and whatever. I haven't spent a dime there in six years and they don't seem to care. Like theirs, my reaction is: ha!

APRIL 1974
An Ad Man's Lament

THERE'S A LITTLE LARCENY IN THE SOUL of every ad man. The profession seems to demand giddy claims of greatness and "proof positive" that product A is better than product B. Sometimes the effect is amusing – as when, years ago *Zenith* regally proclaimed a radio with a output of "1000 milliwatts." We cognoscenti are all aware that 1000 milliwatts is, sad to say, the same as ONE watt!

And who knows better about the "larceny in the soul" of ad men than Yours Truly who directed our advertising from 1948 to 1970? However, when I became president of the company, I took the pledge of all *reformers, which is – to immediately point an accusing finger at the un-reformed.*

Item: *Zenith* is back at it in a recent ad proclaiming *"deeper, richer sound" via an "innovative speaker system"* featuring what they call a tuned port. Our first *Realistic* speaker, the *Solo-1* of 1955 vintage, also had a tuned port. In short: there's nothing new about tuning ports except perhaps port shape or location; in many ways it's the same as the bass reflex enclosure we dropped when we went into acoustic suspension designs to get more fundamental bass. To be fair, I haven't heard a *Zenith* and I wish them the best of sound. But the latent ad man within me did stir and mutter when I read their copy.

Item: the *JS&A National Sales Group* in a recent *Wall Street Journal* ad proclaimed "the end of the AC adapters" for calculators. Why this miracle? *Because their Model 800 will* "last almost one year on the same set of batteries." What sort of batteries?

Two inexpensive 9V batteries! Actually their machine looked good enough without this silly claim. But then it takes one to recognize one. An Ad Man, that is.

This old reformed ad man freely admits that business would be mighty tough without advertising. So you'll note that *Radio Shack* advertising is earthy but purposefully honest. We don't have to sell our price vs. another's because we don't see their product. Our claims are backed by engineering data. Errors get corrected. Accusations get answered. You can believe what we say. And the puffery has been replaced with salesmanship and service.

Now that the consumer is king, old-style free-swinging ad men like this correspondent have a bitter choice. Retire. Or become a missionary for truth in advertising, darn it!

JULY 1974
Determination

THE SAME WEEK IN JUNE that *RCA* declared its intention to quit its "unprofitable home audio products business next year." *Philco-Ford* announced its scheduled "departure from radios and stereo components." Both quotes are from the *Wall Street Journal*. These moves follow similar steps taken by *Ampex, Motorola, Westinghouse,* and *CBS Masterworks*.

On the second level of importance, we've seen the virtual or actual disappearance of such brands as *Symphonic, Arvin, Scott, Decca, Bogen, Webcor, Emerson, Traveler, Air King,* and others, from the so-called "audio" scene. So many of the famous names of my early working days at *Radio Shack* (1948) have faded and gone that you might think there wasn't a business any more.

And yet by any standard you care to use – units, dollars, dealers, hardware, software, etc., -- the non-TV business we call "consumer electronics" has never been bigger, better, or more fun.

It has become an axiom that our *Realistic* brand is now more important than the above-mentioned brands. "No way," would have been the estimate of our chances in 1964. And in truth it was never our intention to eliminate a competitor, merely to be one!

In my humble opinion, neither *Radio Shack* nor a Japanese label brought these giants to their knees. The answer is to be found within a simple word: *Determination.*

This means the determination to be in a business profitably and on a growth basis, to re-think problems to retain flexibility, to strive to be BEST at what you're doing, to have a business and marketing plan but NOT A QUITTING PLAN.

We've all seen how half-fought wars are losers, how businesses that spend more than they take in are losers. What could *Determination* have done in these cases? How can anyone in his right mind convince *Radio Shack* and *Tandy* that "consumer electronics" isn't a great, logical, growing business with a limitless future?

Somewhere, somehow, the late great drop-outs of our industry lost their determination and, thereby, the will to think through and surmount their difficulties.

For them, frankly, I can say I saw it coming as surely as cloth collars followed celluloid. For us, with the help of every reader and friend, I reiterate *Radio Shack's* determination NOT to let it happen here.

AUGUST 1974
A Memo to Our Managers

(1) ***YOU HAVE JUST RECEIVED*** perhaps the biggest check you've ever held in your life – the Bonus you earned by the sweat of your brow, the time of your life and a little help from your various bosses. Good going!

(2) You are about to make a major decision; what to do with the money. You are, believe me, at a *crossroads* in your life.

(3) You may choose to suddenly become capitalistic by investing this money in stocks, bonds, banks, annuities, or some other investment that looks for yield at some soon or later date. If you are thinking along this line I congratulate you and *you need no read beyond this point.* Good going!

(4) You may choose to suddenly become a consumer by expending this money on furniture, a boat, a larger car, a fur coat – something you've always wanted but don't desperately need. Now (expletive deleted) you're firmly fixed on the road to nowhere and I can guarantee you'll get there. At your age you should know better. At some age you *will* know better but it will be too late.

(5) The man who "gets ahead" in business as in life is also the man who "looks ahead" to what can or may happen. Not only does he usually get the promotions but he also gets the dividend checks; he has *plowed back* a portion of his labor for a future growth; he has resisted the temptation of instant gratification or traded it for peace of mind – either way, he stands twice a tall as the man who has to pass the buck the moment he gets it.

(6) This sermon *will not* be preached again in this space for another year.

(7) In *all* instances where the word "man" is employed, the word "person" is implied.

(8) Your job is *not* in jeopardy if Paragraph 4 describes your handling of your bonus. But *your family* may be.

(9) I am again not trying to sell you anything. Either you get the message or you read it again next year if you are still with us – and I hope you are.

(10) If you have made a bonus you have put something in *every pot* – the stockholder's pot, the corporate pot, everybody's pot including mine. Come to think of it; *pot isn't all bad!*

SEPTEMBER 1974
How to Get a Raise

THIS IS ANOTHER MEMO TO OUR MANAGERS. It begins with the acknow-ledgement of a letter written to our Chairman by a Manager who complained he'd only gotten a raise of something like $2.50 a week in two years.

I'm not normally a violent man but my reaction to this sort of complaint Is full of 4- and 5-letter words which I picked up from President Nixon.

In our abysmal innocence, we'd thought this was the first lesson a Manager got when he joined our team. The point being: by good management, including good sales management, a *Radio Shack* Manager can give himself substantial raises in pay throughout the year!

This privilege is not extended to any of us who are not out there selling. It's exclusive to our Store Managers. It's at the very heart of our system for personal and Company success.

Up to a few deals ago, never in my entire working career have I had the opportunity to write my own raise by the monthly application of improving skills and desire. For me, it was a 100-mile hike to the Boss" office, hat in hand, heart in mouth, and the answer was often No – with or without reason. I would wonder what I had to do to get my values recognized?

Our Managers have no such problem. There is no one saying No. There's instant cash recognition of a better performance, and it echoes all the way up to the top of our commercial pyramid.

What a fabulous opportunity for young people starting out! What a special way to get ahead financially all throughout the year! What a dummy . . . if you don't get the message!

NOVEMBER 1974
Sold: 3,627,627 Units!

IN MY RECENT SWING AROUND ALL OUR REGIONS – the annual Bonus Road Show – I rediscovered a vast credibility gap. Too many of our people STILL don't think *Realistic* is an accepted national band.

Some don't even know what "expletive deleted" means, so I shall rely upon 7-digit figures rather than 4-letter words.

It's a FACT that during the past fiscal year 3,627,627 products visibly bearing the *Realistic* label were sold to customers, an average of over 300,000 a month. This friends and skeptics, is what anyone would call a Bull Number.

Let us speculate. Assuming *Pioneer* and *Fisher* – two names often used when reckoning who's #1 in audio – have sales of about $40,000,000 each and that their average sale (to dealers) is $100, that would give each of them 400,000 unit sales per annum. Using this guesswork and a *Radio Shack* calculator (made in Fort Worth!) nine times more *Realistic* brands get sold than either Pioneer or Fisher, and 4X more than Brand-P and Brand-F combined!

True: *Realistic* sells a wider range of goods than those two competitors, but when it comes to branded products in customer homes *REALISTIC* IS #1 by so far it isn't even funny. We also do more advertising than anyone in the field – probably more than all audio advertisers lumped together.

Realistic is big and growing bigger. Network and spot TV ads are giving *Realistic* an incredible reach into every viewing home in the country. We tell our *Realistic* story in over 600 daily newspapers several times a month. Nobody but NOBODY else can make this claim.

If you're not a *Realistic* believer and booster – get with the Now Generation – do your customers and your 1975 bonus a great big favor.

Show this editorial to your fellow workers and the folks who visit your store. Brag, don't apologize. And remember; you don't have to knock your competition to make the sale., The 3,627,627 "sold by *Realistic*" units – sold in 1974 alone – give 'em more hell than you can imagine, as one by one they quietly give up the ghost and retreat into history.

DECEMBER 1974
Thank You, Mr. Chernicoff

MY ORIGINAL INTENTION for this fifth Christmas Greeting message was a fight-talk about the great first quarter we've had at *Radio Shack*: sales up, profits up, chins up in the face of all the gloomy news fed to us hourly by the press. What a paradox – that good news really isn't newsworthy, that from their commercial point of view the only "good" news is bad news!

My second intention for this column was to discuss why I might have gotten bumped from Page 2 to Page 3 by the *Intercom* and turned a pale blue (picture-wise) in the process. The theme: Is This Progress?

My third idea was to light out after *Consumer Union* which had again, in its *Consumer Reports* magazine, quoted from a private intra-company memo and again grievously misinterpreted by intention. This, however, did not seem exactly appropriate for The Season.

My fourth notion was to tell our people to be on their best behavior for Christmas because not only is it the right thing to do all year but also this period is crucial for the good health of most businesses – particularly ours.

Luckily, a Mr. Chernicoff provided me with the fuel to ignite notion #4 far more brilliantly than I could ever had done because his message comes directly from the playing field.

He writes: "It has really been most gratifying to find . . . old-fashioned sincerity and service from any type of service company, but when you find this attitude repeating itself through all of your stores, the pleasure of finding it is multiplied many times over. You can be sure I will continue to do business with the **Radio Shack** stores." He itemized three of our stores in Virginia. His letter is my files for inspection.

How many Chernicoff's do we have in our 12-million name mailing list? How many will walk in tomorrow, looking for old-fashioned sincerity and service? I'll tell you this for sure: a Company of our size and importance and visibility had better find a Cheernicoff every working day in every department, everywhere we raise our flag.

Until then, and anyway: Merry Christmas!

JANUARY 1975
J. Paul Getty Revisited

IN OUR SOCIETY – FAMOUS FOR FREEDOM OF CHOICE – it has been Capitalism and Profits, not Bureaucracy, that have given the thrust that made the wheels turn. If we don't recognize this, our freedom of choice may eventually be between Obedience and Punishment.

If the words "capitalist" and "profits" are frightening, substitute "investment" and "dividends on investment."

If the word "Getty" alarms you, try substituting "Marx." Neither word will make you a billionaire automatically. But one of them won't under any conditions, and this you'd better believe.

While many will view J. Paul Getty and others of his breed as tycoons, minsters from another age, or – as a class—The Enemy, I am too practical to hold these views.

"I believe," said Getty, "that the able industrial leader, who creates wealth and employment, is as worthy of historical notice as the politician or soldier who spends an ever-increasing share of the wealth created by industrial initiative and courage."

To bring this observation home to roost, unless *Radio Shack* gets into some business-school's "case method" textbook, our achievements won't rank with even the smallest war, or Watergate, or recession, or President Ford's exploits on the gridiron. Yet the fact remains that we have created "Wealth and employment" and certainly qualify as historically important by Mr. Getty's standards.

I don't think that Mr. Getty (or in our case, Mr. Tandy) desire to have statues of themselves erected in public places. Rather I think the basic message is to put values into perspective.

The only time business really makes news is when it's bad. You read about layoffs, rarely about hirings. You hear about defects, never about quality. You're told about bankruptcies, seldom about fresh starts. And eventually you begin to question the very fundamentals of being in business.

But finally you discover something like Getty's little paragraph, and you start one again to sense the historicity of everything we're doing!

FEBRUARY 1975
Looking Backward

THIS PAST CHRISTMAS SEASON WAS LOWLIGHTED (antonym for "highlighted") by the Great Free Flashlight Debacle. Since this occurred at the store level, this piece is written to Store Managers. The rest of us have all eaten enough crow to last a lifetime.

To explain briefly: our supplier failed miserably to fulfil his commitments – an American supplier by the way; our warehouse in Columbus lost 100,000 units due to the Great Roof Cave-In; and we used faulty judgement in believing that 1-plus million units, together with continuing receipts, would cover the promotion.

One cannot guarantee that events of this nature will never happen again. One can only try harder. Every "freebe" is meant to be available in good supply, just as every Blockbuster is meant to be fully available and meant to sell out 100%. We do not, in brief, subscribe either to the theory of bait-advertising or switch-out advertising.

Much, however, can be learned from disaster if the latter does not destroy one's equilibrium. Rain checks can be issued. Names and phone numbers can be collected for future personal contacts. Substitutes can be cheerfully offered. And apologies can be turned into warmer relations if the apologist treats the problem as an opening, rather than a closing.

I have been answering complaints by mail for 26 years and have never – assuming I felt the plaintiff justified, as he/she is in 95% of the cases – lost a customer or failed to make a friend for *Radio Shack*. The reason is elementary. Desire!

And my desire to make a friend has never forced me to "knock" our Company. Far from it. When I get through, the company appears more warm, human and personal than ever before. Humanity includes frailty. This season the free flashlight was the perfect example of our humanity.

The next time we goof, don't hang up a sign that says "out of flashlights." Instead, make it your job to salvage another unusual opportunity to win friends and influence customers.

Turning failure into success has been our "finest hour" at Radio Shak. I can assure you it wasn't done by crying over spilled advertising!

MARCH 1975
"Every Crisis is an Opportunity"

A POPULAR SELF-MADE ECONOMIST named Harry Browne wrote these words in the prologue of his latest book. Right up near the front. Because that's the reason for the book. The book is a best-seller. Mr. Browne will make a killing by doing a very simple thing: telling you how to turn bad news into good news. And now it's my turn.

SALES GAINS: while everybody's sliding, we're ascending. That says a lot about our policies of (1) holding the line on prices, (2) extra price cuts to keep things humming, (3) extra ads to let people know, (4) opening new stores and creating new sales-management jobs.

MORE SATISFIED CUSTOMERS: we're improving our sales training and repair and delivery services, and not cutting any corners to do so. Complaints that didn't get handled in the field get fast action from your Management and you get notified on how you failed to save us (and eventually) the trouble. The number of "very pleased" letters I get is gratifying. Glad or mad, every customer-crisis letter is an opportunity.

STOCK PRICE RISES: when the market turned it recognized *Tandy* Corporation and we more than doubled our "low." Your next Savings Plan statement should restore your faith in investing in yourself. Plenty of our alleged competition failed to duplicate our performance on Wall Street.

DEALER BUSINESS IMPROVES: despite the crisis you read about in the papers concerning retail sales in general, our dealers in the ASC program – over 800 independent small-town businessmen – are buying more of our products than ever before and for cash, not credit. This tells me that the grass roots of our country are far from dormant. You don't re-order when goods aren't selling. Maybe we're replacing some of the vanishing American and Japanese brands? Maybe we're simply filling a void? Either way there's action in Podunk, and I don't mean to belittle the hinterlands. Most folks out there wouldn't trade what they've got for love or money.

SHORTAGES ARE VANISHING: when backlogs dry up a funny thing happens – costs stabilize and begin to fall. Our Buyers are no longer desperate to hold the line. Our vendors are desperate to hold our business! All this in 12 short months! More opportunity born of crisis!

They don't give me nearly enough space to illustrate all of the opportunities we've scrounged from all the crises we've faced in recent years, Maybe it's because paper is too expensive? Ah, so? Next month it may be too cheap!

APRIL 1975
How to Sell a Dog

A DOG IN RETAIL-ESE IS A PRODUCT THAT WON'T MOVE when the salesman says "Sic 'em." A dog is product nobody asks for. And there are always too many in stock even if one should sell by accident. And finally, dogs are created – not just born; a dog is the creation of a merchandiser who couldn't say "No."

But the usual dog is simply an item priced above the general market's notion of the right price. The minute the "right price" is arrived at, the dog suddenly becomes a different animal altogether. And thereby – pun intended – hangs a tale. In 1964 we had a surfeit of teak speakers. Walnut had taken over the speaker cabinet scene. Mahogany was a dog. Blond was a dog. Unfinished was a dog. But teak was the dog we owned and it was, again in retail-ese, coming out of our ears. That's the way retailers talk: picturesque, tough, and overstocked.

The simple combination of a salesman's spiff and a small discount sold us out of teak speakers so fast you wanted to try maple or white, two of the greatest no-nos in the audio business.

What happened? Our salesmen suddenly found their tongues. Instead of trying to take an order they started trying to MAKE an order. Briefly, teak speakers became the rage at *Radio Shack*.

I've often wished we had re-ordered them because teak is a beautiful wood. Never mind. We'll create another dog and repeat the cycle. I'm almost inclined to think dogs are necessary in any inventory. Because they make salesmen reach and exercise their skills. There's nothing that weakens salesmanship like an easy sell which can be credited to (a) the customer's actual stated need, or (b) the pull of advertising.

You sell a dog by pure unalloyed desire, not by standing around hoping for miracles and taking orders for best-sellers. In everyone's store – just as in everyone's basement or garage – there's a dog waiting patiently for his master's voice.

So speak up! Or man's best friend will be around you for a long, long time,, patiently waiting for its value to go to zero.

MAY 1975
The Distaff Side

THIS IS JUST ABOUT MY 5TH ANNIVERSARY MESSAGE — the fifth year I've been in this office – and I figure it's about time I recognized *Radio Shack's* wives. Yours and mine. They put up with a lot. You and me.

The "little woman" of a retailer has to expect to see her husband less often than what's normal for many white collar families. If she doesn't know this – tell her.

I have countless friends who haven't worked a Saturday in their entire lives, thus in my 26½ years at *Radio Shack* I've worked at least a part of 1325 days longer than they have. An extra 3.6 years longer. Some have had, as teachers, sabbaticals in addition to more and longer vacations.

If you want a lot of time off, friends, don't get into retailing. Be sure your wife knows the kind of business you're in! Long hours don't necessarily make you heroic. When I was overseas in WWII I had nothing but hours and I sure wasn't heroic. You just have to put out or change the game you are playing. And the lady of your house can make a whale of a difference in the way she accepts these realities. And the different impact on you as well as her.

None of us has to become a retailer. Or remain one. Those of us who have made it a lifetime career think the compensation far outweigh the overtime.

The benefits include job security, eventual better pay, more opportunities for creativity, an unusual amount of independence, and the chance to succeed far beyond the average of our peers.

No doubt about it – The Love of Your Life can make yours a rather hollow victory. But she can also drive you to succeed in ways more subtle than those available to your superior on the corporate stepladder who is supposed to motivate you onward and upward.

I don't really care where your drive comes from so long as you have it. But my bet hunch is that behind most of our winners there's a woman. And both of you are to be congratulated on your good taste and judgement.

JULY 1975
Received "With Interest"

ON APRIL 12, 1961, A CERTAIN MR. HILL of Alabama was sent a letter by the then *Allied Radio Corporation* asking him to remit a balance due of $2.27 on a mail order. *Allied* was never again to hear from Mr. Hill and the $2.27 debt on a $7.27 purchase was never received.

Never received, that is, until May 13, 1975, when the same Mr. Hill mailed us the *Allied* bill and enclosed the $2.27 owed. Plus 73¢ interest.

Almost 15 years late to the day, Mr. Hill wrote this very moving line; "Sorry I did not have the money at the time this (invoice) was mailed, then it got lost in my papers. Please accept my apology, with interest."

I am much impressed by the nature of Mr. Hill's papers; they must be unusually comprehensive to go back a decade and a half. But it's quite clear that the quintessence of humanity we call "conscience" is of supreme importance to his man. The $2.27 debt was heavy. The 73¢ interest – which should have been perhaps $2.04 – had great meaning to him.

One may speculate about a number of things. (a) What if the debt was $227.00 instead of $2.27? (b) is the $2.27 – now $3.00 – the property of *Allied Radio Shack Electronics, Radio Shack*, or even? (c) How much more could be collected in this manner if all *ex-Allied/Shack* non-payers paid up?

The answer to (c) is easy: *Radio Shack* is $3.00 richer because the cost to take it away from us would exceed that amount in the lawyer's letter.

The answer to (a) is moot. One would like to believe in a nation of Mr. Hills but, alas, reality prevails and our security people are encouraged not to wait for a second coming.

In this respect I am reminded that when Diogenes went out in search of an honest man it took him a hell of while to find even one. Less than 15 years . . . but how much less?

AUGUST 1975
Thank You, Mr. *Tandy*!

I DON'T THINK IT'S TOO LATE to throw a bouquet in the specific direction of our Chairman. He would be the last person to claim authorship of the employee's stock purchase plan. Therefore, I'm taking the liberty to tell the facts as I see them. Programs such as the stock plan don't just happen. Somebody has to want them to happen. As long as I have been with the Corporation I've observed that somebody is Mr. T.

Many companies, including the "old" *Radio Shack*, have benefits like stock options. The latter are almost always for the so-called chosen few. We don't have any stock options. We don't have any chosen few.

Tandy savings and stock-purchase plans are for everyone who's qualified. YOU do the choosing. This has caused some of you to wonder what's in it for the Corporation. Because, frankly, you're not exactly accustomed to being included in the distribution of "goodies" where you have been before. These belonged to The Boss. But not to THIS Boss. And that's a fact.

The idea behind these programs is to help employees plan: primarily for retirement, secondarily for dire emergency, thirdly for general peace of mind. Mr. Tandy sees us all as part of a family to which he has supreme responsibility: not to lead you automatically into The Promised Land, but rather into a land with real promise, with you doing your part to make it happen.

Our collective efforts have helped him build a large, profitable, growing business. The several plans are simply his way of recognizing our contribution. And he has said many times that there's no way under our tax system of building an estate merely from earned wages.

If you are not in BOTH plans you are less likely to build an estate for the distant future. Perhaps you're not aware of this? Or perhaps you don't care enough to make the effort? I hope you'll review the situation with your supervisor.

But this essay is not a harangue on your need for taking care of yourself. In the last analysis, that's a private matter. I want to finish what I started out to do – pay tribute to someone who really cares about people and puts his concern right out on the table for all to see and share.

In his chair . . . would you have done it? Would I?

SEPTEMBER 1975
Learn to Please

SOMEWHERE THE FIGHTING BRITISH PRIME MINISTER, Sir Winston Churchill, is supposed to have said: *"If you mean to profit, learn to please."* This is particularly potent advice for businessmen. But it is also heavy with meaning for individuals and groups engaged in any endeavor – be it preaching, politicking, or even romancing.

Learning to please some types of customers is a genuine problem. Explaining why we are out of CB, for example. Or why they had to wait so long for a repair. Our manuals don't always explain these things.

Learning to please the customer who bought something – but at another store, not yours – and wants immediate service, is a typical situation requiring you to think twice about Winnie's little aphorism. It needs to be repeated here that no customer is YOUR customer . . . but all of them are OUR customers, regardless of whether our customer comes from a company, franchise, ASC, or other store near you or remote from you. Please him and you will profit. Send him back to Store X and we'll lose. It's that simple.

The phone calls and letters received by Mr. Tandy or myself invariably relate to store personnel who have failed to please. And invariably they GET PLEASED, often in a manner more costly to the company than it would have been had you "pleased" the first time you had the chance.

Some failures result from a direct breach of policy – not honoring a battery card or a sales price. But most are the result of broken communications between the customer's alleged problem and your alleged interest in its solution. A customer is only interested in himself, not in your difficulties or those occurring somewhere in The System. When we tell him he can get served at ANY store, we mean it, and there's a way to do it. Sooner or later, you too will believe it and ultimately reap the rewards of pleasing.

The place that pleases is the place that gets returned to. *Radio Shack* hasn't become #1 by giving lip service. Learn how to please. Learn today. Tomorrow is 24 hours too late.

OCTOBER 1975
The Game Plan

ABOUT A YEAR AGO I WROTE in this space something to the effect that *Radio Shack* was not going to have a recession just because the latter was in vogue. We didn't, thanks to the power of positive thinking and your extra efforts. And in case you're wondering: we're not going to have one this year either!

We've already gone through a quarter of the fiscal year with excellent results. However, our second quarter, October through December, is crucial to any retailer's full year results and we are no exception. If you're a seller: SELL. If you're in a factory: BUILD AND SHIP. If you're not exactly either – like most of us – then think of *Radio Shack* for all your gift giving, and, since you're going to be a buyer: BUY OUR GOODS.

If you're in doubt as to what *Radio Shack* is planning to help the antirecessionary forces in this country:

-- We intend to open 500 new stores to continue our efforts to bring each market area up to the standards of the best markets.

-- We intend to open another 400 ASC stores. Often called dealer stores, these are located in towns under 20,000 population and retain the original operator's store name. ASC means Authorized Sales Center.

-- We intend to do about $120,000,000 in company-owned manufacturing here and abroad, a 50% increase.

-- The above involve several thousand new jobs; more leases and signs and fixtures and inventory.

-- And we intend to soar in retail sales in North America to well above $600,000,000.

If this isn't a Game Plan for lots of activity and no recession, I'll eat my *Tandy* stock in Independence Square.

NOVEMBER 1975
A Loss of Innocence?

A "LOSS OF INNOCENCE" ABOUT AMERICA'S GROWTH potential and invincibility is the concern of a professor of marketing at USC. This means simply that large numbers of Americans no longer believe we can keep up with our needs of a progressive (in numbers) society, or defend our principles and our allies anywhere in the world – perhaps not even at home.

He cites the following additional phenomena: a rise in cynicism for authority; a desire to hang loose and await the outcome of events; a change in aspirations from power and acquisitiveness to natural simplicity and sensuality; a trend toward complying about goods and services and away from practical remedies.

There's a little bit of truth in all of the above. And a large bit of baloney. In the *Wall Street Journal* another guy thinks we're all suffering from "an overdose of perpetual fault-finding." There's a lot of truth in that, and hardly any baloney.

These sentiments, however, affect every one of us in the way we feel about our country, our democratic way of life, our outlook on private vs government management of money and the creation of jobs.

I happen to think that acquiring things and owning things isn't vulgar and is an inherent right of every person. If that makes me a materialist, so be it.

In my heart of hearts I happen to have a smidgen of jealousy for the "flower children" of recent times – not the ones who scar and maim, but the ones who dare and dream. If that makes me somewhat sympathetic toward the Pepsi generation, so be that as well.

I also happen to like a little mythology with my everyday cold, alleged facts. Even with proof positive that you can't throw a buck across the Potomac or that all Presidents were liars, womanizers, megalomaniacs, and tools of big business, I think The System is still working.

If that makes me a naïve American, or even an ugly American, well let's face it – I've got to stand for something!

DECEMBER 1975
The Whole World's Watching

RADIO SHACK IN THE WEEK OF SEPTEMBER 7, 1975 opened its first and only store in France; in Toulouse, to be exact. And in December we will open two stores in Tokyo, Japan. As of the week ending 9/13/75 we had 357 overseas shops in operation and these had achieved sales of $6,318,507 since July 1.

By our way of reckoning these are not big numbers. Yet *Radio Shack* probably didn't hit a sales number that big until about 1956 – after 33 years of trying to amount to something in the world of electronics.

In the few years we've been trying to master the intricacies of marketing in foreign countries with their differing customs, language and regulations, we have yet to make our first nickel of profit. Au contraire: we've lost money.

We are now in the process, painful to some and progressive to others, of changing some of our coaches and players. You'll read the news or hear about it through the gossip mill. But one thing's for certain: we've lost neither heart nor determination.

Without even opening a shop in Rome we know full well that Rome wasn't built in a day or even a year. We will have to be patient, even as we were with Canadian operations; even as *Tandy* Corporation was with the 1963 to 1967 *Radio Shack*; even as we were when we first ventured seriously into manufacturing in Fort Worth, in Iowa, in New Jersey, in Canada, in Japan, and finally in Korea.

A receptive audience for *Radio Shack's* product line and business technique exists in every country we've entered. The combined populations of overseas locations is far bigger than that of the USA and Canada together. Who's to say it can't be done?

Our company hasn't gotten to its present size and shape without taking very substantial risks. And without plowing back profits to finance these risks. On balance, all of our risks and risk-takers have been well rewarded by our achievements.

They say: a good thing is worth waiting for. Companies that sit back on their duffs really don't have anything to wait for. Except perhaps the Hereafter. And by the time they get there they may – quien sabe? – find a few hundred *Radio Shack* stores open for business despite the extreme heat!

JANUARY 1976
How to Make Money

THE FOLLOWING NOT-TOO-BRILLIANT STATEMENT comes from a recent article in Forbes magazine: "Concepts by themselves to not make money. You make money sale by sale and order by order."

No! No! That's what W. T. Grant did – sale by sale and order by order. *Grant's* went into Chapter XI substantially because of a poor concept which culminated in the loss of enormous sums of money.

If the writer meant that "pure" concepts – ideas that are verbalized but not executed – can't make money then, of course he was correct. You can't do much by just talking, only by putting plans into action. It seems to me that the entire discount-store concept isn't such a great concept even though sales are made in large numbers.

Sears, Ward, Penney and – yes – *Radio Shack*, have proven rather conclusively that good concepts make good business. Good business, in turn, is intensely involved with the making of money. What, I wonder, is the basic concept of New York City? – they certainly have plenty of sales!

Radio Shack's concept is deceptively simple: (1) lots of small stores, (2) small numbers of stockkeeping units continually weeded for losers, (3) tight control of the numbers, (4) a carefully controlled and profitable product line, (5) competitive pricing, (6) aggressive advertising, and (7) good, honest, hard-working, well-rewarded people. Every reader of this piece is in some way tied into every segment of the concept.

As we enter our bicentennial year, we can be thankful we have a concept that really works – both in our business and in our nation. Other businesses and other nations are not so fortunate, regardless of their GNP and conceptualized endeavors.

Keep it working, and the sales and orders will – almost – take care of themselves.

FEBRUARY 1976
The Naked Truth

NOW THAT RADIO SHACK IS A BIG-TIME SPENDER in media advertising in the country – media being newspapers, television, radio and magazines – I get asked a lot of questions which deserve answers. For example:

(1) Why don't we use Larry Czonka instead of Arthur Fiedler to endorse our hi-fi? Answer: the latter is a bona fide, believable music personality, the former is simply an unbelievable bull of an athlete. Note: this answer doesn't satisfy young people, but I like it.

(2) Why don't we use someone more famous (or tougher, etc.) than Paul Burke on TV? Answer: Burke fulfills our requirements – he's neither too young nor too old, he's neither too retiring or too brash, he's neither unknown nor so well known that his presence detracts from our merchandise offering, nobody can totally dislike him, and he has reasonable "class" – an undefinable aura of achievable good breeding.

(3) Why don't we advertise a line of items instead of a single item? Answer: My permanent instinct is to ask for an order for a specific item because it produces measurable results. Note: to be specific you also have to quote a price.

(4) Why don't we use beautiful women I our ads? Answer: how can you ask for an order for a piece of merchandise when you are distracted by pulchritude?

(5) Why don't we advertise on radio? Answer: aside from the fact that we usually spend 100% of our budget in other media, use of radio has seemed ineffective either because we misused it, or it actually wasn't a good medium. However, on December 26, 1975, we went on the Paul Harvey News morning drive-time show for 52 weeks at the rate of one 60-second spot per week, 641 stations, 4-kilobucks per spot or $66.67 per second, so now we'll see.

(6) Why don't we advertise in *Penthouse* and other girl/boy magazines? Answer: we're in Playboy which, compared to other sexy publications is relatively tame. But I don't even like *Playboy*, really, as a place to be seen. The rest of the hi-fi industry appears in most of them, regardless of the actual or implied promiscuity.

Somehow, in the final analysis, I guess I'm more of a prude than I's thought I was when, years back, I desired D. H. Lawrence, Joyce and Henry Miller to be openly distributed. They were artists and I haven't changed on that. But since their time, "freedom to publish" has gone far, far beyond my ability to rationalize it. And that's what I mean: the naked truth.

MARCH 1976
You Gotta Have Heart

REMEMBER THAT MUSICAL COMEDY SONG? Tandy Corporation eminently qualifies as a Big Business with a big heart. Not just a bleeding heart filled with corn and sympathy. *"Today is one of the proudest days in my business life"* said your Chairman in his February 9 letter to *"over 7,000 employees receiving shares (of stock) who had the foresight to plan for their future."*

Our Stock Purchase Program – whether the stock is in orbit or hitting new lows – is positive proof that your Company has a heart where you're concerned. From May to December of 1975 participants bought over 243,000 shares on the Plan. The Company contributed matching funds of not less than 40% to your purchase. Cash, not promises. Instantly vested in you, not withheld until your antiquity. Yes, Ethyl, I got my share and it's resting very comfortably in our safety deposit box.

Did you get your share? Or are you among the group which thinks there's a catch in it somewhere? Or are you among the group which couldn't possibly put away 1% to 19% of your earnings for some (I'm forced to say "lousy") reason? You should have *your* heart examined! And your head, too, because *you've turned down a raise.*

A raise? Here's how. You make $5,000 a year gross. You invest 5% or $250 in the Plan. You've worked less than 4 years for the Company so the Company's contribution is 40% of yours, or $100. That's a raise of 2%. If you'd been with us 4 years, the contribution would have been 60% or $150. That's a raise of 3%. If you'd worked just one more year, the contribution would have been 80% or $200, a raise of 4%. People who don't like raises aren't my kind of people. And people who can convince themselves that saving money is impossible at ANY age or ANY salary level are unfair both to themselves and their families. Heartless, in fact.

You gotta have heart! Miles and miles of heart. There are over 7,000 fine people in the various *Tandy* companies who'll tell you exactly where to find it. And since I'm one, don't be bashful – phone me *COLLECT* at (817) 335-3711 and ask me!

APRIL 1976
An Open Letter to Mrs. Selma Reeves

DEAR MRS. REEVES:

Our Chairman has given me your letter to answer. I am taking the liberty of publishing both your letter and my response in The *Intercom.*

As of the February 21 sales report your new store is running at a better rate than the average of our new "company" stores. Neither of us can complain about that. Typically an SMIA store will yield a better volume of sales than our other types of outlets. In this instance it's nice to be typical!

I have previously written an editorial in praise of Manager's wives. I should know . . . my only daughter-in-law is among this group. And, as is obviously the case with you, she's a great boon to her husband and his store. Praise is not; however, what we're working for, delightful as it is. We work for two things: (1) a living, hopefully better than average and, (2) satisfaction in our work. Fulfillment of these two motives is something only observable by the fulfilled.

We have never assumed that women are second-class citizens. First-class citizenship is guaranteed to all of us by the Constitution and Bill of Rights. Sometimes the difference between second-class and first-class is society's fault. But sometimes the fault lies with the citizen who *feels* down-rated. The best response is to do something about it. One hopes, also, that society will improve its perceptions of class B.

If you'll pardon my feeble attempt at witticism, we have not, judging from the birth notices, *pregnantly omitted working wives."* As William Shakespeare once said: "Tis a consummation devoutly to be wished."

In fact, Mrs. Reeves, we *never* omit wives – working or otherwise. Some nationalities feel we *include* them too much. Maybe the reason for this is that women like you have succeeded even better than your realize?

Appreciatively,

Lewis Kornfeld
(Mr. Ethel Kornfeld)

MAY 1975
Another Kudo for CDT

SINCE 1902, THE MAGAZINE FINANCIAL WORLD has been a faithful observer of the world of commerce including the securities market and the men behind the companies whose success makes it possible for there to be a meaningful "financial world" in America. It has just selected (3/15/76 issue) Charles D. Tandy as one of the top 10 chief executive officers of 1976. And #1 in the category of Specialty and Other Retail Stores.

"One business that intrigued him in 1962," says the magazine, "has become the company's mainstay today – electronics. He turned *Radio Shack*, a sickly company in the early sixties, into the world's largest electronics specialty-retail chain."

The winning of awards is nothing new to Mr. Tandy, but this sort of acclaim, from professionals in the nation's business press, is a bit novel. Surely it must be gratifying to the guy who came to Boston in 1963 and told the few of us there assembled at *Radio Shack* (few, because that's all he said he needed and could afford) three most unusual things.

First: "Call me Charles." Second: "We're going to open a lot of stores." Third: "I won't settle for less than being Number One in this business."

We called him Charles right away. The other two items took us quite a bit longer. But achieve them we did – we and you – and it's a fair statement that we have substantially exceeded the bravest dream of April 4, 1963, the day on which it all began for the modern *Radio Shack*.

The word kudo which I used in the title of this piece comes from the Greek word kydos, which means glory. We all get a little when someone in our Company is recognized for meritorious conduct. But as our award-winning CEO would say, we don't add any points to our stock by standing around congratulating ourselves. So let's get back to work and beat the hell out of last June. Okay?

JUNE 1976
Who Needs a Secret?

IN A RECENT INTERVIEW WITH THE YOUTHFUL EDITOR of *Chain Store Age* magazine, I was asked: What is the real secret of *Radio Shack's* success?" My answer was – as it has been ever since we became famous –that there isn't any secret. We've told everyone exactly what we are going to do before we did it. We've done everything we said we were going to do.

To some people this sort of consistent behavior is quite surprising. They will be surprised when we do it next year in fiscal 1977. They are surprised by CB too.

No one really wants to believe we've been in CB since 1959. They'd prefer to think we latched onto it in 1974 or 1975, because that's what so many other businesses have done. And they already want to know what's going to replace CB after it drops dead.

Why should CB drop dead? It shouldn't and it won't. But the quick-buck crowd will have many fatalities when history inexorably repeats itself and zeros out businesses whose "secret" is to be opportunistic and inconsistent. Stereo isn't going to drop dead either, nor will calculators, but these are notions firmly held by grown-up people.

There's quite a bit of morbid curiosity about what will happen when "*Shack* has opened all the stores it can in the USA?" There are several ways of looking at this intriguing question, not the cleverest being that the earth stopped growing 4- or 40-million years ago but it keeps on getting bigger. I can say with certainty that we will not have any secrets beyond a consistent plan that can be executed by normal human beings capable of deducting themselves to success, via hard work. Period.

Much of the above applies to this country which, contrary to early and recent expectations, hasn't dropped dead in any of the past 200 years. Likewise America has no secrets; and those it intended to have seem to get published anyway. America's plan was laid out in black and white in 1776. Anyone could have copied most of it, but nobody did, and it has become a silly notion that American democracy is too delicate to travel. Okay then, let's have a happy 200th birthday all by our lonesome. Believe me there's a lot to celebrate, not the least of which is that nobody's going to catch up with us in your lifetime.

JULY 1976
One Hundred Years from Now

I'VE DEBATED WITH MYSELF FOR MANY MONTHS on the question of what (if anything) to say in this space about the 200th birthday of this country. It should be obvious by not that any reader that this is the best and safest place in the world for working, saving, learning, medical care, bringing up families, and for thinking, saying, and publishing anything that comes to mind. There shouldn't be any need to discuss anything so obvious as the foregoing. But, alas, there is.

The memory of man is pathetically short. He forgets two centuries of progress. He doesn't see himself as a link in a never-ending chain. He has no historic sense of gratitude. He knows more about Tom Jones than Tom Paine. He hasn't the faintest idea about what keeps his society on the tracks, but it can hardly be politicians because "they're all crooks." And as for patriotism, that's embarrassing and undignified: pornography, on the other hand, well, that's a human right.

Fortunately, America is more than people. No person has lived for 200 years. But America has. America is people too; and it is also ideas, places, things, myths and beliefs. In a world where results count, America is No. 1 by a country mile.

My late, old, unhappy Aunt used to say: "It will not all be the same a hundred years from now." In line with these sentiments if not that meaning, I think it's about time we make plans for America's tercentenary and start celebrating just a little bit at a time from July 5th on. What could be more certain than the USA in 2076, still out front with egg all over its shirt, ever the envy and wonder of this incredible planet?

AUGUST 1976
About the New FCC Rules Concerning CB Radio

BECAUSE CB HAS BECOME such an important part of our business, it's IMPORTANT to sort out the facts and fancies surrounding the late July FCC rule changes based on data available July 29, 1976.

The most significant change increases the number of channels from 23 to 40 on radios which may *not* be offered for sale prior to January 1, 1977 and which first must be FCC type accepted not earlier than September 10, 1976.

FACT: 1-channel to 40-channel radios whose manufacture began prior to January 1, 1977 must meet some very stringent new FCC requirements, particularly in respect to the receiver section. Such sets cannot be manufactured after August 1, 1977 unless or until they met the new specs. This means that all sets in all CB lines, including *Realisitic*, must be altered in some respect if their manufacture is to continue after August 1, 1977. Unaltered radios in this group may be sold up to February 1, 1978 – meaning the balance of 1976 and all of 1977.

FANCY: Sets in current or prior manufacture can't be used after February 1, 1978. This is NOT TRUE. All such sets may be used by owners now, next year, and probably for all time to come. There is NO reason to fear the obsolescence of ANY CB RADIOS ever sold by us or sold by us at any future permissible time.

FACT: CB radios whose manufacture begins after December 31, 1976 will have to meet new FCC specs. Sets introduced after 1/31/78 will have to meet even tougher requirements.

FANCY: Sets whose first-time manufacture occurred before January 1, 1977 can continue being made as-is until August 1, 1977 and continue being sold through January 31, 1978.

FACT: The number of permissible channels has been increased from 23 to 40.

FANCY: This means that 23-channel sets won't be as useful and won't sell. This is NOT TRUE. Most CB users employ Channel 19 for road conditions and general listening and this will continue indefinitely. They use Channel 9 for emergency calls and this will continue indefinitely. Thus even a 3-chanel TRC-9A is as useful and saleable now as it ever was.

FACT: All sets made after 12/31/77 will have permanently affixed serial numbers.

FACT: Channel 11 is released from call-only to general purpose.

SEPTEMBER 1976
5,000 = 1,000,000,000

NOW HERE'S A FORMULA ANYONE CAN UNDERSTAND: 5,000 = 1,000,000,000. The five "grand" is the number of *Radio Shack* outlets recently reached, including dealer and overseas stores. The billion is the amount of retail sales dollars we anticipate doing in the year July 1, 1976 through June 30, 1977.

These are staggering numbers. These are numbers of which we can all be extremely proud, because they have been achieved by people, not the chance discovery of oil fields or the accidental good fortune of inheritance. They have been achieved by the reinvestment of earnings and the investment of outsider's' dollars, not by government loans or frequent acquisitions.

Assuming our shops are open 365 days of the year, the sale of a billion dollars' worth of goods will be painstakingly arrived at by selling $2,739,726 of goods per day, 7 days a week. I want to remind you that when I arrived at *Radio Shack* (fiscal 1949) our sales were just short of $1,000,000 a year – or $2,739.73 a day! Don't bother figuring . . . we're each 1,000 times better than the *Shack* of 27 years ago.

But there's a funny thing about the right-hand side of my equation: the billion in sales doesn't come automatically or easily. Every day is a new ball game, a new threat, a new challenge. Unlike manufacturing, retailing does not have the blessing of a backlog; there's not a single buck of backlog in retail selling.

After a brief pat on the back for what we've done for all of our 20,075 yesterdays, all Wall Street really cares about is what we're going to do tomorrow. And if you tell them "a billion," sure as hell they'll say, "and then what?"

"And then what?"

That's the neat way life has of never letting a winner rest on his laurels. And so . . . please don't. Even billionaires have to run scared!

OCTOBER 1976
Find a Taller One

FROM A MAGAZINE STORY I GLEAN this exceptionally quotable quote: "After you've climbed one peak, the next goal should be obvious: find a taller one." This is not too far from Oscar Hammerstein's desire that you "climb every mountain 'till you find your dream." But there is a difference.

Our unknown author is more practical, less idealistic. Instead of seeing life as a never-ending search for the grail of grails, he offers a pathway built of one achievement after another, a blueprint for living that is well within the limitations of folks like ourselves.

I think the essence of both statements is the necessity of having a plan, a daily plan, a several-year plan, and a master plan.

If you don't know what you're going to do today – until you've started doing it – you are living in a random manner that will get you nowhere but part way tomorrow, that will find you no better off than yesterday and very uneasy about next week.

Make lists – written or tape recorded. Make agendas for doing. Make reviews of everything up to now. Then establish acceptable and reasonable goals for tomorrow, next week, next month, the current year. Don't keep these goals a secret. A shared goal becomes a meaningful challenge. A secret goal is like a calendar without numbers. Nothing motivates like a spoken or written promise.

This is why we publish sales goals. This is why each period's goals are a bit (or a lot) higher than previous goals. This is why we have savings and stock purchase plans: to reach and then surpass previous plateaus of security.

The first thing you tell a child is that she or he "can do better" and on this point you are extremely specific. Not instantly better in ALL things. Instantly better in ONE thing.

In terms of making our Billion Dollar Breakthrough happen, what is your part of the plan? Can you describe the taller peak that is your "obvious" goal? Write it down where your associates can see it. It won't happen unless you find the courage and character to "go public."

DECEMBER 1976
Santa Claus?

DON'T GIVE ME YOUR NITPICKERS who say the rock in Plymouth really isn't THE rock the Pilgrims stepped on in 1620. I have seen and touched this rock and I have been well satisfied with it for 60 years from all points of view: size, shape, material, color and location.

Please spare me confrontation with the expert who can prove that George Washington couldn't have thrown a silver dollar across the Potomac, and that the whole cherry tree incident was made up by somebody with a deadline to meet.

I never hope, as a matter of fact, to meet either the alleged mistresses of our rather recently past President or to know the whole truth and nothing but the truth concerning these antics even if directly from the lips of those who made the discoveries plus 16 x 20" color enlargements of the alleged trysters and trysting places. There are important beliefs and unimportant beliefs – it's just that simple.

And so you can bet "bet your sweet bippy" (quotation from an anonymous source, exact meaning unknown) I believe in Santa Claus.

It is utterly irrelevant to try to persuade me that Santa Claus does not exist, and exist in the exact manner as perceived by me. The dictionary blathers on about how his name is "corrupted" from a Russian patron saint, who was a bishop in Myra, Asia Minor, died in about 345 A.D, and was named Saint Nicholas. Humbug! I am not the least bit interested. My Santa Claus was born about Zero B.C./A.D. And, as previously noted, he is very much alive.

So alive is Santa Claus in this yet incomplete year of 1976, he sends to all (albeit through me, since I am fluent in Clausese) his "heartiest greetings" The Season and best wishes for your fiscal and physical well-being during The New Year." This is exactly what he said during our most recent interview, no an approximate translation. I doubt if I could top that. So I won't try.

JANUARY 1977
Money Grows in Texas

THE THEME OF THIS HAPPY NEW YEAR card from me to you is the title of a book written by Dallas stockbroker James Walker Davis. He took some 270 Texas-based companies and did some math on what would have happened had a person invested $1000 in any one of their stocks when first issued.

Well, dear *Tandy* person. $1000 put into *Tandy Corporation* stock in 1960, when "the company was initially available to the public," had a June 30, 1976 market value of precisely $80,390.62.

To say it simply: each of those 1960 dollars invested in *Tandy* common stock had grown by 1976 to $8.04. Your profit would have been $79,390.62. Further, since *Tandy* pays no dividend, you would have paid zero taxes to date on this gain.

Had you put $1000 into a 5% interest-paying bank account in 1960, and left the interest in the bank to compound, it would have had a 1976 value of $2182.87. Further, because bank interest is taxable, you would have paid an income tax on each year's interest for 16 years.

To say it simply: each of those 1960 dollars invested in TC stock in 1960, and $1000 invested in a savings bank in 1960 would look about like this:

```
1976 value of stock  . . . . . . . . . . . . . . . . . $80,390.62
1976 value of bank account . . . . . . . . . . . $  2,182.87
Difference . . . . . . . . . . . . . . . . . . . . . . . . . $78,207.75
```

Granted that on actual sale of the stock you would have plenty of taxes to pay. But the time and amount of sale is up to you. This is called "estate planning." And if you have a number like $78,207.75 to plan for, that, Good Buddy, is an estate" in anyone's language.

Granted that the June 30, 1976 stock value isn't a fixed , but a moving number, its 16-year record is a significant sample (over one-third of a person's working life!) of what could happen in the future if we do our jobs properly. Whereas the fixed $2,182.87 won't pay for either a proper pregnancy or a proper funeral.

Turn over 1977's new leaf and see what's on the other side. There may be something there for you that 'til now you hadn't thought about. Tomorrow!

FEBRUARY 1977
The Hager Proposition

FEW OF YOU KNOW HIM, BUT BOB HAGER is District Manager of 0535 in California, an ambitious man of relatively many words. He recently sent to six persons in your Management a 4–page single-spaced typed letter and a 240-page $1.95 book, mostly to make a single point.

The Hager Proposition is that by correct dress during working hours you can achieve "25% in additional sales in all stores." Not to listen to such a notion is to confess you're just not interested in a low-cost way of doing better. I have yielded to desire by reading both letter and (*Dress For Success*) book.

Let's forget about the little details such as pin-stripe width, tie color and sock length – author Molloy says never Never NEVER wear 'em ankle length. Let's play down the fabrics, textures and cuts. Let's go to the mat with plain old big/little/medium you.

When you are facing the public you are representing a billion-dollar worldwide Corporation. You may be the only representative of our Company your "trade" will ever see. What's equally important, assuming you're in one of our great employee estate-building programs, you're also an important stockholder.

Are YOU looking like what YOU expect YOU to look like under such conditions?

Are you looking like a guy or gal whom some consuming soul is likely to entrust with the details of a $500 audio system? Would you feel comfortable in *Tiffany's*? Would you buy a used car from YOU?

Not if you look like a clod, a waif, a GI reject, a down-at-the-heel amateur poet, or an up-on-the-heel faddist who just doesn't dare look square. If that's the way some or many of your customers look it's because they're still trying to avoid looking like Dad – a physiological problem you solved when you seriously considered the Hagar Proposition!

Clothes include such things as posture, hands and hair – both cut and length.

Unlike Bob, I'm not guaranteeing you a 25% sales gain. But a gain. A measurable gain. A gain in self-respect after the first shock of going conventional. And a gain in the way others see you and think about you, including your fitness for a promotion up the leadership and income ladder. Maybe a small gain. Then again, maybe 100%

March 1977
They Laughed When I Sat Down
to Play the *STA-2000*

WHEN I WAS A KID (AND BREAD WAS A DIME) there was a famous magazine ad whose headline read: "They Laughed When I Sat Down To Play The Piano . . . "You see (the ad said) they didn't know I'd been taking lessons in private, so quite naturally they laughed when I said I'd play." The ad was about learning to play in a hurry. This piece is about learning to overcome an obstacle.

For some time we believed *Radio Shack* couldn't sell anything – not one item – For $499.95. *Yes* if we block-busted it out for $299. *No* if we wanted to sell it at our regular unbusted price. Note: if you believe something long enough it's apt to become true. Note: so we didn't even try.

And then along came *TC Electronics*, our company-owned and company-operated factory in Tokyo. They needed an order – anything, so long as it was big. We dreamed up something we really didn't need, a hi-fi receiver to sell at $499.95, exactly $100 over our top (pre-markdown) price. In retrospect, TCE's need was to become our mutual gain.

So, *TC Electronics* entered into an unprecedented project and, in turn, *Radio Shack* entered into an unprecedented price point. We told *TCE*: your quality must be beyond reproach. We told our Managers: get out and sell it for $500, it CAN be done. There were plenty of disbelievers.

The project was put to R&D in May 1975; its nickname: *The Mach One Receiver*. Some 17 months later, in late October of 1976, it arrived in stock. Its real-life name: The *STA-2000.*

Here's what *High Fidelity* magazine (3/77 issue) concludes: "The *Realistic SA-2000* must be taken seriously, both in performance and appearance . . . its standing relative to other members of its price class is fully competitive . . . a receiver that neither the competition nor the value-conscious buyer should ignore.

Now perceive that reviews like this and products like *STA-2000* are exactly what *Radio Shack* needs to put *Realistic* into the new, higher orbit it deserves. And if they laugh when you try to sell 'em a stereo receiver for $499.95 without a discount, give 'em a sly look, bit of the buck and wing and some nifty soft shoe. And then you can tell it like it is: "IT'S SELLING!"

APRIL 1977
Next to Godliness

ONE OF THE GREATEST DIFFERENCES between our many *Radio Shack* stores is the way they look. Their appearance runs the gamut from super to super-sloppy. It may or may not show up on the P&L, the return on investment, or the Manager's bonus. But a super-sloppy store affects each and every one of us in the way that the outside world views *Radio Shack,* and this editorial is to remind those concerned that cleanliness is next to Godliness, as the saying goes.

What's the cause of bad housekeeping in a store? First, it may be a sign that the person responsible was badly brought up, had a family situation in which keeping things net wasn't important. Surely our sloppy Manager and our Laissez-faire District Manager haven't learned this bad habit from observing the décor of the neighboring stores: most of their neighbors are neat as a pin regardless of the traffic they serve or the number of stock keeping units they house..

Secondly, it may be that they just don't give a damn. Okay. Go mess up a K-Mart or a *True Value* store. We'll count our blessings.

There is a third possibility. Perhaps you just need help and don't know how to get it. My phone number is (817) 390-3212 and Bill Nugent's is 390-3211. What's next to Godliness is cleanliness, and by gosh nobody's ever said what's next to cleanliness. It's Management, old pal, so don't say you don't know if you get asked.

Of course, if you're running a *Radio Shack* you ARE management. And it's Management's determination that you shall and must clean up your act. Get your Christmas signs down and – mercy! – get those toys outta there even if you only get a dime on the dollar. When we hit that billion-dollar mark next July, feel sharp, be sharp, and LOOK SHARP. Oh, Bob, oh Charlie, Marvin, Dean and Jim – Hope this is the last time I'll ever have to write this piece!

MAY 1977
Moving Advertised Merchandise

AS MOST OF THE FOLKS IN OUR STORE SYSTEM know, what's advertised in our monthly flyer is usually advertised during the same month in newspaper ads and often on network television as well. The biggest problem we have is NOT having the advertised merchandise in stock in the stores. And when it's not the fault of a delay in shipping from the factories or warehouses, the fault is yours, Mr. or Ms. Manager.

But there's another fault that's entirely yours, assuming you do have the merchandise. That's when you don't prominently display the items featured each and every month.

You're not supposed to hide these goods, not even supposed to display them in their traditional places within your store. They're supposed to be PUT OUT FRONT and made EASILY AVAILABLE to the traffic these ads are designed to bring in.

When we run a newspaper ad, it costs your Company anywhere from $350,000 to $650,000. When we run a TV ad we've spent about $400,000 in four days. When we run an insert we've laid out over $1,000,000 in a single day. When we mail a flyer you can kiss goodbye to over $1,200,000. And Jimmy – that ain't peanuts!

I haven't looked this matter up in the Store Operating Manual because from where I sit typing these notes (at home) it's just plain common sense, and the dumbest, greenest merchant is supposed to know it. So here is all the advice you need to become a Pro in five minutes:

Get that ad merchandise OUT FRONT TODAY! And at the end of the month, put it away and put next month's ad merchandise OUT FRONT!

Take down the old signs. Put up the new signs! First you'll make your supervisor look good. And next you'll find that when you AFTO it won't take up much of your valuable time. In fact it might not take any time at all, because your customer will lay it right on your warranty mat and all you'll have to do is write the order. Lots of people have become millionaires just by learning how to merchandise. If you don't believe me, just ask the Chairman. But just don't ask him more than once.

JUNE 1977
Fiscal 1977: A Great Year

SOME PEOPLE DON'T KNOW there's an "r" in FebRuary. And some don't know the difference between a "fiscal year" and a "physical" year. Well there's no such thing as a physical year. But our fiscal year ends on June 30, 1977. Some fiscal years end on December 31. Ours doesn't. Fiscal means "of or pertaining to financial matters generally." The day after June 30, 1977 is July 1, 1977. The latter is the first day of our 1978 fiscal year. And are we going to do better than fiscal 1977 — better believe it!

But let's not allow fiscal 1977 to pass into oblivion without a fond and proud farewell look. Considering the fact that most CB-related companies cratered during the past few months, with a fantastic drop in sales and a fabulous shower of red ink, we did pretty well. Our plan for leaving 23ch radios and getting into 40ch radios was appropriate to the situation forced upon us by the government's double shuffle of last July and the industry's glut. Our unmerited (unplanned) drop in the stock market was inappropriate to our results in sales and earnings.

Radio Shack also continued to open new outlets at a breakneck pace, finding both acceptable locations and ambitious new Managers in quantities unknown to business of any size. So welcome to all you new executives and your new places!

If we had a disappointment it was not breaking through the billion-dollar-sales mark; we missed it by 30 days of business, but in fiscal 1978, we'll go through it like a knife through butter.

Our business overseas finally looks like it is turning the corner, led by Australia and Belgium. And our company-owned manufacturing sales are now bigger than our fiscal 1971 retail sales; an incredible achievement any way you look at it.

Radio Shack has a lot going for it — and for you! So starting today; we won't look back, we won't rest on our laurels, we won't tolerate being No. 1 in a few categories of endeavor when we want, deserve, and have enough invested in products and people to become THE WORLD'S LARGEST ELECRONIC COMPANY in your lifetime!

JULY 1977
"When You're Through Innovating, You're Through"

THIS HEADLINE, BORROWED FROM another company's ad, says something extremely important to everyone at *Radio Shack*. We are a company and a product line that cannot be put on "automatic pilot." Too many have crashed as a result of complacency!

That's why I am delighted to report that our made-in-Texas, made by us, Micro Computer, the *Radio Shack TRS-80*, will be introduced in August as an innovative state-of-the-art product.

Industry experts who have seen the *TRS-80* say it will be a break-through in price (by at least 50% at this time) and are enthusiastic about its appearance, functions and timeliness.

We are enthusiastic for another reason. *TRS-80* will show the world that *Radio Shack* has an engineering and design capability far beyond the typical outsider's perception of us.

We get a lot of innovation via combining our merchandising know-how with the technical capabilities of non-owned vendors in many countries. But *TRS-80* is the first sweet fruit of company-operated, company-owned manufacturing in a new consumer electronic business: microcomputers. There is absolutely no question that micro computers are here, now and forever. There is no question in my mind that *TRS-80* is the most important product ever marketed by your Company.

Quite aside from the dollars we may invest or harvest, and not withstanding the number of units we produce and sell, *TRS-80* will enhance our technical image in a way no amount of TV or newspaper advertising could do.

You've seen it happen in a small way with the *STA-2000*. You ain't heard nuthin yet! *TRS-80* will be upgraded and added to (the buzz word is "peripherals"). And as the title implies, the entire world will soon know we're not through. Not Through! Only getting started!

AUGUST 1977
They Also Serve

DURING THE COURSE OF A YEAR, many people in the *Tandy* and *Radio Shack* organizations get public recognition in the form of press releases and quotations and awards. And yet, aside from the patient wives and families we've mentioned before, there are many key people whose important roles in the drama of our everyday business life goes entirely unnoticed.

For example, our VP Corporate Treasurer, Charles Tindall, is probably unknown to you. Yet "Charlie" is involved in every dollar we employ, every yen, every franc, every pound, mark or guilder used anywhere for any reason by your Company. In addition, he's our tax expert and most articulate (and informed) on matters of corporate inter-relationship, financial reporting and the like. He is never quoted publicly, seldom seen by employees – even local Fort Worth employees. The same is true of folks on his staff with names like Bock, Harding, Hughes, Cross and others.

I doubt many of you have seen or heard of our "legal lights" – Herschel Winn and Louis Neumann. The former is also VP Corporate Secretary. Lawyers are private people, eschewing advertising of their name and trade, seldom praised, often maligned. And yet the amount of *TC/RS* business in which they are heavily involved is really quite staggering. Chances are you wouldn't know them should they pass you in our hallowed halls.

To avoid hurt feelings – since even the anonymous are sensitive to slight – I'll drop no more names and close with the observation that for each of us who do get the PR and the plaques, there's an "unknown soldier" waging our battles, winning most of them.

It was John Milton who remarked, "They also serve who only stand and wait." We want to express our awareness of these many unsung notables who move the scenery, rent the halls, and prompt us when we forget our lines. Our awareness, ladies and gentlemen, and our gratitude.

SEPTEMBER
The $1,000,000 Challenge

DURING OUR 11 REGIONAL MEETINGS in August (nine in the USA and two in Canada) the Company has made the following offer to its "Company" Store Managers: Sell $1,000,000 worth of *Radio Shack* merchandise during fiscal year 1978 and make yourself an extra $10,000 – that's 10G on top of ALL other earnings and bonus!

The idea, like so many other good ones, is the brainchild of Charles Tandy. He's the kind of guy who believes there's nothing like a carrot to make a racehorse run faster. SO the question is – are you motivated by a $10,000 carrot? And incidentally, we'd like to have more than one winner. Many times more.

It's only natural to wonder if a store of ours – yours in particular – can do a megabuck's worth of business in 12 months. Many of our shops are now in the over $500 M range; the majority are below. Personally, I don't think the hurdle is too high, having been around when the 730 Commonwealth Avenue (Boston) exceeded that number and at 1961 prices, not inflated 1977-78 prices.

No one told Babe Ruth it was "impossible" to hit 60 home runs in a 20 home run league. No one told Jimmy Carter he couldn't go from Mr. Zero to Mr. President. He just kept on running.

And how's this for unmitigated gall: I'm TELLING YOU you can do a million this year. Here's how. First, you stop saying it can't be done – leave your mind open. Second, you start selling – make up your mind to add to the size of every sales ticket, any amount just as long as it's bigger than what the customer thinks you're writing. Third, you sell just TWO MORE HI-FI SYSTEMS PER WEEK – that notion alone will get you an extra $60,000 in sales. Fourth, you back every blockbuster with inventory – not just a token guesstimate. Fifth, you clean out your discontinued merchandise – that'll free up open to buy. Sixth, you display your goods like a merchant – not like a pawn-shop owner. Seventh, you HUSTLE – do everything faster than you did last year. Eighth, you believe in Santa Claus – believe me, pal, he's coming. Ninth, you believe in *Radio Shack* – the best game in town. Tenth – you believe in YOU – the lad who puts bread on the table.

My Ten Commandments will put Ten Grand in your pocket next August if you rise to the $1,000,000 challenge. And if you miss, you'll still (by trying) make the biggest bonus you've ever made. Man . . . or mouse? Fiscal-78 is the year you find out something very, very, VERY decisive about yourself!

NOVEMBER 1977
One Tandy Center

My first *Radio Shack* office was a place right out in the open. No walls. No windows. No doors. Everything that went on in my first office was entirely unprivate. Not knowing any better, I thoroughly enjoyed it. My second office had walls, a window and a door, but it was very small and radiator hissed and leaked. I liked that office, too, but no better than the first one. I spent 10 year in the first office and 13 years in the second; both were in old buildings in Boston.

My third office was also in an old building, but in Fort Worth, not Boston. A cut above the others in size and fittings, it still had a few problems. The ceiling leaked, the air-conditioner was erratic, the noise level was high due to machinery on the floor above, and it was occasionally visit by rats – large Texas style rats which ate pieces of the lower décor instead of the neatly laid out rat poison which no rat, not even a giant Texan, is dumb enough to eat. In something over 6 years I learned to like this office as well as the two previous offices. All of this liking, as you now perceive, has gone on over a period of 29-plus years, or just about the entire span of Percy Bysshe Shelley.

That brings us to my fourth office. October being the month we moved into our new 19-floor building at One Tandy Center in Fort Worth. It is mostly glass and, contrary to my prior office history, everything in it is as new as the building itself, perhaps embarrassingly so. Nevertheless, I expect to like it. Hopefully, from time to time I will reflect on all that our employees and investors and customers have contributed to this slow elevation from comparative rags to comparative riches.

Please come visit me. Each new office finds me just a little bit farther removed from the bustle and the hustle (but I still know where to find it).

Over these nearly three decades I've repeatedly observed something about people. If they don't like their specific place of work, be it an area or an office, and if they don't like their bosses, they're unhappy. And probably always will be. The glamor of One Tandy Center will be extremely fleeting for you if you are disenchanted; likewise the next meal, the next car, the next mate and next and next job.

But to those of us who like what we're doing and want to do more if it, the move to this or any other building is just like . . . going back home!

DECEMBER 1977
The Ultimate Battery Card

Should an attractive blue-eyed gentleman present the Free Battery Card in your store, my instructions are quite simple: HONOT IT. The card is unique. It's sealed in plastic. The basic difference between this card and our usual card is that instead of saying "1 Battery Each Month for 1 Year" it says "1 Battery Each Month for Life." There will be no similar card issued to anyone who is not, at the date of issue, President of the United States of America.

To further identify the cardholder, he will be about 5'11" in height, wearing a wedding ring. He is the President of the United States. He does have the card. He received it from me, personally, at the White House on November 10, 1977. Do not punch this card if it shows up in your store; we will have to take the small risk that it might be used more than the allotted once in any particular month. Having spent a bit more than an hour with this cardholder, I feel I can vouch for his character.

Now, friends, for the explanation. About a week prior to 11/7/77 I received a telegram invitation from Pres. Carter to visit with him and members of his staff – along with 29 other businessmen from around the country – for a buffet lunch and conference from 12:30 TO 3:30 P.M., ON THE 10TH. This being a signal honor for *Radio Shack* and *Tandy* Corporation, I passed up our annual stockholder's meeting and went, instead, to the White House. Getting in was not exactly easy, but after two misses I finally found the right gate and presented by Texas driver's license to the guards as identification (via a drive-in-bank type metal drawer). I walked to the front door of the West Wing and entered.

The President's cabinet-rank international trade advisor, the former Chairman of the Democratic Party, Robert Strauss, was our initial host. Affable, charming, homey, poised, and very dedicated. "A measure of this President's interest in reducing the cost of government," Strauss later quipped, "may be seen from the luncheon he serves." Sandwiches', egg or potato salad, relish tray, chocolate cake, white wine, coffee. Secretary Schlesinger sat at one end of the table. My old friend Sidney Harman (ex *Harmon-Kardon*, *Jervis* and *Bogen*), now Under Secretary of Commerce, greeted me warmly. At my request he introduced me to *Motorola* Chairman Galvin. That's the sort of day it was.

Lunch over, we walked past the Oval Office to the Cabinet Room; the latter is where we met and talked. Portraits of Truman, Lincoln and Jefferson. Two chandeliers and perhaps 28 round spotlights over a long oval table. Tall chairs, each with a small brass back=plate bearing the title of its permanent occupant and his date of accession. I sat along the wall just behind Mondale's chair. When the President arrived at 2:25 p.m. he sat directly opposite me.

"Be brutally frank," said Sec. Strauss, "the President wants input. This is the first such meeting . . . a mixed bag of people. I am here because the forces of protectionism, raging as they are in this country . . . require someone like me to deal with Congress, someone with credibility. I am for free trade." Secretary Schultz (Chairman of Economic Advisors) spoke. Others too, myself included.

Secretary (Energy) Dr. James Schlesinger spoke about the "seven or eight years of grace" left before a real disaster if energy problems aren't attended to promptly, but "nobody . . . wants change." I said I thought that a part of his problem was lack of awareness on the part of the public, offering suggestions. When he handled but didn't light his famous pipe, I suddenly noted I was the only person in the room who was smoking. "Okay," I said to myself, "there are ashtrays all around and I wasn't invited here to be cured of my bad habits."

Secretary (Treasury) Blumenthal spoke next. His most potent statement: "We would have a $15 billion trade surplus without the energy problem." Who's aware of this, I wondered? Certainly a remark worth remembering.

The President entered from a side door. Blue suit, shirt and tie. The famous smile. We stood. He came to the middle of the table, his regular place and chair. (The President speaks much more rapidly and firmly in person than from a prepared speech on TV or radio; he radiates force and good humor – usually these are not found together). Moments after he arrived and began speaking, without notes, a rear door opened with a clatter of reflectors and other photographic hardware. At least 15 youthful media people entered in a file and photographed and recorded Jimmy Carter for about two minutes; they were scruffy and busy, he was totally composed, probably accustomed to this astonishing clatter after 10 months in office.

Pres. Carter spoke of the "importance of jobs in the private sector." We businessmen "should see Local Labor Department people . . . take them to lunch . . . be overt . . . take a direct local initiative in this matter." And let him know of our results.

He asked for a vote (among those present) on our choice between "a permanent reduction in the corporate tax rate" or an "investment tax credit." By a show of hands, the latter won. To myself I said, "Look, you all came all this way, don't just sit there, do something." I raised my hand and was pointed to.

"Mr. President," I said aloud, "my name is Kornfeld."

"Yes," said Jimmy Carter, "you're from *Radio Shack*, aren't you?"

"Yes Sir," I replied, proceeding to request that along with such a (tax credit for investment) program we should have a very strong program for encouraging exports. "What can the Department of Commerce do?" he asked quickly. I doubt if my answer was memorable.

To the group Pres. Carter pointed out youthful John McIntyre of OMB ("He took Bert Lance's place.") and began talking about reducing the paperwork burden placed on industry by government. "If you were President," he asked, "what would you do?" An exchange followed.

Finally President Carter remarked that he "always came out of meetings with leaders of other (foreign) governments feeling good about the United States." This was the up-beat end of his stay in the room of just over one hour.

I have left out many quotes and observations. But from the bare bones of this mini summit meeting a few facts may be derived: (1) that the President of the USA, cabinet officers, and many top businessmen are aware if *Radio Shack* and consider us sufficiently important to be consulted on trade and labor matters, (2) that the President is trying to interface government with business or at least give us the feeling there is an open door policy in Washington, and (3) that it is at least partly our responsibility to keep the door open rather than continue playing America's favorite game . . . Monday Morning Quarterback. Shall we give it a try? I think so, I hope so, I pledge to do so.

I told the President that the Ultimate Battery Card was a gift from our employees. Now we can give him this one more thing – local action, letters to congressmen, more interest in government, more attention to politics including voting in every election, better understanding of the issues. The importance of the foregoing preempted my usual Christmas Greetings, but only in length. Have a merry one, lots of success and togetherness! You've earned it!

JANUARY 1978
Waste Not, Want Not

I HOPE YOU LIKE THE "NEW" INTERCOM. Twenty regional newsletters were eliminated when we put each region's special news inside the pages of Intercom, plus 20 separate printings and a few people better employed elsewhere. If the presently allocated space doesn't suffice, we'll add more Intercom pages.

The Merchandising Newsletter, a wonderfully useful monthly publication written by Dave Gunzel et al., is now included in Intercom as a pullout center section. This eliminated another separate mailing and handling waste area and made Intercom a more useful Company document.

I hope that when you go home at night you turn out all the lights in your work area. Electricity costs money; misuse of it is wasteful of cash and energy. You do it at home, so what's different about your store, office, lab or rest room? You say it's not yours personally? Well, if you're on a bonus schedule and/or if you're a stockholder, the waste of anything "owned" by *Radio Shack* or *Tandy* Corporation definitely does affect the cost of doing business and, therefore, your bonus figure and stock value.

At a recent management meeting we eliminated over 50% of the printed material going to new stores, and about 25% of the printed material going to all stores each month in connection with items advertised in the flyer.

I am a great re-user of paper clips. It makes me feel good not to throw away those little pieces of bent metal that come to me daily in substantial number. It's not a fetish, nor is it an important area of savings; it's a symptom of my awareness of waste, actually my dislike of it. If you can learn to Harte waste you may be able to learn to love thrift.

The greatest natural resource is Time. I appreciate the wonderfully American saying that advises: "Don't just sit there, DO something!" Employees who can't find anything to do when nothing seems to be happening are wasting an opportunity to make things look or work better. A good healthy guilt feeling is indicated!

Leftover 1977 materials, now that it's 1978, are a classic example of waste. Throw them out if they're dated and obsolete. And make a resolution: if you see Company waste that isn't being cleaned up . . . let me know. Waste of material things. Waste of time. Waste of talent. I'll give the best waste-finder a monetary reward and write about it in a future Intercom editorial. Happy New Year and may it not be wasted upon anyone who doesn't care!

FEBRUARY 1978
Follow Up: *TRS-80*

MANY OF OUR PEOPLE IN THE FIELD and many of us who answer telephone complaints have been perplexed by the large number of apparently unresolved issues concerning the *Radio Shack TRS-80* Microcomputer. Here are a few explanations.

1. *Back Orders.* At this writing we are still behind in shipments at the rate of about one back order for every one shipment. Waiting time is about 4 weeks.

2. *Floor Samples.* Our original plan was to have one in the largest store in every district, plus one in every store which sold 3 or more systems. Because of (1), this plan has yet to be implemented; our advertising has been almost zero not to put the Company in the position of advertising an item not available from stock.

3. *Peripheral Equipment.* Announcement will be made in February of add-on gear to go on sale in March. This will include hardware and software. Hardware: 6 basic microcomputers from $400 to $789, plus video display; two printers; one floppy disc. Software: 11 items, $4.95 to $29.95, plus a $9.95 manual.

4. *Tandy Computers.* This is a new division consisting of one store in Fort Worth, plus inside and outside salesmen to handle large and complex system inquiries involving *TRS-80* and also other-brand material. Its future will depend upon what happens in the next six months.

You may recall that I once said the *TRS-80* is "the most important new product ever developed by *Radio Shack.*" It is also the most complex and the slowest to manufacture. It is also getting us more good free publicity than anything we've ever done. It is also proving to the financial and technical and business community that *Radio Shack* is a quality electronics company. It is also a fine indication of American ingenuity and know-how are still alive and kicking. And also it's OURS . . . alone!

In contrast, the rest of the electronics giants are busting their humps to sell Betamax or equivalent VTR equipment, and true to form, they're also busting the price and profit potential. *Zenith* went with *Sony. RCA* went with *Matsushita.* But neither Mr. *Tandy* nor yours truly ever liked to go with anyone if we could go it alone. And that, folks, is why *TRS-80* is a computer instead of a video tape recorder. Amen!

MARCH 1978
Work Ethos. Going or Gone?

I'M SORRY TO BORE YOU WITH LOOKING BACK, particularly with looking back fondly – a universal disease known as nostalgia. But there was a time, damn it, when people really worked their butts off in this country and didn't complain about every little fault and inequity in our society, real or imagined. The boss was the boss. The job was important. I might even say vital. And the options were limited. Did I say that was bad or good? No. I said that that was the way it was.

One of the reasons that that was the way it was is that the concept of the world owing you a living had not matured to the full-grown skunk it is today. The world does NOT owe you a living, not the government, nor the Company. But of the three, the Company is the most dependable and the most sympathetic.

In the legendary "good old days" it was really difficult to pick up, pack up and get out of town. There was the uncertainty. There was the breaking up of the large family unit, the togetherness that has suffered so much attrition from TV and too much cheap mobility. You came from an environment where the need to work was not more important than the desire to work, and not more important than the innate good sense about work being an important part of the definition of life itself. The last part of that sentence explains what a Work Ethos is; the first part explains how you got it if you have it. I'm not bragging when I say I've got it, I'm saying it was built-in when I was born, like a front tooth.

How you know you have it is when there's "nothing" to do. You feel there IS something to do, and you do something about the feeling. There is always something to do. I've never been in a *Radio Shack* store or office (mine included) where what needed doing wasn't painfully, shamefully obvious. Look behind any counter, open any drawer.

Do you have a Work Ethos? Score yourself on the following list. (1) You feel ripped-off. (2) The country's going to hell. (3) Nobody tries to do things well any more. (4) The profit system stinks. (5) The company doesn't offer any opportunity. (6) You write a lot of complaint letters. (7) There's nothing to look forward to.
Score each item one point if the answer is Yes, zero if he answer is No. If your total is one (1) or more, you've got a problem. Boy, have you got a problem! The text-book cure is hard work and no play. It may kill you, but we've all got to go sometime or other and it's a better way to go than emphysema.

MAY 1978
Wage and Price Controls?

IN A NEARBY SECTION OF THIS MAGAZINE is a piece written by Senator Bentsen, D-Texas, which ran untitled in the *Wall Street Journal* and which I, therefore, have chosen to call "Wage and Price Controls?" If you will read Senator Bentsen's remarks you'll discover two things: (1) that the Joint Economic Committee which Bentsen vice chairs has FOR TWO CONSECUTIVE YEARS approved a recommendation for mandatory wage and price controls, and (2) that he believes, and fully amplifies his belief, "the recommendation is a serious mistake."

Read Senator Bentsen's article and learn for yourself why these controls are bad policy. Get to know more about government and business by reading and thinking, not, for heaven's sake, by hearsay and sentiment.

My reason for bringing u this obnoxious subject is because I have a "gut feel" our present government is likely to impose these controls despite pious claims to the contrary. Recall, please, when Pres. Nixon did exactly this not too many years ago in the name of controlling inflation.

President Carter and/or his administration have not shown the kind of firmness in staying with declaring programs that would; indicate an exceptional talent for leadership. Let me bring this home to roost.

On March 28, 1978, Mr. Carter yielded to pressure by raising the tariff on imported CB base and mobile radios from 6 percent as follows: first year 6 percent plus 15 percent; second year 6 percent plus 12 percent; third year 6 percent plus 9 percent; fourth year – back to 6 percent.

The only viable present beneficiary is wealthy old *Motorola*. The only obvious result is more inflation. More is MORE, Jimmy, not less. We fought a very hard battle to prevent this. We lost, we are told, "in the 11th hour at the Cabinet level." No tariffs had been increased in many years, but, we are told, the government, in view of future trade battles, had to have some evidence of increasing tariffs in order to demonstrate flexibility on the issue.

And so, alas, beleaguered Citizens Band Radio was "beheaded" in order to show that our leaders, after all, are flexible on the death penalty. In my book such softness will lead up to wage and price controls if we are not exceptionally vigilant. Vigilance is voting. Vigilance is writing letters to people in power. Vigilance is being inflexible where history and logic endlessly make examples of those who thought to achieve stability in the marketplace either by being rubber stamps or . . . rubber men!

JUNE 1978
The Fine Art of Survival

IT GIVES US NO SATISFACTION to see an erstwhile competitor, *Lafayette Radio*, losing both sales and money over their recent fiscal periods, or to see an erstwhile competitor and one-time supplier, *Hy-Gain*, in dire financial straits. We are not in business to defeat competitors and of course neither of these particular two competitors is in trouble because of us.

Trouble, short of an act of God or nature, is self-made by an untimely combination of miscalculated action or inaction. When it occurs the harvest of blame is reaped by Management, and it is a heavy burden indeed. Although we are taught early in life that "it's not whether you win or lose but how you play the game," there is absolutely no satisfaction in losing gracefully.

One must indeed be very careful not to confuse loss of an inning with loss of a game. Business is a game of infinite numbers of innings and which theoretically goes on until the end of time. I can think of no business that has not, on occasion, had a set-back of a temporary sort. And I can think of many which have stopped short of fatality and risen to new heights of success, not ones but several times.

The same process of loss and rejuvenation apply equally to races, nations, and just plain ordinary individuals. The bottom line requirement is a willingness to break with the past, to face the present and future with a "game plan" that simply replaces bad habits with better ones.

Being creatures of habit, we find this over-simplified solution easier to say than to do. Even so, the machine that made 78-rpm records can be rebuilt to make 33-1/3-rpm records, and the worker easily retrained. The factory that made calculators can be quite rapidly rejuvenated by being converted to make scanners, smoke detectors, intercoms, or even computers.

How does an individual person start this conversion? You break every habit. Drive a different way to work. Wear blue if you've always worn brown. Eat what you don't like. Say what you think, not what you're expected to say. Trade your old TV or a box of books. Vote for the opposite party. Find a new hero. Quit something old. Join something new.

Our one and only world does not stand still for wounded individuals or corporations. But it does offer repeated chances for revival. While we sympathetically watch our troubled competitors search for fresh beginnings, we are sure to see new companies (and people) spring up from "out of nowhere" to do the seemingly impossible with the instinctive grace of youth. That's where, old friend, we should constantly be looking for ourselves!

JULY 1978
Excerpts from the Ivory Tower

MUCH AS I LOVE TO WRITE THIS COLUMN, the following remarks are not mine, but those of E. G. Harness, Board Chairman of the *Proctor & Gamble Company*, with deletions made by me to conserve space. Obviously I like what Mr. Harness has said and believe his message is good medicine (not soft soap) for *Intercom* readers:

Let's start with a little history. What really is a corporation for profit in the free world? How did the corporation come into being? And why?

"The publicly-owned corporation for profit had its origins in Great Britain. In all countries where such corporations exist, the right to that existence rests on legislation created by government to achieve a very few simple aims for the common good. Prior to the passage of such enabling legislation, one person could join with another in a business venture only through the route of unlimited partnership. In such partnerships, the risk of failure was too great in many instances. Each partner was liable for all of his or her personal assets in the event of collapse.

"Thus, the first purpose in the creation of corporations, which is really nothing more than a 'paper citizen,' was to enable the individual to invest to the limit of his desires or capability without the risk that failure would wipe out other personal assets.

"In addition, the creation of this paper citizen, the corporation, allowed an entity to exist which could be relatively free from the mortality of man. As the investors died off, the paper entity could live on and continue to perform its intended function.

"Society saw a need and responded with laws to make the corporation possible. The corporation was required in order to get bigger jobs done – jobs which society needed doing – than *individuals alone could do.* Said another way, the state created the corporation to advance society's economic well being.

"The state provides a corporation with the *opportunity* to earn a profit *if* it meets society's needs. It follows inevitably that reported profits are the primary scorecard that tells the world how well a corporation is meeting its basic responsibility to society.

"However, in recent times critics of our business structure seem to be losing sight of the primary purposes of the corporation and some want to blame the corporation for all of society's ills – real and imaginary.

"I guess this is not surprising. The corporation for profit has been one of the most phenomenal success stories in the organizational evolution of the free world. It is perfectly natural that the progress of corporations over the past century has raised the expectations of mankind in general and of government, educators and thought-leaders in particular. This is understandable, considering some of the roles that corporations have come to fill in the non-Communist world.

"For example, corporations in the United States *pay nearly 40 percent of all taxes collected at the federal, state and local levels.*

Corporations in this country *furnish over half of all the jobs;* generate about two-thirds of the gross national product, and a similar share of the payroll dollars.

"The only way in which corporations can carry their huge and increasing burden of obligations to society is for them to earn satisfactory profits. If we cannot earn a return on equity investment which is more attractive than other forms of investment, we die. I am not aware of any bankrupt corporations which are making important social contributions."

AUGUST 1978
Going Public with the Computer

*Speech delivered by **Radio Shack** President Lewis F. Kornfeld at the National Computer Conference, June 6, 1978, in Anaheim, California.*

IN OUR TANDY CORPORATION ANNUAL REPORT for the year ending June 30, 1977, I wrote an industry perspective which described the *Radio Shack TRS-80* as "the most important product we've ever built in a company factory." I said, "The market we foresee is businesses, schools, services and hobbyists." And that "the market others apparently foresee is in-home (uses) for recipes, income taxes, games, etc."

On February 2, 1978 at the Morgan Stanley Personal Computer Conference, I said that our intention has been to produce a system which could also be used "at home or . . . at any location with an AC outlet."

The press, indulging in its predictable fantasies, earnestly desires *TRS-80* to be a *"home computer"* presumably because there are more homes than institutions, and surely everyone lives in a home! Nevertheless, I choose to cling to our original intent and conception of a primary user group consisting of business and institutional users. This, despite that the Morgan Stanley Conference revealed that none of us could put hard numbers on the unit sales potential of any market where the microcomputer would be used at this time.

In the ensuing months I came up with a new description of our product – this microcomputer that the industry has labeled "personal" and the press has labeled "home". My new better idea is that the *TRS-80* is *portable,* a transportable computer. We have developed two suitcases to substantiate this breakthrough!

While you are contemplating the closing of the gap between people and I/O programming, I want to quote a very eminent scholar who wrote to me on 4/24/78 as follows:

"I want to congratulate you and your *Tandy* team for the visionary perspective and drive you are bringing to bear on this challenge. The potential of the task you are taking – literally taking computing to the masses, is only beginning to be appreciated, even by the knowledgeable people in our field. I believe its potential rivals that of some of the great technological developments of our time. I say this advisedly because you are not only providing an advanced technology to the public; you are actually making possible, the tapping of human innovation and creativity on an unprecedented scale."

Now I want to quote from a highly placed businessman who wrote to us on 5/26/78:

"Just a short note to express my complete satisfaction with my *TRS-80 Level-II* 16K microcomputer. I have written a complete inventory control program for the products my company sells and five programs for use in sales surveys, all of which I have used profitably.

"Again, I want to express my delight with your product. As one involved in professional sales for over 15 years, I expect the *TRS-80* to enable me to increase my income and that of my company tremendously."

These letters indicate, aside from our order backlog, that something is brewing that is quite separate and apart from the 1978 National Computer Conference program's page 12 vision of:

"A device . . . which can be used by persons technically disinterested and incompetent to turn a knob or two."

In short, the *TRS-80* has no knobs and was never intended to compete with TV games, oven timers, or *Cuisinart*, and is not a product for incompetents.

However, the computer is indeed invading every corner of everyone's life – but it bits and pieces – not in the precise total shape of computers and terminals as abundantly displayed in the many acres of this (NCCC) convention. Here in a wristwatch . . . here in an automobile's viscera . . . here in a micro-processed CB or scanner or hi-fi radio . . . and there in a system using home wiring or the telephone line to do some task that perhaps got "computerized" because it was available on a chip, regardless, it often seems, of whether it represents actual progress or – to use my recent favorite word – overkill.

Back to basics, what is our game plan for *TRS-80*? The formula is brutally simple. *Radio Shack* had 7,040 places to potentially demonstrate and sell *TRS-80* computer systems and peripherals on May 15, 1978: 4,463 stores in nine countries, and 2,577 dealers in strategically located small communities principally in the USA and Canada.

As of June 6, 1978, despite our best production efforts, only an estimate 33 percent of these stores had one or more units in stock due to our continuing backlog, although well over 50 percent had sold one or more systems.

Radio Shack, in the USA alone, has a current customer list of over 20 million persons, over 50 percent of whom – on a running average – receive a mailing piece from us each month.

Radio Shack has been credited by *Advertising Age* magazine as being perhaps "the first network TV advertising of a company system.

Radio Shack advertises in over 1,000 USA newspapers at least three times a month.

Radio Shack distributes 9 to 12 million catalogs buy hand to store visitors per annum.

Radio Shack is believed to be the only billion-dollar-sales-retailer specializing in consumer electronics in the entire world.

Radio Shack has 20 company-operated factories, 5,000 factory employees, over one million square feet of manufacturing space, over 7,000 selling locations, over

$80 million of annual advertising funds to devote largely to this cause should the potential become evident and desirable.

This is the muscle that, in my opinion, will achieve complete awareness of the Personal Computer in this country by the end of 1979 at the latest.

Therefore, the very difficult task I perceive for 1980 and beyond is to back up this awareness with perception of *benefits* if the microcomputer, which we call "Personal" today, is really to become a "mass consumer market" item tomorrow.

We do not think this will come about via a bookshelf of ROM cartridges, but rather by dynamic interaction between people and information, interfaced by technology on a two-way street that can, that already has, led us to the near stars and back.

Radio Shack's unparalleled, undreamed of (in 1921 when we began) distribution network is the sharpest part of the leading edge that is cutting through the cords of complexity that have innocently kept the computer's *multiplication of brain power* away from the public and preserved it – until now – for the scientific elite.

We intend to intensify, to expand, and to simplify, our advantage in the distribution of this technology and in the creation of this awareness.

It is a privilege to share and debate these potentials with you today, and – to be a bit chauvinistic – here in the Far West rather than the Far or Middle East.

SEPTEMBER 1978
The Computer on Main Street, USA

A BUSINESS COLLEGE HAS WRITTEN to thank me (meaning us) "for bringing the computer to Main Street, USA." Historians will probably note that, "*Radio Shack* did to the computer what Henry Ford did to the automobile. The computer is now in the mainstream of America."

We have received many similar letters; some even predicting *Radio Shack* will be the next IBM. Fact or myth or somewhere in between, commentary like this should enhance everything we do. Everything! But only if we do a few things in return:

-- We must all do some homework on computing in general and *TRS-80* in particular. Don't guess when you talk to people. Most questioners know more than you do about the subject.

-- We must continue to grow the *TRS-80* line, and plans for this are well under way. Don't discuss plans until they become products. Don't guess. Don't gossip.

-- We, must get quickly into stock position on everything in the announced *TRS-80* line and have sensible explanations for unanticipated delays that are quite typical of new, high-technology products.

-- We must be prepared to encounter competition, some of it real and some phony. Our fantastic head start makes concern over competition diverting, but not constructive in public contacts.

-- We must remind people that the Company able to make the *TRS-80* certainly ought to be able to make very high grade – (and then show them what else we actually manufacture).

-- We must remember we have 2,399 other things to sell and that selling does not mean just showing up at the store – it means more than merely writing up orders – it means a 100 percent effort to write at least two lines on a sales slip for each person you talk to on the floor.

Well, let's end on a high note with another quote, this from the manager of a lab in Michigan; "I never thought I'd be spending the money at *Radio Shack* as I have in the last year or so. How did I ever make it this far without products from *Radio Shack*? I'll never know. I am looking forward to your latest contribution with excitement."

This is what happens when you put the computer on Main Street. You make sales! You create excitement! Fiscal 1979 (meaning NOW) offers opportunities which I am sure some of you thought disappeared when CB became just another fine product line. How wrong you were! HOW GREAT IS IT!

OCTOBER 1978
A Man for All Seasons

OUR EXECUTIVE VICE PRESIDENT, F. R. "Bill" Nugent, has once again left *Radio Shack* – this time probably for good – and once again will be missed. But I am happy to report that "GRN" has new worlds to conquer in his new position as President of *Tandycrafts*, a New York Stock Exchange listed company which is in the process of spinning off its most profitable division, Color Tile, leaving Bill in charge of a group of companies which have 47 percent of Crafts' sales and 29 percent of its profits.

The outfits remaining under the *Tandycrafts* banner include *Tandy Leather Company* – the original *Tandy* success story; *American Handicrafts* and *Merribee* – two divisions dealing chiefly with things bought by women, neither, as yet, a *Tandy*-style winner; *Magee*, a profitable Arkansas manufacturer of picture frames; and *Bona Allen*, a leather manufacturer which the old-time Texans call "Boneyallan" with wry affection. This is the lot which Bill has inherited and which, when offered the top spot, he accepted with alacrity and with, as a poet once said of the end of the world, a bang – not a whimper.

Bill is unquestionably the best-trained *Tandy* executive available for a challenge of this magnitude. In addition he has an ample supply of wisdom, drive, ambition, ego, and guts. Enduring the recent past he has risen above open-heart surgery, and the loss of his wife, Hilreth, whose like doesn't come along every day – or every decade.

Despite that he vanished from the 16th floor of Tandy Center to the 17th within 24 hours of his promotion, taking all his office furniture with him, he will be remembered by all of us for his friendship and countless contributions to the system which has built *Radio Shack* (and thereby *Tandy Corp.*) from a midget to a giant in 15 years.

Naturally his successors and peers at *The Shack* will claim as their own all the good (and none of the unfinished) things Bill Nugent set in motion. But if *Intercom* is maintained as an historical document, this entry will testify for the record that GRN is one of our true Company pioneers, and let no one say otherwise. The vote is unanimous!

For the rest of 1978 at least, GRN's (the G in GRN, incidentally, stands for George) office will remain empty. During the interim his duties will be undertaken by Mr. *Tandy* and your correspondent. Neither of us is deceived into believing that filling his chair, even with double occupancy, will be an easy task. We've walked a lot of hard, great miles with this man Nugent. That they finally moved to *Tandycraft's* corner office is *Tandycrafts'* gain. And our loss.

NOVEMBER 1978
Charles David *Tandy*, 1918 – 1978

OUR GIFTED AND BELOVED CHAIRMAN passed away in his sleep on Saturday, November 4, 1978, at age 60. In those six decades he lived 120 years in comparison to ordinary mortals. He thought more thoughts, dreamed more dreams, planned and executed more plans, talked more words to more people, and affected more lives than anyone you and I will ever meet.

In Addition to being a man of extraordinary natural talent, Mr. Tandy was able to convert this talent into success – success not only for himself, but for the many thousands who worked with him, who invested in his enterprises, who sold him goods or services.

That others shared his success was by design, not by coincidence. It will sound a bit incredible when I say that he wanted his associates to succeed even more than many of them were willing to, meaning simply that some perfectly capable people lacked the drive and ambition to fully capitalize on the golden opportunities Mr. Tandy offered them. Hard to believe? Believe it!

The Chairman was a man whose leadership qualities absolutely dwarf those of any leader, owner, or boss I've ever met. He stood tall in any group of distinguished people, radiating intelligence, class, good will, humor. He was always himself. He was always approachable in person or by telephone, a facet of his personality that astounded people who imagine persons of high rank as being unavailable, distant, secluded, too "important" to make time for strangers or subordinates. He drove his own car. He answered his own phone. He smoked 30-cent cigars. He served coffee from a thermos jug on his desk (and the cups were plastic).

All but the most recent of our employees have seen Mr. Tandy, so the above comments are mostly directed at our newer folks who now will never have the chance. He believed that everyone's' duty was to teach . . . to teach someone down the line to be a better businessperson, how to build an estate, how to communicate and follow up, how to contribute to the corporation and to the community.

What he expected from us at this particular moment in time – the Christmas selling season – was to break every record in the book. If we don't, it won't be for lack of having been taught how. If we do, it will be the most fitting parting gift to this formidable (but gentle), excellent, eloquent man who considered each of us as "one of the family" and expected nothing but an honest effort in return.

DECEMBER 1978
I'm Dreaming of a Green Christmas

IT'S APPROPRIATE FOR ME TO LET IRVING BERLIN DREAM of a white Christmas while I pick a color that's more appealing to all of us who labor in behalf of ourselves and our great Corporation. Green is the color of money.

It may be, on the other hand, inappropriate to be talking about money when I could (or should?) be talking about holly, hearthside and heavenly matters. So be it. This is the chosen message for my 1978 Christmas card.

Radio Shack is not as Yule-dependent as many companies. Nevertheless, we make about 33 percent of our sales in the December quarter and (according to *Value Line*, Page 1576) an earnings-per-share figure substantially above the 22 percent range. Confusing? All it means is that the October/November/December quarter is about 50% more potent than our other quarters.

And what all THAT means is that the best time of the year to make money is the Christmas season. Not only Company money, but YOUR money if you're involved with making sales. OF course you are affected even if you don't have a thing to do with sales: the better we do as a group, the more secure your job; the more healthy your stock, the greater our chances for expansion both personally and corporately; the more likely that somewhere along the line you'll be justified in expecting higher earnings or bonuses.

Even so small a service (and joy) as giving a gift bought at Radio Shack, the Telephone Booth or Safe House, all Company companies, is important. Why give a *GE* or a *Panasonic* when you can help your fellow workers and stockholders and get an extra 10% off? It's absolutely the wrong time of year for heresy!

The main thing is not to think of the commercial aspect of Christmas as if it were "just another" selling season. It's THE season for the retail business and your behavior should reflects its timeliness and urgency. By shaping up your store. By speeding up your service. By putting on a happy face. By creative salesmanship. By remembering everyone you meet is a gift-giver and the time to dream green is NOW.

JANUARY 1979
"If YOU Can't Get It Done, I Can"

MY NEXT SEVERAL EDITORIALS in this space will be in an attempt to enrich my customary efforts at motivation with memories of Mr. Tandy. Old friends of the late Chairman may be entertained (which he would have appreciated) or saddened (which is not my intent). And those who never knew him, but considered him a legend who was, yes, a legend in his time – a legend we are not prepared to let fade away anytime soon, if ever.

Whatever the problem, Charles Tandy, in his own mind, always had a large number of solutions. Bringing him an unsolved problem was a poor way of approaching him because it meant per se that you didn't have your own strong recommendation plus a well-documented list of options.

In other words: you, as one of his chosen Lieutenants, were not performing up to snuff, using experience and common sense to get this problem whipped and get on to the next one. One trick was to bring him a solution you knew wouldn't be totally appropriate so that, after a bit of chewing-out, you could get the benefit of his best thinking. The time required to achieve this was seldom less than two hours and could be more than eight hours; it depended upon the number of intervening phone calls, document signings, unexpected guests, delays due to a luncheon date at a bank or a university, and so on.

Often a second or third Lieutenant with a problem would appear, and your position in the solution-pecking order would change (deteriorate) without notice! But whether the problem was one you brought or one you developed during a "rap: session – the location of the session being absolutely random – the advice, or rather, the admonition, was always the same:

"Just tell me you're not going to do it because you don't know how, and I'll do it, *because I know how to get it done."*

Nothing was insoluble to CDT. Nothing was impossible of solution. Nothing was a bigger pain in the psyche than a problem left hanging for want of an excellent timely solution. Nothing was more aggravating than a Lieutenant who couldn't belly up to a problem and solve it.

There is, however, this nagging suspicion. It could well be that Mr. Tandy *enjoyed* being brought into your situation. Because it gave him another insight regarding your thinking process. And another chance to teach his lesson in *Positive Radiant Optimism.*

Nobody, but NOBODY, but Charles Tandy could do it so well. But there are still some of us around who remember, and will try.

FEBRUARY 1979
How Fortunes are Made

A FAMOUS FINANCIAL ADVISER SAYS he learned early in life "that most of the big fortunes of the country were made *by people retaining ownership of successful business enterprises* that continued to grow and prosper over a long period of years." This message is aimed squarely at every *Radio Shack* employee who is also stockholder. That's a lot of fine people!

"Retaining" means KEEPING. "Ownership" means STOCK HOLDING. "Successful business and enterprise" means *TANDY CORP.*, a Company that has "continued to grow and prosper" over many, many years. You betcha! We fit the description of the business and you fit the description of the owner like the proverbial "T"!

Every February you get the stock you bought through the prior year under the Stock Purchase Plan. And thereby you get another shot at remaining an owner or selling yourself down the river (perhaps for the second or third time).

A retiring employee at one of our factories thanks us for her "TIP" check which "added greatly to my retirement." In this instance, over just six years, her $3,588.15 grew to $8,456.69. An increase of nearly 136 percent. Had she put $3,588.15 in one lump sum into an eight percent CD, for example, she would have ended up with $5,693.94. A 59 percent increase – less yearly taxes. Small numbers, small amount of time, but an owner who retained her ownership. An owner who got 136 percent on her money, instead of 49 percent before taxes.

Traders are most investors who STAY PUT usually come out on top.. Young people in particular have a tendency to think that a quick buck makes more sense than a patient buck. So they quit, swap, move, change, and otherwise ineptly run their affairs. If that's true because no one ever told you differently, I'm telling you now.

Build your estate by *retaining ownership* in your Company. When you get your stock – no matter how few the shares, no matter what the gain or loss – hang in there! You get precious few chances in life to build a net worth. This is one of them.

MARCH 1979
"Make a Noise Like a Cheese"

BACK A FEW YEARS, OUR LATE CHAIRMAN employed in his speech a great many homilies, metaphors, and analogies which vastly amused his listeners and which nearly always related to some kind of animal.

In discussing advertising, particularly efforts in building store traffic – known in the trade as "bringing in warm bodies" – his most memorable aphorism was the following:

"If you want to catch a mouse, you've got to make a noise like a cheese."

What is the origin of this remark so worthy of Casey Stengel or Samuel Goldwin? Older friends may know. I don't. All I know is that it instantly makes a point most advertisers either never learn or seldom consistently practice. I have tried to teach advertising for over 30 years and still find it just about impossible to convince practitioners that:

(1) – Mice like cheese.

(2) – To find it, mice have to be told it *is cheese* and where it's located.

(3) – Hence and Q.E.D., a cheeselike noise must be made wherever particular mice congregate!

There will now be a brief pause while any of my readers who deny that "a noise like cheese" can be made to go back to their backgammon boards.

"What would you do?" Mr. Tandy once asked an employee who had let a bad thing happen *for a second time,* "if a horse came into your kitchen and bleeped on your floor?" The employee sat there silently, thinking thoughts about the nearest exits.

"You'd get him OUT!" the Chairman roared.

"And you wouldn't let him back in."

There was, of course, the frequent, "If that's true, I'll kiss your sweet bippy." My lexicons do not define a bippy. Perhaps I should look into the dictionary on which I am sitting?

And the threat to have your bleep "kicked 'til it barks like a fox," is yet another dandy *Tandy*ism that got delivered with a deep, almost fond chuckle. IF you want to know why so many of us are prolific in Fox Bark, don't hesitate to inquire.

A strong plea for better ideas, solutions and understanding somehow seems more human when an animal is personified in the process. Mice, horses and little foxes are neat devices for a Boss who never one came out and said, "You're an ass and you're fired."

APRIL 1979
Take the Last Step by Yourself

EVER THE PATIENT TEACHER, our late Chairman would spend any length of time attempting to bring one of his disciples up to a higher level of creative activity where the Company Is concerned. He never stopped teaching. But some of his students took a long time learning. And many never did.

To one of us he once complained: *"I've almost drug you to the top of the hill . . . WON'T you take the last step by yourself?"*

The meaning is crystal clear. I've coached you. I've shown you a variety of living samples including failures and successes. I've brought you to within two feet of the top of Mt. Everest. And still you're leaning on me, you're a burden, a dependent, WILL YOU PLEASE now show me you've learned enough to go the rest of the way under your own steam?

While we're waiting for that to sink in, to become personally meaningful, here's another *Tandy*ism with a similar plea:

"You've fought success so much that you've almost won."

This means, old pal, that you have courted failure so persistently you have almost succeeded in failing permanently. Professor Tandy had a way of putting up with employees – or shall I say "associates" – who had a keen instinct for making the wrong decision, even were there were only two choices. But no teacher enjoys seeing his pupils fail.

Similarly, many people do what my Marine Corps drill instructors used to call "fighting the problem." You fight a problem when you feel the teacher or the situation is trying to trick you. And the way to fight a problem is to try to solve it by an unusual method, rather than the A- to Z- method you were taught and which is invariably correct. I've seen plenty of guys in business who thought that only dopes and squares went from A to C via B. It's a perfect way to fight success.'

No teacher in this company wants you to fail. If you do, it will be either because you're self-taught or too lazy (OR SKEPTICAL) to listen.

MAY 1979
Success is a Matter of Degree

OCCASIONALLY A MANAGER IN A POSITION to get a bonus based upon sales improvement, will, on making the improvement, think he has really done something fantastic. And of course he has. But then, it's also a matter of degree.

One such individual bragged about his achievement to our late Chairman. "D'ya know what I've got Boss," he confided, "I've got a 35 percent sales gain!"

Mr. Tandy knew very well that this individual had been given a store with extremely low sales, a place from which there was almost no way to go but up. He responded to our pal in the following manner and without even pausing to reflect.

"Hell, when you're sleeping on the floor it's hard to fall out of bed." I guess one of the many possible morals is that any gain over a zero base has to be a big percentage gain. For example, our so-called "W" Store Program gives a Manager a stellar opportunity to rack up a big improvement; while at the same time the top store in the district may have to fight like mad to go ahead 10 percent, and the latter may well be more vital to that month's Company bottom line.

Winning being a matter of degree, it gets clearer every day why C. D. Tandy (and Vince Lombardi, the Green Bay giant) were never satisfied with marginal victories. Winning big is the only sort of triumph worthwhile; after all, little victories are almost borderline defeats.

And yet, this outstanding leader, this man to whom being less than Number One was totally boring, was the same guy who told a defeated associate: "Get up, dust yourself off, and get back in the game. We all make mistakes. The test of a man is what he does to recover."

So you see – even loss is a matter of degree. And there are two things about loss worth recalling. (1) Don't repeat a losing technique. (2) Don't just sit there in your puddle of spiked milk; dry yourself off and "get back in the game."

Radio Shack never repeated its annual habit of operating the month of May at a loss once Mr. Tandy got back in the game of selling at a profit between the end of April and the beginning of June. If memory serves me right, that was about 12 years ago.

"No big deal," Tandy later remarked, "after we got our minds right." Just a matter of degree: the result of improving an insufficient profit plan!

JUNE 1979
Music to My Ears

THE LATE AND NOT VERY WELL-KNOWN American composer, Henry Cowell (1869 – 1964), once said: "I believe that each human being should have the liberty to be an individual, and that everyone who wins the right to act in his own way must, in return to society, behave ethically."

If you want to "do your own thing" then you must repay the society that permit this and makes it possible. The price is ethical behavior. My dictionary defines "ethical" as "conforming to professional standards of conduct." While not a perfect explanation, it's quite understandable.

Many countries offer their citizens very few rights while requiring much, much more than "ethical behavior" in return. In fact, in exchange for the "right" to live under highly restrictive conditions, they insist on virtually robotic behavior. You cannot make demands. You cannot publically hope for "the better way of life" that is the built-in ongoing dream of every American regardless of origin, creed or race.

The paradox of the American dream is that it required what on paper would appear to be unethical behavior – to get our country going in its present direction. But, thanks to Mr. Cowell, the answer to the paradox is one that should make everyone comfortable in his own mind about the American Revolution. He said "in return to society" – not in return to government – we must behave ethically. Society, not government! Society is "we, the people," whereas government is merely its designated operating system.

Henry Cowell abhorred totalitarianism because it makes "individualism impossible and expression of liberal thought punishable." And also "its right-wing counterpart, under which liberals fears persecution and reprisals . . . if they express their sincere ideas for the betterment of the government."

Come July 4 of every year, I like to review the process by which the United States has fared so well during the past two centuries of change, upheaval, and innovation. It has never been so clear to me that the intellectual appeal of a totally ordered social system that enfolds one "from the cradle to the grave" is, aside from being unaffordable, a cruel, inhuman and mischievous delusion.

JULY 1979
The Million Dollar Baby

WELL, WE DIDN'T FIND OUR FIRST MILLION dollar baby (read: *Radio Shack*) at the five and ten cent store. We found it in San Antonio, Texas. In May 1979. According to our most recent *SMSA Market Report*, San Antonio's national ranking among the cities of the USA is 38th; but being 29th in our Company's sales ranking, it's a better than average place for us or else it would be 38th in our ranking as well.

Most businesses think that Baghdad-on-Hudson or Smoggy-Bottom-California are where the big bucks come from. And so they do. But the bigger, safer, friendlier bucks come from places like San Antonio.

Most businesses think an employee has got to be a graybeard or a whizkid from the B-School (or at least somebody qualified to work for Proctor & Gamble) to run a million dollar business. But Jim Savoie, our first million dollar Manager, is a paltry 29 years of age. In addition, though a part-timer for five years, he has only been a *Shack Manager* for three years. So much for the old myths, the conventional wisdom, and all that bleep.

As I tell the Manager Classes that pass through Fort Worth: the first year I worked for *Radio Shack* (1948) we just missed doing a megabuck for the whole year. With Presidents and Vice Presidents galore; an Ad Manager (me); mail orders; an individual sales department; and something like 60 employees, all working their tails off. Rumor has it we had upwards of 30,000 stock keeping units. Fact has it the Company, *Radio Shack*, was a sprightly upstart of 27, meaning 2.7 decades old.

The prize – that is: the extra prize – for running a million dollar *Shack* in FY '79 is $10,000. Double my 1948 salary, friend, just for doing The Possible.

James Savoie, 29, and Store #8202, you're the first. First, in the millionaire run for the money. First in the hearts of everyone at *Tandy Corporation* and *Radio Shack*

Thank you!

AUGUST 1979
On Being Created Unequal

DESPITE THE FOUNDING FATHERS of this country having proclaimed that "all men are created equal," my Authority for this editorial proclaimed — frequently publicly and loudly – exactly to the contrary, allowing, graciously for a period of actual equality which extended from Mother's delivery to Baby's first cry. This grace period may be considered as one minute, plus or minus 30 seconds.

"No two people are equal," thundered my Authority, "and that includes you and me." I might add that I hadn't considered myself as being equal or unequal, only different.

Thus, while each American has certain inalienable rights, such as the right to vote, travel around the country, quit one job and take another, and select a lifestyle, neither the government nor the heavenly hosts (said my Authority) ever perfected the art of cloning. "Don't give me that malarkey about equal rights," in other words, "because we have to earn every right we get and no two people do it the same way, and some lose out."

And further, no two people are as "good" as each other, therefore equality will out and those who have the votes on relative equality do the electing. Naturally the electors have to share the blame in the event of an erroneous choice: however a very keen elector will have several clever and well-rehearsed alibis.

Well, the moral may be: don't tell me you're as good as I am, tell me you're better or (which would be choice indeed) almost as good. We were NOT created equal, merely equally created. We have more or less power, influence, assets, social standing, and so on, due to being created unequal. At the very least, this should induce everyone to try harder!

Marching in a straight line, i.e. – from A to B – would seem the natural thing to do to get to B most directly. But we don't, being unequal, all see it that way. Not only is there a consideration of space and direction, but also one of time. My Authority often observed that a certain party "wasn't marching straight because he had two left feet." (He was unusually unequal.)

My Authority, being the late Charles D Tandy and the least equal man I've ever met, never got an argument from me on these matters. Now, since I'll never get the chance, I thought the next best thing would be to keep the dialog alive!

SEPTEMBER 1979
Memo to Store Managers

IT WAS A PLEASURE TO BE WITH YOU in August at our big regional meetings. You are the hope of this company as it forges ahead through the years. The meetings are supposed to give you a horizon beyond that of your store door; to let you see what award winners and executives look like (and how much similarity there is between you and them); to promote your sense of belonging to an organization that, although enormous, is extremely dependent on even its smallest components; to allow you an educated glimpse into the coming year's programs; to give you an opportunity to ask penetrating questions of management.

One of our newest employees told me they were the best meetings of any meeting of any kind he'd ever attended, and he came to us from a very large company. At any rate, that series of meetings cost us stockholders over $1,000,000. So you can see the annual price of togetherness and motivation is more than many men make in a lifetime of work.

Your questions at the second-day meetings with management were sort of run-of-the-mill. For example – what's our stock going up to this year? My typical, wise-guy answer is: go up and down. But aside from the fact that nobody knows, much of the answer to that question resides in your attitude when you're in your store. The "stock market" is interested in sales growth (which it typically rewards with stock price improvement), and not in sales-loss excuses (which it rewards with stock price declines). Spiff program questions could have been asked of your DM. Questions about merger rumors indicate you don't, perhaps, trust us to keep you informed; rumors are not worth discussing when we meet only once each year.

A well-worn question is "Why do we run out of blockbusters sometimes?" But no one asks "What happens if we don't run out?" – which is often the case. Pal, when you're throwing a party and you don't know how many guests will come, how much Scotch do you lay away and how much ice? Most everything in life is an educated guess, except how much money you have in the bank, how often do you ask if, in 10 years, it'll be worth as much as it is today? (The answer is "no" by at least 50 percent.)

I hope we have bonus meetings next year. I hope you'll come. I hope you'll ask questions that either stump or better inform the experts. I hope you'll let me know if you come up with a better way to run these meetings. We've come a long way doing what we're doing, but I hope you'll remember that our programs are not carved in granite . . . they can be altered whenever a better idea presents itself. And I hope, if you think you've got one, you'll let me know!

OCTOBER 1979
A Crisis of Confidence

ANYONE WHO HAS EVER PLAYED A SPORT, made a public presentation or tried to make a sale knows one thing well: confidence is essential to success. The reverse is also true: lack of confidence is a basic ingredient of failure.

Our more than 3,100 Company Store Managers who shared a fiscal 1979 bonus pool of over $20,000,000 had to be confident in order to earn this money. Our several Million-Dollar-Store Managers had to be supremely confident to pocket the additional $10,000 prize for performing that special feat. The hurdle for this achievement has been raised for fiscal 1980: to $15,000 for running a $1.5 million store, and to $25,000 for running a $2.0 million store. Will confidence make the difference? Believe it!

Your Company is displaying amazing confidence in producing and marketing he *TRS-80 Model II*. To compete with folks like *IBM, Hewlett-Packard* and *Wang,* you've got to have implicit faith in your ability to survive and excel. Assuming you have the skill, you need CONFIDENCE to close the look . . . and I do not mean just plain guts or one-upmanship.

We agreed at our August regional meetings that *Radio Shack* WILL NOT have a recession this year; we are confident nothing will happen between July1, 1979 ad June 30, 1980 to put a crimp in our business.

We therefore DO NOT AGREE with our government in Washington and the news media (practically everywhere) that we're in for trouble. In fact, we're confident we're going to have another record year.

Sadly, the other thing we're confident of is the government's lack of confidence in itself. The government, via Mr. Carter, has actually blamed its problems on us, the oil companies, OPEC and a few other chosen targets. And the news media picks on every bit of bad economic news as if it were the choicest morsel of immediacy, supporting, in effect, the government's crisis of confidence.

I have no doubt Mr. Carter will fail, primarily because he cannot conceptualize and personify success. Equally, I have no doubt our 1979 winning managers will repeat in 1980, primarily because they are success oriented and have no intention of letting the President or the networks and news publications talk them into lower take-home pay.

Nobody in *Radio Shack* or *Tandy Corporation* has a crisis of confidence; but it gives us no pleasure to be part of a seemingly ever-shrinking minority in this country. No Pleasure. But a considerable amount of personal; security derived from believing we know how to achieve The Possible.

NOVEMBER 1979
Our Immovable Feast

OTHER HOLIDAYS HAVE, DURING MY LIFETIME, suffered the indignity of being moved to a Monday or, as with Armistice Day, having their name changed and their meaning altered. Not so with Thanksgiving Day. It's the fourth Thursday of November. It's a genuine holiday. It's a day of gratitude for the many bounties served up by a land that somehow keeps on giving despite our devastation, waste and relentless urge to cover it with asphalt.

Please reconsider the history of this peculiarly American day and pass along its reason to all those who share in whatever festivities you have planned. Don't let it become yet another fleeting affair with food and football.

Thanksgiving is surely not just another day off. Neither is it merely an excuse to dissect a turkey. Nor is it the only day ordained for serving kumquats or assembling families. Its meanings are spelled out in the name. Don't be bashful about finding something to be thankful for, and don't keep it a secret.

Despite that they are cultural treasures, our holidays, like certain special animals, have an ominous habit of threatening to become extinct. You can help keep the fourth Thursday of every November alive, meaningful and American. A day when simple gratitude is rediscovered precisely how, when and where we've done it since the 17th century: at home!

DECEMBER 1979
Why I Believe in Santa Claus

RECENTLY, I HAD A VERY SERIOUS CONVERSATION with a little girl, the child of one of our co-workers. It soon developed that she didn't believe in Superman but she did believe in Santa Claus. After severe cross-examination, I admitted agreement on both points. Unfortunately, we never did discuss our reasoning, only our conclusion. If I'd been asked why I believe in Santa Claus, I might have said something like this.

Personally, I've had a raft of unanticipated success, and a lot of it has been just plain luck. Back in 1963, when *Radio Shack's* fortunes were tumbling, the late Charles Tandy came into the picture instead of someone with a dimmer vision and a smaller heart. My whole 16-year experience with *Tandy Corporation* has been well above any reasonable level of expectation. Santa-stic? Well, er, yah!

Then there was the CB affair, a classic study in boom and bust. All day I could name you companies that never got put back together again after CB crashed, and one that just kept getting better: us. On Donder!

Some trustworthy souls theorize that we had the *TRS-80* all dressed up and ready to go the minute CB faded. But of course that's a lot of bull. Our first timid order to our factory was for 1,000 systems; then we upped it to 3,000; a far cry from genius. But O' the great lucky timing! Tell me St. Nick didn't play a little teeny role in getting us into computers, and I'll tell you you're a Grinch.

The reason, my children, that there were no other electronics shops in most of the town we entered after 1963 was really quite obvious. Nobody thought that the world's zillion towns could support a *Radio Shack*, much less 5, 10 or 100. And that included us. So, sort of like Topsy, we grew; and the numbers kept hinting that saturation was still hanging out there like a carrot we couldn't seem to get close to. I submit that this is the Clausian Phenomenon in rare full bloom.

Out there, out where the cogitation over commercial success and corporate pecking orders is at their most frantic, is a whole small army of guys trying to figure out why *Tandy*'s still doing okay after the loss of our namesake on Nov. 4, 1978. Whereas most of us figured we were well trained to carry on and grow, they stuck with their doomsday scenario and probably sold out their client's stock for a two buck gain or loss. These are the descendants of Scrooge; they wouldn't bet on Old Claus on stack of Krugerrands, but they'd bail out *Chrysler* "one more time."

You're dern right I do believe in Santa Claus. Maybe not each and every day; but then, again, maybe I do. But show me December on a calendar . . . that's when my belief really comes on strong! Like now!

JANUARY 1980
You, Too, Can Save $415,000

I HAVE A THEORY. IF EVERY YEAR I can develop a project that will save the Company a lot of money, and IF it does, then I can rest easier in my conscience about how much money the Company pays me.

My project for 1979-80 to save the Company some money and reassure my conscience was to zero in on the way we order, stock and distribute forms and packaging martial. Envelopes. Stationary. Order forms. Bags. The lot! My target amount of savings, since our Company is large and spread all over hell and gone was $500,000.

Two of our Vice Presidents have been working on this matter since last February and on Sept. 18, 1979, one of them sent me a memo to the effect that "at least $415,000" will be saved. Naturally I'll check back on this pledge, but for now I'll assume it's correct. And I'll settle for the $415K.

Down, conscience, down! You can rest another 12 months. You can forget about the 96 ball point pens you once saw in the back office of a store in Minneapolis while the Manager was attending one of our meetings. You can stop wondering where all those pads come from that suddenly appear at meetings, and whether there's too much toilet paper tucked away somewhere where it's dry, and why people JUST MUST leave their office lights on a the end of a working day. Forget it!

Is it true some people use our letterheads for writing personal letters? Maybe that's part of a 1981 savings scheme. Would anyone fail to distribute catalogs that cost 35¢ each and annual reports that cost triple that amount, that is – until they'd expired. Or throw away bright new paper clips? Hey, that's the stuff saving campaign are all about!

You, too can save $415,000 if you'll join my little crusade and let me know where you perceive a big pile of waste. To do this, as the song says, *ya gotta have heart!*

FEBRUARY 1980
Thanatopsis on a Sloppy Store

WILD HORSES COULDN'T GET ME TO GO BACK to Store # _____ (name withheld to spare the management) after my visit last December, just a few weeks before Christmas. It looked like a businessman's nightmare of "Chapter 10" of the bankruptcy process.

I have made this point known to our establishment folks; they will thin, on reading this, that I like to beat a dead horse. I don't. I like to see horses running free and wild. But even a wild horse won't get me back into Store _____ where I finally lost my naive notion that people will generally run shops as neatly as they run their homes. Now I know they won't . . . I know they'll tolerate crud on the floor, the walls, the stockroom, display windows, and on their desks.

But I know even more. They'll tolerate crud in partial darkness and over indefinite periods of time. And more! They'll not only tolerate crud but think "it looks pretty good," meaning, I guess, they don't know the difference between crud and clean, unacceptable and adequate.

This much is true: consumer electronics merchandise has an almost built-in propensity to become disorderly in a short time. But this much is also true: we have a while pyramid or professional people to monitor our stores and keep them shaped up to some sort of standard of decency and hospitability. Here's the Salesmaker, the Managers, the District Manager, the Regional Manager, the Divisional Manager. There's a whole host of other trained executives eyes as well. And there's me.

Gents, I think I'd better admit that the buck stops here. Before I hang up my cleats, my friends, I'm gonna lean very hard on my mop, broom, pegboards, light fixtures, displays, signs, floorway, vacuum cleaner, and the pyramid of business. I'm just too old to take lying down the shock of seeing Store # _____. I'm too experienced to believe that even a profitable dirty shop can't win more sales and influence more customers by changing from a tenement into a showplace..

Now don't try to snow me with how successful we've been with crummy looking Shacks and the occasional schlocky ad. Don't try to con your Uncle Lew that our customers love us just the way we are. I said in a recent editorial that I believe in Santa, but I didn't say I believe in craperoo. We'll destroy a lot of youngsters in our stores if we train them to overlook the obviously bad, to accept as our norm the trashed-up look of Store # _____ and its peers. My office was upstairs over # _____ for over 10 years, and the store was always a flagship. Now it's a wreck. And with it sinks my theory that our partners in labor could never find sloppiness an environment capable of being lived in (and ignored) for 300 days a year.

MARCH 1980
Is Government "For the Birds"?

NOTE: AS YOU KNOW, I LIKE TO WRITE THIS COLUMN myself. But Manager Jim Lockley of #1752 in High Point, N.C., sent me this material which, it seems, has been published in a number of banking journals and the author's name is not available. The title is my own. The answer to its question is: when it's too much. And the time: is now.

There was once a little girl who went to see the loan officer at her local bank, and said: "Mister, I want to get a loan to buy some bird seed."

To which the loan officer replied: "I'm sorry, young lady, but in order to take a loan application I have to give you a statement that says we treat girl applicants the same way that we treat boy applicants. I am out of them today, could you come back tomorrow?"

The little girl returned the next day and said, "Mister, I want to get a loan to buy some bird seed."

To which the loan officer replied: "Here is your Equal Credit Opportunity notice. However, I have just been informed by the Examiners that our promissory notes do not have the interest rate printed in terms of Annual Percentage Rate and it is not conspicuous enough. Could you come back tomorrow?"

The little girl returned the next day and said: "Mister, I want to get a loan to buy some bird seed."

To which the loan officer replied: "Your application is now correct showing the 6-percent loan to have an Annual Percentage Rate of 10.90. However, the Examiners have just informed us that on all bird seed loans, the customer has to wait three days before receiving the funds. Could you come back in three days?"

The little girl returned in three days and the loan officer said: "Congratulations! Your loan has been approved, all forms are in compliance and I have a check here for 60 cents."

To which he little girl replied: "Mister, you want to buy a dead bird?"

APRIL 1980
What's in It for Me?

THE SELLING OF SATISFACTION IS ONE of the world's oldest professions. But too many salesmen persist in trying to peddle product instead of satisfaction, with the result that they work harder than necessary and sell less than enough.

Whoever came up with *Chesterfields'* old slogan – "It satisfies" – had it exactly right. Right, that's why, until *Chesterfields* no longer satisfied changed tastes and conditions. "It" because you smoked them one at a time. "Satisfies" because the product was artlessly obvious, but people's perception of it needed perpetual enhancement.

So the prospect who couldn't care less about owning a computer might be able to care a lot if he were offered satisfaction instead of hardware. So the customer who wanted magnetic tape for his $30 cassette recorder might have bought *Supertape* instead of *Concertape*, if our salesman had offered a benefit instead of a box.

"What's in it for me?" is a natural question everyone asks – usually silently – every time an object or a proposition is offered. You asked yourself that question when you came to work for us, when you joined the stock purchase plan, and again today when you decided on the color of your clothing or accessories.

Some people will buy from us because we're NOT *Sears* or *K-Mart*. Some will buy *Realistic* because it's NOT *Panasonic*. They have perceived a benefit that probably has nothing to do with the product. Our store is more accessible. Our product is easier to get serviced. Our salesmen make 'em feel at home. They saw an article in *Fortune* about *Tandy Corporation*. They watch our stock. It's easier to find a parking space. They bought that radio regardless of quality . . . because somehow they found "something in it for them" they didn't find elsewhere, assuming they looked.

The next time you're in the mood to make a deal (instead of writing up an order) see if you can discover what's in it for the other guy. Entertainment? Education? Thrift? The solution to a problem?

The legendary, "better mousetrap" isn't a product, Pal; it is the easily sold benefit of a dead mouse!

MAY 1980
Waste Not, Want Not?

NO, NOT EXACTLY WANT "NOT", I've never met anyone who wanted not. So let's say: want less. So far, two Managers responded to my recent editorial about water with practical suggestions.

Stephen Jones of #8733 in Mableton, Georgia addresses THE PAYROLL DIVISION (my capitals). In respect to mailing payroll information to "payroll 5" he says he has always sent it special delivery as he was told to do. But the post office tells Stephen that since the address is to a P.O. Box they handle it the same as regular mail, "a waste of $1.85 or $48.10 a store a year." I'm memoing (this is a memo) Payroll to inform me tomorrow if Mr. Jones of right or wrong.

Ted Paul or #4365 in Dunkirk, New York has a raft of ideas. (1) The ad package has contents that are mostly irrelevant to him. Waste not! (2) Thermostats in stores should be trimmed back to 65°F and Company sweaters given out or sold to offset the colder environment. Customers be damned, I guess. Also the lights should be turned off. Yes! Mailings should be consolidated – he gets many separate letters in the same week whose separate postage clearly adds up to more than one batched envelope. Right on. Maybe (this is a memo) John McDaniel can save our dough here? Certain forms could perhaps be consolidated . . ." an ICST with an ISCT, a twice yearly revision of the Store Operations Manual instead of the present random manner." Can you hear the applause, Ted? It's for a Paul, not a Kennedy.

The way things are trending in the world, my fellow workers, we had all better be thinking of ways to do more for less. I'm talking transportation. I'm talking productivity. I'm talking about sickness prevention rather than cure, which may mean more physical exercise and less eating. I'm talking fossil fuel. I'm talking about complaining less and converting that energy and hostility into more useful avenues.

Would you walk off and leave the water running in the sink? Then why walk off and leave the lights on? Please don't tell me. Turn off the lights! And also please lock the doors when you go out and lock your car when you're not in it. Don't ask me why. Just do these two simple things.

I'm probably old enough to be your father. It seldom pays to argue with the Old Man, even when he's wrong (and even if he's not your father). I've been that way myself, and I can tell you that on the subject of waste you'll be wasting your time.

JUNE 1980
It's a Lotta Baloney!

A MANAGER WITH SIX YEAR OF SERVICE to the Company resigned last December at the end of the month. Funny. That's when a lot of people pull up their tent pegs and head West looking for pastures that never turn brown. Anyway, he thinks I should know he has a tape of (presumably) his last conversation with his DM. Presumeably our tape too.

However, his point in letting me know about his departure was that "it seem so sad that all the principles that Mr. Tandy stood for are so rapidly fading away in his absence."

You know what I say to that? I say it's a lotta baloney!

We do have, certainly, some things that often are a lotta steak and potatoes. For example: number-battered DMs can forget the value of a guy or gal who has put in six years with us. Plenty of irate Managers forget the same thing. And practically all of us at one time or another, hates his boss (please remember that that's a feeling as well understood on the 19th floor of *Tandy* Center as it is in Indiana, and as normal as apple pie?.

Principles are another thing. Plenty of Managers quit when CDT was around. But our principles have never changed and are not about to change. Contribute to our mutual cause and get rewarded basically on the weight of your contribution. Even so, we've lost a few very well rewarded contributors through the years, usually because they got disenchanted, tired or thought they had a better idea (Note: very few had one that paid as well).

Aside for the morality of it, whoinhell wants to change a winning formula?

We've won so many battles against the odds of becoming a billion dollar baby in consumer electronics. We've pleased so many stockholders, landlords, bankers and just plain folks. How? By doing it our way, consistently, and with heart and a good conscience.

I'll listen to your gripes. I'll debate the reasons you're no longer to play on our team. I'll probably be extremely sympathetic. Just don't ask me to believe we've turned away from operating on the "people principle" that made this outfit All Pro. Because we both know that although your problem is real and its cause is change, the explanation is infinitely more fragile and complex.

JULY 1980
Running Scared

WE CLOSED THE BOOKS ON THE FISCAL 1980 selling year on June 30th. It was another record-setting year for *Radio Shack* and for the *Tandy Corporation*, thank you.

You may not know it but the figures for *Tandy* are the same as those for *Radio Shack*; we are the only operating division of the Corporation. *Tandy* is NOT in the leather business, the tile business, the crafts business, the belt business, the sewing business. *Tandy* is electronics, pure and simple.

Once in 1987 I suggested to Mr. T that we change the name of *Tandy* Corp. to *Radio Shack* "because that's the way people know us." He gave me his piercing look and replied: "Over my dead body, Buster." That probably set a new record for brevity in a dialog with the late Chairman.

With Penny's, Wards and Sears slumping in sales and earnings, *Radio Shack* – or if it please you, *Tandy* – has become something of an anomaly in the retail world; the wolves are waiting for us to fall behind the herd. But we have never felt comfortable playing a catch up role. Even as the audio shop (with which we are so often erroneously compared) flirt with disaster; we just keep doing our thing which, in its humblest terms, is known as "beating last year."

It's a tradition to say our people make all the difference. Without disagreeing, I'd like to mention a few seldom-mentioned differences: (a) our merchandise line; (2) our sales and marketing plan; (3)our financial accounting and legal; departments; (4) our transportation, warehousing and repairing system; (5) our manufacturing section; (6) our A&A import-export program. Trying to break a record without these elements of our business would be tougher than running a three-minute mile.

Sung and unsung, you heroes of fiscal 1980 are as popular on Wall Street as you are here at home. But since bulls turn into bears on elixir no stronger than a jigger of softness in sales, the program for fiscal 1981 should be self-evident. Running scared will just mean you'll get to the bank that much sooner!

AUGUST 1980
Quod Est Demonstrandum

SOME OF MY LETTERS FROM CUSTOMERS are wonderful – love that salesman, your Chats should be published in book form, everything works like a charm, thanks for helping me out when I needed help, and so on.

Some of my letters, well – you could fry eggs on them. The gist is that Nagasaki Hardware is a rip-off, and anyone who likes Jane Fonda is either a freak or an idiot (remind me to ask Henry if that's the way his cookie crumbles).

And then there's the kind that really help. Because they put a finger on a sore spot that can easily be made painless. *"With the hundreds of thousands of dollars that Radio Shack must spend annually just to get me into a store, it always amazes me when I see equipment on display that (a) doesn't work, or (b) isn't even hooked up."*

This is an excerpt from a letter from a Biomedical Equipment Technician who, in general, likes to shop his Vermont *Radio Shack* and, in prior paragraphs, said some very nice things about our equipment.

He said those things about our equipment, not about people, and certainly not about the way our stores are fine-tuned to serve him.

If my reader is a Store Manager, or Salesman, or District Manager, or Regional Manager, or Division Vice President or Senior Vice President of Retailing (I have just called out 175 lucrative positions above store level), I ask you to look at me, your aging chief executive.

I am on my hands and knees, facing all of the great directions of the world (including Mecca), praying that you will hook up your display models and plug in your electrical equipment, and fill your non-AC display models with appropriate batteries or plug-in power supplies.

That which is demonstrated (from the title of the same title) ain't worth a bleep unless it plays. We have thoughtfully provided dials, pilot lights and "on" knobs to overcome this problem. And now I've provided a dissatisfied customer to further identify an area worthy of your attention. In all, it's been quite a busy day.

SEPTEMBER 1980
The Santa Barbara Caper

HERE I GO . . . ABOUT TO HURT SOMEONE'S feeling again. Nut when you've heard me through; let's come back to that notion for another look.

First, how do you like the idea of a customer who finally has to call your chief executive to place a $5,000 order because none of his local *Radio Shack* stores can give him the perfectly reasonable *TRS-80* demonstration that he wants, needs, deserves?

You don't like it? That makes us Pen-Pals, 'cause I don't like it either. This is a first-time computer buyer, mind you, a guy who runs a company with 20 employees, so he wants to be right, he wants to get precisely what he needs; he's convinced *TRS-80* is the way to go. But the poor chap can't get the right time of day from our team. He won't demonstrate our Payroll disc software. They will demo their own little Mailing List system . . . okay, except that's not what he wants. Then they fiddle for an hour trying to run Payroll on a cassette – not the requested disc – and can't seem to load it. "Well," they said, or something like it, "cassettes aren't much good anyway."

In desperation, this small company president phones this large one. "I read your column," he said, "and instinctively liked you."

"I like you too, I said, "and I intend to satisfy you on this problem, no matter what." He was beginning to wonder how we sold computers if simple requests can't be handled in the field.

"I thought you ought to know," he said, "and I don't want to have to drive down to Los Angeles to get an intelligent demonstration. Then I might end up with an Apple, or who knows what."

So I called Mr. Cash. Mr. Cash called the customer and arranged for an in-office demo of whatever he wanted to see and at a time of his choosing. And almost for certain stores that didn't satisfy and didn't even pass him along to CMR or an RSCC won't get any of the rewards. But these same stores would bust their humps if a customer offered to buy ten $500 audio systems for the same $5000.

If the problem is laziness, combined with insufficient training, combined with insufficient sympathy, combined with insufficient desire, I'll hurt a feeling any time . . . if I can start a fire. And listen, my friends, great as a $5,000 order is, a $5 order deserves THE BEST that's in you and in us . . . a thought to hold onto tightly from now to December 25th . . . and then forever.

OCTOBER 1980
Is There Anything Else I Can Show You

THIS BEING THE SELLING SEASON, it behooves a peddler like me to give our salespeople some vintage advice on the care and feeding of prospective customers so that we may peddle enough to soundly defeat last year's numbers. Actually, I'm going to make this lecture exceedingly simple by only giving you one piece of advice instead of my usual three. It is to NEVER ask a prospect "Is there anything else I can show you?"

The reason this advice is so important is that 99 out of every 100 salesmen in 99 out of 100 stores of any kind – including *Radio Shack* – use that awful line as an accompaniment to the writing up of a sales ticket.

DO NOT DO THIS!

First, its's insulting to the customer. The customer has already determined the nature of the purchase; to question its sufficiency is the same as saying: "It would seem, Sir, that you have forgotten something." This on its face is a no-no. And second, in many cases, and to be brutally frank, you haven't shown the customer anything! The customer has made a selection and brought it to you along with some form of payment. Right? – right!

Your intent, of course, is totally admissible. You want the customer to increase her purchase. HAVE THIS FEELING EVERY TIME YOU WRITE UP A SALES TICKET! But do not ask if there's anything else you can show the customer for the reasons developed in the paragraph above.

Now we get down to the nub of my dissertation: How to increase the sale without insulting the customer's intelligence. The answer is embarrassingly simple. MAKE THE CUSTOMER A TANGIBLE OFFER OF SOMETHING SPECIFIC!

Examples of specificity: (1) Do you need any X batteries *(point to them)* for your Y? (2) May I show you our *TRS-80 Pocket Computer* before you go? (3) We have a Z radio on sale that you should really look at *(show it)* because it is as interesting as it is cheap. (4) Maybe you or a friend uses a cassette tape deck or recorder? And if you do *(put in hand)* a blank cassette makes a great gift. (5) I'd like to show you *(do so)* our latest in a calculator that's also an electronic watch.

Well, now that I have shown you a technique that has taken me about 12 years to learn, there's just one more thing I'd like to do before we go our separate ways. And that's to ask you *is there anything else I can show you?* I have the patience, if you have the urge.

NOVEMBER 1980
Two Years Later

CONSIDERING THE PLIGHT OF WARRING NATIONS, and those whose citizens would like to partition themselves off from their brothers (Scotland, Canada, Belgium, etc.), considering the state of things in general; around the world and at home, we at *Tandy Corporation* have a lot to be thankful for this year. More, in point of fact, than usual. Even though our "usual" is quite a lot indeed.

A thing to be extremely thankful for—now for the second year—is that our enterprise didn't falter or fail after the untimely death of its founder, Charles D. Tandy. His passing on November 4, 1978, certainly gave rise in many minds that *Tandy Corp.* and *Radio Shack* were bound to stumble soon.

What we proved to ourselves and to the world was that a well-built structure almost always outlasts its architect. We can be grateful -- as our common stock price attests — that we have passed all the building code requirements once again, and our house is in good order. Mr. T will never know it, but then again Wilbur Wright never flew in a 747.

We can be thankful that our business philosophy has survived amid the tribulations of many of our erstwhile competitors. One of the most conspicuous differences between our way and theirs is the matter of the products we offer. We sell only our own brands. They sell mostly "national" brands. I'm not about to write a lecture on this subject, but the difference between exclusive product marketing and me-too product marketing may be reduced to two very simple words. Pride. Profits. You have more of each when you do it our way. I'm thankful to have had this opportunity that most merchants never get unless they sell Big Macs or gasoline.

I'm thankful for a neat trick I learned from Mr. Tandy. Once, when he complained about a warehouse, I said, "Y'know something, Charles, I can't remember the last time I heard you praise anything around here."

"Buster," he said, albeit with a grim, "if you want to be a Boss you look for what's wrong — not for what's right. You take 'right' for granted because that's what you pay people to do."

Well regardless, enough has been done right during the past two years around here to make a lot of us better off in material things and peace of mind. Thanksgiving Day, 1980, just seemed to me to be the right moment to make public note of it.

DECEMBER 1980
WHILE THE MUSIC LASTS

ONE OF MY FAVORITE POETS WROTE of "music heard so deeply that it I not heard at all, but you are the music while the music lasts."

I find, in this my last Christmas editorial for this space, a message eminently suitable for the season and the occasion. To my mind, the Christmas I celebrate is precisely as substantive as music. Not more. Not less. And only while it lasts.

It's not the business of poets to be specific and this poet (T. S. Eliot) has been more than usually generous in my selection. For once there's no question of interpretation, no little feat of scholarship required. But still, yes, a matter of faith in the ability of the written word to transmigrate into an essence, and all this within the outer limits of a human body, one body at a time; and now, in fact, because tomorrow is definitely too late.

How long "the music lasts — that which I call Christmas — is a private matter, as is the question of any music "being heard at all." My hopes go with you: for a little day music, a little night music. That's what this 1980 Christmas card is all about.

It's my last December one in this particular forum because, as you know, I've set my 65th birthday as my retirement date (July) and done my best to see that "insiders" will continue to run this Company. Meanwhile, I am honored to be your Vice Chairman, despite the theory held in various places that "vice chairmen don't do anything" (a quotation from real life, albeit not from a poet), and I will seek to be the exception.

My particular poet has another uncharacteristically simple thing to say that combines the quintessential music of Christmas with more mundane glory we can all share—the beautiful record our Company has made at a time when a stumble and a fumble might have been excusable.

He said we are "only undefeated because we have gone on trying." No matter how many years he lived in England, Eliot was, as you can now see, born in America and never quite got over it.

DECEMBER AWARDS 1980
Our $1,500,000 Gamble

FOR A COMPANY THAT CONCERNS ITSELF about saving envelopes and stamps—and I hope we never change—to risk 1½ million dollars on our annual divisional meetings takes ignoring a real possibility of failure.

If we fail to motivate our team to desire to win bigger in fiscal 1981, the meetings aren't worth their cost.

If we fail to give our players a total, credible an exciting game plan for fiscal 1981, kiss goodbye our second reason for holding these costly get-togethers.

If we fail to express our gratitude for the harvest of the prior year, then we'd reach a new level of callousness for some future management to cope with.

If our management group should fair to impress our people with its character, intellect, determination, appearance and game plan, then why parade it all over the country at the stockholders' expense?

I started these meetings 11 years ago and ever since, I've defended their value to the folks at *Tandy* and *Radio Shack*. Along the way there were some powerful "no" votes, but my concept has prevailed at least through September 1980.

I also think it's fair to repeat that, in the opinion of most people I've talked to, the FY 80 sessions were well worth the cost and effort to stage them, in Canada as well as in the USA.

Once again you got to see the award winners to whom this issue of Intercom is dedicated. You could see that on the basis of looks alone you can't tell a winner from a loser, so looks (size, shape, sex, color, age) don't win prizes at *Radio Shack*. Location and experience aren't always vital to winning, either, as the record proved.

Edison was supposed to have said that success is 10% inspiration and 80% perspiration. I'd score it 10% luck, 41% desire, and 49% perspiration. But I'd add a footnote to the effect that most people who win don't only do it in public. They wake up in the morning feeling good about themselves and what they're doing. That's the kind of winner I like most to see at our meetings. And I see more of them with every passing year.

JANUARY 1981
Our New "Who's Who"

RADIO SHACK HAS ITS OWN WHO'S WHO and, to make it even more exciting our edition goes well beyond America. What this editorial is all about is our New Who's Who — people we've promoted during the recent game of musical chairs which, in part, was prompted by my retirement in mind-1982.

Of principal importance—young tigers please note! — is that all promotions came from within the Company. None of the heads was hunted (grammatical note: I used "was" because "none" means "not one," a fact that escaped most people who persistently that "were" can now be used.)

There is a nice mix of elder and younger heads, so you can see we don't discriminate due to age or length of service. But, alas, no new female VPs, so some will think in terms of discrimination. And be dead wrong. (Practical note: some of my best friends are women, and some our best employees; and we do have two female VPs, neither of whom is a "token" officer.)

To all of the newly promoted: my most sincere congratulations, in case I haven't gotten around to giving them in person. And to all those who feel they should have been promoted, should have been given the jobs that went to others, my sincerest congratulations for having weathered the disappointment and concluded that truth will (and it will!) out, justice be done, patience rewarded. (Experience note: Some of the most permanent-looking appointments turn out to be the least permanent. Don't ask me why. It just works out that way.)

Finally, it's a pleasure to discuss management changes that aren't brought about by hard times. Our changes are due to good times. Good times meaning good things. Good things like expansion and evolution. We're lucky to have an ever- growing pool of trained peoplepower on which to draw when the going gets good (and the good get going)!

FEBRUARY 1981
Good Management

I'VE KEPT HANDY ON THE TOP OF MY DESK a *New York Times* feature article published last June on the success of a retailing consultant who makes it his affair to get paid for telling other folks how to run their affairs. My experience with management consultants has been very, very bad, so essentially we've bought and sold, hired and fired, leased and vacated, borrowed and paid, without recourse to the many glib Think Tanks available for hire. Nevertheless, when *The Times* publishes a few glittering generalities for the price of the paper, I stop, look and take note.

"It will be a rough year. I think retail earning may be down as much as 15 percent. But good management will help. What's good management? One that takes it's markdown on sores, people and merchandise," said this consultant.

As I write this on 1/13/81, I've just returned from telling our monthly Managers' Class that management isn't just something to a business . . . it's EVERYTHING. Management puts business into business. And it puts them out. Whatever *GM* and *Ford* may have done to remain viable, Chrysler failed to do; it's all in the record we call hindsight. Most corporate catastrophes are the result of a lot of ravished time and invisible jungle rot in the "corner offices." *Radio Shack* and *Tandy* are not responsible for the demise of our erstwhile larger competitors — *Allied* and *Lafayette* — than we were responsible for the Iranian hostage fiasco,.

Taking markdowns on stores means to get out of losers and into winners without waiting for the nine more years on the lease to expire. Taking markdowns on people means to help the losers help themselves to different positions or employers whereby both sides stand a better chance to enjoy the fruits of their labors. Taking markdowns on merchandise is one of the world's oldest professions; it's the result to thinking shopworn, discontinued and overstocked goods as money that slowly self-destructs . . . and that it's YOUR money. (If you just wave at it every day, and do nothing, consider our love affair OVER.)

So in the end, Your Honor, I again respectfully submit we do not need a consultant to tell us how to manage better. What we need is better managers managing better. And that, again for 1981, is predictably what we'll get if we can keep narcissism down to 1971 levels and remember what it was like when all we could brag about was our dream being bigger than anyone's.

APRIL 1981
The Open Door Policy

A LOT OF EMPLOYEES DON'T LISTEN TO US when —at every annual meeting and many in between—we say we have an open door policy.

An open door policy means you can talk to ANY person in the Company about ANY subject at ANY time without fear of revenge, reassignment or release (the three Rs of the corporate world, the academic world, and just about any world you care to dream of except OUR world.

I wouldn't have to knock out these paragraphs if everyone believed or remembered that we have an open door policy. But the pathetic fact is . . . they don't. Instead, they get all squirreled up in their minds about whom to turn to when things turn sour. The typical end results are hysteria, panic and extremely inappropriate action.

Fear of people in high places appears to be instinctive, a natural impulse requiring an artificial antidote. Since common sense does not seem to be instinctive, try common sense. It's common sense that all people are physically pretty much alike—often aging with minor cases of pettiness, jealousy, fear of the known and unknown, and insecurity. Common sense, should tell you that a millimeter before the title there's a person not very different from yourself. Maybe luckier or smarter, maybe not, but certainly not all times and about all things.

If you're afraid of calling me, Mr. Roach, Mr. Keto, Mr. Berger, etc., reach down for a little common sense and try it anyway, The numbers are (all 817-) (all 390-) 3212, 3214, 3372, 3219, respectively. Common sense should tell you that if we're in we'll accept the call, if we're out, and you leave your number, we'll return it.

While I'm not encouraging meaningless calls, it takes only a few meaningful calls per day to keep progress in high gear. We've been telling you to buy Company stock and own a piece of the rock for at least the last 18 years, and 11,778 of you do. If you don't think your bosses listen to stockholders, friends, you've got another think coming. But the open door policy isn't only for those employees who've bet on themselves by investing in *Tandy*. It's for ALL employees. Use it!

May 1981
Our 350th Market

TO SHOW YOU HOW FIGURES LIE and not how liars figure, our 350th market in the USA is a very interesting place. It, with its 349 predecessors counts for 90% of our "company store" business!

Yes, Junior, the other 342 markets (metro areas) in our parade only account for 10% of the business. And there are lots of similar quixotisms in retailing, like the old saying "you do 80% of your business on 10% of your items." Things like that. (little quixotisms — a forced second chance to use that word! — of this nature are actually all some people know of the mysteries of commerce.)

If it really takes 32 markets to do the last measly 10% of our business, why, you might ask, go to all that bother? Why not just run the lovely 350 and do the lovely 90% of our business, and do it all at 10% of our current cost?

It's not exactly like playing the piano with 8 fingers, but something like that analogy will suffice to get you to Kornfeld's First Law of Sufficiency. It reads like this: *All is usually more than most.* There is also a subset: *All is usually better than some.*

And that reminds me of the pie-shaped circles they often use to depict what portions of an enterprise go to which cost-center. For example: cost of goods 60%, labor 25%. And so on. The last, smallest piece is usually what is called profit. Unfortunately for pie-eaters and dividers, you have to go through all the agonies of division just to get that teeny residual slice. You can't get it first, and then cut and run.

Our size provides "economies of scale" — a phrase borrowed from the eastern establishment — that would, at the level of 350 markets, make our business lifestyle unaffordable. You get the whole man (woman) when you marry, not just the preferred parts. So it is with our system.

We had he most *stores* in any market in 1980 in Los Angeles — 142. But in a one-store market in a certain New England state we have a store that does about three times the sales of the average L.A. store.

If you really want to help our cause, *tell me* (tell anyone) *how to triple our L.A. per-store sales volume.* The employee with the winning answer gets to write the next editorial on this page and a quite enormous cash prize. That's the kind of attention fabulous ideas get when they get to your home office's 19th floor!

JUNE 1981
Say it with Numbers!

ABOUT ELEVEN DOZEN MONTHS AGO I wrote my first editorial for *Intercom* as president of your company. It's high time I turn the quill pen over to you, JR, this being the end of our fiscal year.

And WHAT a year! As Mr. Tandy once said: "When we get there, everybody else will look up at us and say . . . . I could have done it!" How true it is that anybody could have done it. *Could have* opened little stores all over the country and beyond.. *Could have* worked out a number of great employee incentive plans. *Could have* reduced the number of stockkeeping units to a manageable 2400. *Could have* found courageous investors, lenders and landlords. *Could have* convinced young trainees that the knowledge of electronics wasn't essential to running a profitable store. *Could have* gone into manufacturing, a project which ultimately led to our crowning commercial success—the TRS80 personal computer.

Dante Russetti, once wrote": "My name is Might-have-been; I am also called No-more (and) Too-late." The columnist, Milt Moskowitz, recently wrote: "Today there are some pretty big companies trying to figure out what *Radio Shack* did and how. Once they figure it out, they would like to do it themselves. O yeah? Like I would like to figure out how to have been John D. Rockefeller's favorite kid!

We have kept fewer things secret than any company I know. For example, at one time we used to figure it cost about $75,000 in various things to open a company store. Okay, Milt, you multiply $75,000 x 4096 company-owned *Radio Shacks* and you get $307,200,000. Then you have to back that up with buildings full of merchandise, employees, factories; then you add selling and administrative costs.

Pretty soon you get a number you can write down on a piece of paper, say $666,666,666, because "6" is my lucky number. Then you have to understand our business (which few do, though we tell 'em many times a year). Then you have to get your products designed, and rent 4096 stores. Along about the year 1986 you can ask yourself if you're where Shack was in 1981, although naturally, we'll be pretty far out of sight again by then.

Our worst kept secret is: there's no such thing as a Sure Thing. You have to work your butt off, first, to stay up with the parade; second, to stay ahead of it; third, to surpass last year. Lately our worst competitor has been inflation, but there's always another adversary. . . . . and another.

That's why I've tried so hard to motivate you in my eleven dozen president's messages. And, boyoboy, you've responded! It stands to reason, friends, that a 42-year old motivator will have more oomph than a sexagenarian-plus fiver. So don't write me. *Say it with numbers.* As a continuing member of our Board of Directors,

I'll be watching you and your numbers more carefully than your average fellow shareholder. And that's a promise!

Part II
Flyer-Side Chats

WHEN YOU PURCHASED SOMETHING at a *Radio Shack* store, the salesman always asked for and usually recorded your name and address. Over the years Radio-Shack mailed millions of flyers to its customers. Additional flyers were distributed to the thousands of *Radio Shack* stores and were inserted in local newspapers.

In addition to featured sale items, bargains of the month, and the latest electronics gadgets, a *Flyer-Side Chat* – a column designed and intended to grab the electronics hobbyist and get him to see all the latest featured items – was a part of the flyer. They were all written by Lewis F. Kornfeld and appeared regularly. In this section of this book we have captured these columns, arranged them in date order.

Sometimes, presented a similar theme to those that appeared in the President's Messages. But they were always aimed at the buyer, the customer. And they were always carefully designed to increase sales. It is my opinion, that these *Flyer-Side Chats* played a huge part in the every expanding sales and growth of *Radio Shack*.

They represent and demonstrate a unique quite successful marketing technique that was responsible for much of the continuous sales growth of *Radio Shack*. They date back to the 1970's and 1980's, yet even today it illustrates and teaches a technique of advertising salesmanship that every advertising/merchandising executive could learn from. -- *Editor*

APRIL 1974
Specials

FROM TIME TO TIME I'M GOING TO HAVE a flyer-side chat with our readers so you can know its *people* who run *Radio Shack* — not machines. My first essay coincides with our 51st birthday. The *Shack* was born when I was seven. I've been with it 25½ years. Those are my credentials.

Sometimes when we run out of a "sale" item we get accused of (1) bait-and-switch tactics, (2) never had it in the first place, (3) only had a few to sell. The plain truth is (1) we rarely sell out of an item although it's *always* our intention, and (2) there are over 2500 places that had to be stocked so you know we had at least several thousand to begin with, (3) we've never used bait and switch tactics in our lives — and like the Miami Dolphins — just win by plugging away at the line.

I apologize to any and all of our customers who have missed out on a "sale" bargain because of our stock position. Can you *please believe* we love to sell you what we advertise? Will you give me a chance to find it for you if we let you down? Now I don't promise to search overseas for that sold-out special. Too much red tape! By year's end we had eight stores in Belgium, one in Holland, nine in England, four in Australia, 162 in Canada, promises in Germany but no action . . . *ach du libe* our Chairman is mad!

As a last word on "specials" I can promise you they're real and — what with shortages, currency changes and inflation — usually irreplaceable at the price. But, our industry, loosely known as "consumer electronics," has a great way of coming up with price-saving technology that keeps our merchandise in the bargain category no matter what. And I think you'll perceive that our particular candy bar doesn't get shorter and shorter. When newspapers were 2¢ apiece and hamburger 33¢ a pound, radios were more expensive and less reliable than they are today in 1974.

JUNE 1974
We Make a Lot of What We Sell

LAST MONTH I PROMISED OUR READERS I'd invade their privacy in these pages by occasionally inserting a personal message. The purpose is not gratification of my ego. The way I see it: you pay my salary and are entitled to know what I'm doing to earn it.

My pet project for the last few and next many years is company-owned manufacturing. From a little platoon back in 1970 when I took office, we now have over 2000 people exclusively engaged in making things we sell. Over half these folks are located in the USA, others in Canada, Japan, and South Korea.

We now make most or all of the following *Radio Shack* product lines: magnetic tape, wire and cable, intercoms, multitesters, small walkie-talkies, AM-FM stereo and quadraphonic receivers, VHF-UHF and CB crystals, television and FM antenna, communications antenna, Science Fair P-Box kits. And other products including our own store signs and fixtures!

Two new factories are just coming on stream here in Fort Worth: one for loudspeaker manufacture—*speakers,* not just boxes; and one for *digital products.* I can promise pleasant surprises before Christmas.

Most of our non-company-made equipment is actually *custom made* for us alone using our designs, features, engineers, and tooling. Prominent among these: speaker systems, CB transceivers, scanners, top-price audio receivers, Science-Fair products, headphones, phonographs, numerous radios and recorders. *Radio Shack does not* sell "private label" goods where our name is merely stuck on in place of somebody else's!

Naturally there are some "look alike" products, just as a gold plated watch "looks like" one of solid gold. Our rigid quality and production standards make many of our suppliers wince with real pain. They say: S****** and M****** have bought them, how come *Radio Shack* won't?

Now bear in mind that S****** and the others are names I've made up to stay out of trouble, and besides that they're all nice people. But the fact is, we won't buy unless we're certain *all doubts* as to reliability and performance have been removed per our specifications. A good example is our aversion to radios made in Hong Kong, where over half the world's radios come from and the price is right. When we can get a Hong Konger to do it *Radio Shack's* way, we might join the parade. *Price*, old friend, is only a *part* of how you keep customers coming back!

JULY 1974
Speakers from Our Fort Worth Factory

THE 28TH OF MARCH WAS AN IMPORTANT DATE. That was when our first *company-built* loudspeaker rolled down the line in our new factory in Fort Worth, USA. Our factory, incidentally, is the newest speaker factory in the world, let alone Texas.

The first speaker was a 6 x 9" acoustic suspension model with a 10-oz. magnet, cloth suspension, and a navy blue cone. Blue doesn't sound better than black, but it matches the décor of our new anechoic chamber. Among the hidden (invisible) benefits we've built-in is *exact* impedance. Our experts point out that (a) it is important, and (b) it's unusual to be this accurate because, perhaps, nobody cares. But *we care*, and we care that you know we care!

Frankly, we could buy speakers "cheaper" than the speakers we'll be making from March 18 on. But we couldn't control what we'd get. We couldn't innovate. We've seen cheaper speakers in Singapore and Mexico, but what we saw we didn't care to sell. We can and will compete with the best of the USA, Japan and Europe. And since we started after they did, we think we've profited by all their errors and omissions. And as a by-product, created some brand new American jobs.

When *Radio Shack* opened the world's newest magnetic tape factory, also in Fort Worth, a lot of people thought we were crazy because tape is difficult to make and easy to buy. Now that we've got a tape as good or better (better we think) than anybody's, people think maybe we're not crazy — just audacious. It's selling quite nicely in our stores in Europe, right under BASF's nose, so to speak. Why not? *They're* selling under *our* nose!

When you see that 6 x 9" speaker with the blue cone, black surround, and *Realistic* on the box, think of the company that isn't crazy — just audacious. We dare to do anything in electronics that has the prospect of making life a bit more pleasant for all the great folks who work for — and buy from *Radio Shack*.

AUGUST 1974
We Control Our Quality

FOR THE MONTH OF FEBRUARY 1974 our figure for Repair Expense at our stress was 0.52% of sales, an improvement of 0.02% over last year. I have no way of knowing exactly what other folks do, but in my book it's a good number. It proves what we'd like to say about *Quality* if anyone believed in advertising.

Aside from our natural desire to produce and distribute the best possible merchandise at all price levels, we have a built-in need for being extra careful about what we make and sell: *all 11,000.000 of our current customers!*

We probably waited on 3,000,000 customers that particular month; about 125,000 people every working day. Imagine the catastrophe if 5% had product failures — we would have had 150,000 things to fix in February alone!

So you can see we don't rely on luck, fate or providence to assure ourselves (and you) of stuff that works the moment you plug it in, and keeps on working. I won't bore you with the number of engineers, labs, check and rechecks we employ to keep us (and you) out of trouble. But it may well be the biggest secret of our success.

Back in the good-old bad-old days when The Shack was an all-brands house, our repair problem was worse with only 9 stores than it is today with over 2000. *We have full control over our quality.* We don't leave it to the heroes of the slick magazine ads and consumer reports and the guys who used to say "well you're the only one having this trouble." We have the old-fashioned Model-T approach that *our* basic transportation will get you there and back, every day, without fail.

And when something goes awry, we back it up with original parts and service in every nook and corner of this country. Now I won't say you'll "never" have to wait. But compared to any other brand I've ever heard of ours' look like "the winged seraphs of heaven" in Mr. Poe's poem.

So now you know why I wake up every morning feeling good about our *Realistic, Archer, Micronta, Science Fair* and other famous brands. Like the man in the ads said: *they're working!*

SEPTEMBER 1974
We Sell ONLY Our Own Products

WITH RCA, PHILCO-FORD, WESTINGHOUSE, *Ampex, Motorola, Columbia Masterworks* and many of the famous old American brands gone or going from the American "Audio" scene, our own very dynamic *Realistic* brand seems to be one of the inheritors of their mantle. For us, and I hope for you, it's all for the best. Looking back down the years and being, perhaps, a bit superficial, I think I can explain our rise and their fall. It contains some interesting lessons.

(1) Competition isn't merely "meeting" somebody else's price. That's a confession that your product is identical to their product, or that ingenuity has no intrinsic value.

(2) Two-step distribution through middlemen is archaic; the public won't pay the price, neither will the dealer.

(3) Small purchases equal small sales. If not enough is bought to sell, it's impossible to turn around fast enough to meet demand. Large risks must be taken in terms of inventory, sales plan, and design.

(4) The radio-phono-tape business is not easy and shouldn't be treated as a sideline to activities such as TV.

(5) Reliability, regardless of an item's price, should take priority to any other consideration including demand and novelty.

Radio Shack has done a number of interesting things that most of the others can't or won't do. We sell ONLY our own products. Our ads have addresses. We don't sell to discount stores with zero service and nothing to sell but price. We run conveniently located small stores. We publish a catalog containing everything we sell. We manufacture as well as buy. We've meant something to lots of people for 51 years. We don't take you or ourselves for granted.

While I'm truly sorry to see the Big Names drop by the wayside after all those years, all that advertising, all that R&D expense, I'll recover — just as I did from Pierce-Arrow and Old Dutch Cleanser. So will you. *Radio Shack* and *Realistic* promise to continue to grow the way you'd like and to continue earning the respect required to do business in the USA. It's more than a promise. It's a *determination.* And isn't that what those other Companies may have lacked, when you analyze the facts?

OCTOBER 1974
Our Catalog – Our Prices

THIS SPRING I PROMISED TO CONTACT YOU via this column whenever there was news to share with you. Today I have a doubleheader: our catalog, and our prices. A recent *Wall Street Journal* story revealed that *Wrigley's* has raised its wholesale gum prices 15% but is "hopeful" retailers will keep their selling price at a dime per package.

At a dime, the price of gum is double what it used to be. The same story observed that *Life Savers* has recently raised the retail price of their product by 50% to 15 cents a roll. That's triple the familiar nickel price of the recent past.

Radio Shack, in case you haven't noticed, has instituted only nominal price increases and none, I believe, in anything like the 50% to 300% jumps noted above. Our secret has been our ability to pare costs with technical improvements aimed at giving more for less, plus improved line productivity. The growing size of our orders has really helped us offset much of the brutal increases we have seen in raw materials.

Whereas the automobile industry has seen as many as five price hikes in a single season, we've basically held the line with one. And we have not and will not cut corners in performance in order to keep prices in line.

All of our prices are displayed in our new 1975 catalog — just off the press. The catalog now costs us about 50% more than it used to. But the cost to you is still the same: Zero! We spend nearly $2,500,000 to keep you and our Managers precisely informed as to what we sell and for how much — in the USA only; the same is done in Canada and abroad, so the true cost is near $3,500,000.

We hope you will use and appreciate this book. It's just another reason why our people are better acquainted with their product lines than salespersons in other shops. It also lets you study our products in depth. As for prices, we publish them loud and clear, proud of their low profile in this day of abnormal escalation. I Hope "the only catalog that isn't Me Too" will make your shopping easier again this year. We've bet 2½ megabucks it will.

JANUARY 1975
A New Year's Greeting

FROM TIME TO TIME I'VE PROMISED to write a personal note to our customers. And it's that time again. And since it's a retailing tradition to celebrate the New Year with a greeting . . .

To those among you who may think we like to be out of stock on advertised items: please be again advised to the contrary. Our problem is compounded by late deliveries from suppliers and early deadlines by printers, but we NEVER intend not to have what's advertised and not to sell out to the bare walls, so help me!

To those of you who like classical music: may I recommend our *Realistic STA-82*, a receiver I personally use about 5 hours a day for good-music listening and which produces the best FM sound I've ever had in my home.

To those who have stood in line waiting for CB equipment to arrive: your patience is appreciated and our Buyer predicts a steadily improving inventory position during 1975. At present day phone costs, CB is a very satisfying bargain.

To the "other" company which advertises it's "Number One" in CB: Happy New Year but — how's that again?

To the product-review magazines: thanks for the many nice reports on *Realistic* equipment—none in behalf of increased advertising — and especially those from Canada where critics "tell it like it is."

To the FTC: our gratitude for cleaning up the watts (watt-er-gate!) scandal and reducing audio power to disortionless claims.

To our price-conscious friends: we've just gone through six months without raising a single price, so even if you're not grateful, at least be well informed. Our Treasurer thinks we're crazy.

To those curious about our TV ads: they're costing us about $3,500,000. Or about $11,666.67 per every working day of the year. The announcer, actor Paul Burke who is, by the way, a *Realistic* hi-fi system owner. Paul says he enjoys doing the ads. At least (we think) they're a refreshing change from beer and hair-spray. More to come!

To those who wonder why we don't sell TV sets: we're too busy watching the giant manufacurers — *RCA, Zenith, Magnavox* (now *Phillips*), *Motorola* (now *Matsushita/Quasar*), and *Sylvania* (now rumored also to be *Philco*)—kill each other off for the glory of eternally free enterprise and red ink.

To those who bought from Radio Shack in 1974: Thank you each and every one, from each and every one of our more than 9000 employees in 50 states and 11 countries. We may be commercial but gratitude is a VERY real thing at *Radio Shack*.

FEBRUARY 1975
No Price Increases for One Solid Year!

ONCE IN A WHILE I'VE GOT SOMETHING important to convey to you. This is that "once" and I feel certain you'll personally appreciate it as I interpret "important" to mean Something Directly Affecting Your Pocketbook in 1975.

As you must have suspected, almost everything we touched went up in cost since our last pricing period which officially was July 1, 1974. Despite this, we decided to hold the line until our next pricing period, January 1, 1975. Frankly we felt it was a policy we could live with unless the lid really blew off. As we watched other folk's prices go up during the Summer and Fall, we wondered a bit about our fiscal sanity.

As we watched Nixon exit and Ford enter, we wondered a bit about being locked in by a return to price controls. As we heard Mansfield and Albert threaten controls, we watched Ford take off for Japan. We also watched our sales: 34.4% increase from July through October. And we held the line.

As Christmas approached, we held our pricing meeting to prepare for the printing of our Winter Price Book — the one every Manager carries. Numerous categories seemed to scream for increases. A lot had happened in the past 56 months, none of it the least bit deflationary. You'd be astounded at how much the paper, ink and postage used in this Flyer are costing us versus last Spring — maybe they're using too much sugar?

Finally, as we labored over our inflated luncheon and 20¢ cup of dime coffee, we made a decision that was just possibly the least-commercial decision we've made in the last 26 years. Everything we're going to sell from January through June 1975 will be sold at the last-July through last-December price. No increase then. NO INCREASE NOW.

Somebody somewhere had to say it. And we mean it. Just maybe it will start a fad. And as long as we're going to do it. We'll let EVEYBODY know. Heaven knows there's enough bad news in the media . . . are they interested in GOOD NEWS? We'll see. Meanwhile, you, at least, know our position in every company-owned and operated *Radio Shack*. No price increases for ONE SOLID YEAR! But decreases as always. Whenever we have a Sale. Just about always!

APRIL 1975
Free Battery Card

IT HAS FINALLY HAPPENED: a customer has actually *complained* about getting a free battery every month via our famous Battery-a-Month card. His complaint was that he thought he was entitled to the 12 batteries in clusters of, say, two whenever needed and then X-number of random times until 12 were received.

Not so, Sir, and there's no fine print, insurance policy style. You get any ONE of a specified four types during any one month. For 12 months. For absolutely no cost or obligation. Like it says on the card.

The biggest bargain is our 9-volt *#23-464* which sells for 49¢ each, a low price no matter how you figure it. If you picked up one of these at our participating store every month during 1975 you'd save $5.88.

To me $5.88 is still money. And it's money we give away gratis (albeit 1/12th at a time) for a very simple reason. We'd, like to see you that often. Life without you would be lonely indeed. Thus we're willing to gamble that during at least one of your visits you might buy something.

The last thing we had in mind was to rip-off anybody because our giveaway wasn't timed to his actual needs. But now we must in truth record that one citizen out of perhaps 5,000,000 (maybe 10?) is miffed. My question is: have you had the opportunity to test this program?

If not, your nearest *Radio Shack* will be delighted to give you the card entitling you to one battery each month for one year. The card and the batteries are free. There will be no sour looks if all you do is smile and collect your battery and disappear for 31 days. In fact if there isn't a SMILE, let me know!

MAY 1975
Our Parent is *Tandy*

NOT EVERYONE IN THIS BEST OF ALL possible worlds likes his parents. Head-shrinkers spend much of their time working on the quandary. *Radio Shack*, on the other hand, has no such problems.

Our (singular) parent is *Tandy* Corporation and we are very fond of it, him, or her, depending on whatever sex you choose to apply to a corporation. *Tandy* has bankrolled our fantastic growth without a complaint. It's pretty hard to hate a Sugar Daddy.

Tandy borrows and raises equity money to feed our hunger for more stores, more employees. TV programs, a QC Vice President; you name it — we get it. Of course we give some back, but there's no doubt we're indulged and pampered. Who else but Super Mom would let us make calculators in our own factory at a time when other calculator-makers are going broke?

Well we're extremely proud of our parent. Known as TAN on the Big Board (The New York Stock Exchange). *Tandy* has a fabulous track record—for earnings-per-share and other performance figures—that goes back the entire 12 years of our life with the Caliphs of Fort Worth.

In recent months TAN has seen its common stock soar almost 300% from its 1974 low. I say "almost" because that's how it is at this particular moment and Wall Street is not a place where absolutes are in vogue. None of the other socks I watch have done anything like Dear Old TAN. None of the other stocks I own, I might add.

This type of thing makes a parent extremely lovable to its kith and kin and its over 10,l000 stockholders — many of whom are employees. It is also gratifying to see "The Corp" selling off divisions it no longer needs or wants. It takes real guts to de-conglomerate. And it means that the remaining decisions will get more dough to play with. And boy do we love dough.

Please note: this editorial is not an offer to buy or sell or recommend stock. They do that sort of thing in prospectuses (prospecti?) It's merely a paean of praise for *Tandy* Corporation, the determined men who have financed our rise to within a cat's whisker of a half-billion in sales. They used to think the sun rose and set on leather. But now? Now it doesn't work on batteries or AC, they can't work up much interest. And? To be extremely plagiaristic: than to you . . . it's working!

AUGUST 1975
CB Radio is Hot!

THE FAST-BUCK ARTISTS IN AND OUTSIDE of our industry have just discovered Citizens Band 2-way radio and, alas, you'll find all kinds of "shlock" being offered at all kinds of prices in 1975-6. And at all kinds of stores. For example: hi-fi salons! We hear there are 70 new CB manufacturers in Japan alone.

There's just no way these hungry newcomers can do right by this wonderful communications medium. *Radio Shack* entered it as a serious business in 1959. Our first *Realistic* transceiver was produced in 1960. These original ventures were costly indeed: environmental, RF circuit and ruggedness problems sprung up like weeds. Even today the technology is treacherous, the airways so thronged that all parts of a CB system have to be letter-perfect just to be acceptable.

CB manufacturing and sales problems leave little room for amateurs at either game. Of all the companies I'd call professional, *Radio Shack* (in more than just my opinion) stands supreme. We design, we manufacture, we sell, we service. And we have just two brands: *Realistic* and *Archer*. Ours' alone.

Realistic produces mobile, base station and walkie-talkies. Everything requiting it is FCC type-accepted and U.L. listed. We also manufacture our own crystals for sets needing separate plug-ins.

Archer produces all the antennas required for mobile or base station use, and many CB accessories. In a nearby company-owned and operated factory we produce the coax cables. In yet another, the little 100-milli-watt and other walkie-talkies sold as *Archer* products.

Over the years we've sold well over 1,000,000 *Realistic* and *Archer* transceivers, and the end is nowhere in sight. They're used by explorers, businessmen, sailors, farmers, truckers, coaches, hunters, fishermen, contractors, teachers, kids, motorists, grown-ups, nature lovers, mobile home dwellers, students and—who knows — maybe even the Cambodian navy.

People are just crazy about talking to other people, particularly when there's no monthly phone bill to pay and virtually no limit, except terrain, to where and how CB may be used. We recall one helicopter pilot who talked to folks on the ground via our equipment.

If you're thinking of getting a CB — and you should! — take your Uncle Low's advice and get into *Realistic* before you get stuck with a lemon. The Lemon Season is upon us, I'm warning you. Last year it was "cheapie" calculators that conked out. But not ours! See what I mean?

SEPTEMBER 1975
Our Giant Catalog is Free

WHEN I FIRST JOINED RADIO SHACK in September 1948 (as ad manager) my first job was to attend to our annual catalog which was running very late. We had just one store. It was our 25th year of business. And our entire year's sales were a shade UNDER a day's sales today!

Now I have helped publish exactly 28 consecutive annual catalogs, undoubtedly a world's record for electronics companies — Guinness please note. And while the 1949 book leaves much to be desired, and the 1961 book is my favorite, there's no doubt that our new 1976 book is the prettiest and contains the finest product line we've yet produced.

The *Shack* catalog is an industry tradition. Despite its cost ($2.6 million) we still give it away free — this year to over 10 million people. We run out of books around January, except for the few we save for new-store openings. Then you have to wait until Labor Day for the next issue. *Catalog '76* is available now in all our stores and my advice is to get your copy NOW! You won't hurt anyone's feelings if you drop in for a book and leave without buying anything.

But if you do buy something you'll please everyone, including yourself. I'll tell you why. Taking our whole 1976 line and measuring 1975 against it, you'll find that on average our prices have gone up less than 1%. Our Treasurer thinks this is very dumb. But, albeit that he is brilliant, he's not a merchant. Merchants are not known for being brilliant. We rely a lot on intuition, gut-feel, and other indicators rarely used in determining the GNP or world economic conditions. We also, dear friend, depend a lot upon plain old You.

While the recession lingers, we think it's a poor time to reduce the size of our chocolate bar or add 3 sticks of gun and charge double or triple. That's the way our big new free book reads, and I'll be surprised if you don't react favorably.

Our catalog changes quite a bit from year to the next, but in ways difficult to see. Nothing in *Catalog 49* is repeated in *Catalog 76*. Our highest price of hi-fi in 1949 was a *Scott* amplifier (monophonic) at $269. Distortion was 2%. Bottom end was 30 cycles. Power 20 watts. *Meissner* had a monophonic tuner-amplifier (receiver) rated at 18 watts and priced at $198.40 less cabinet. Now you get about double the quality for the same price. Which explains why *Radio Shack* is the Biggest Game in Town. You can see it all "hung out" in our just-published free catalog!

OCTOBER 1975
We're Fixers, not Fakers

BLESS OUR GOVERNMENT, which in its infinite wisdom, deleted the word Guarantee from the vocabulary of purveyor of consumer products after 200 years of successful use by such as us in this country.

As *Nations Business Magazine* puts it: "the word guarantee, although it holds the same meaning as warranty to businessmen, will be dropped, advises FTC, because its use in connection with warranties is said to confuse customers."

Personally, I find the reverse to be true, namely that the word guarantee is much more familiar to us Americans, but then I only have two college degrees in English and am well aware that there are folks with three. I would not, however, expect to find them on the FTC. But that's just a hunch.

What it means to you and me who consume is that there are now three choices: something they call Full Warrantee, something they call Limited Warrantee, and—nothing! At this writing no one is 100% certain of what a Full Warrantee is, in the sense that penalties could be incurred. And who wants penalties for an uncertain ruling.

So we, in our infinite wisdom (no letters on this, please) have decided to drop the word guarantee and substitute the words Limited Warrantee in every instance where we've had a guarantee spelled out. I find it amusing, if a little pathetic, that our Lifetime Tube line will now have a Limited Lifetime Warranty. Forever, as we define that word! Heaven help us if we must further qualify "forever", but don't sell bureaucracy short on dreaming up new ways to tighten the noose.

What's it all about, Alfie? It's to protect the unwary customer. Granted we need protection. But I have always felt that we had recourse when we felt gypped, and our common sense would steer us away from vendors who burnt us once—even a some among us occasionally burn them! This includes ice cream that melts too fast, cars that break down too often, and deals with too much fine type on the back of the contract.

Radio Shack customers may be assured that, as for the past 52 years, we will walk the same extra mile to back up our written promises. There is fast recourse through our hierarchy if one of our young bucks fails to serve you properly. Because we're fixers, not fakers.

I would wish the heirs of the founding fathers would please get us new foreign policy, a new oil policy, a better economic policy, a solution to busing problems, and lean quite a bit less heavily upon us who provide the jobs which in turn provide the taxes which in turn let the government govern. These latter have never been subject either to guarantee or warranty, full or limited. And yet we have to keep buying their "product." Bad as it is, however, I wouldn't swap- it for

Portugal, India, or North Korea. Because their warrantee is not to protect but to guarantee — silence.

DECEMBER 1975
We Wish You A Merry

IT'S A TRADITION AMONG RETAILERS to wish their customers a Merry Christmas in print, usually in a newspaper ad and often in verse form. Their wishes are from the heart, and I'll tell you why: without your activity in December many stores would run a loss for the year. *Radio Shack* does about 15% of its sales this month. Thus on average each of the other 11 months is only 7.7%. Merry Christmas? You Betcha!

Every December I thank my lucky stars I'm in the entertainment business. Because a *Radio Shack* gift is something "that plays all; year." It doesn't wilt at sundown or crunch under the patter of little feet. It's sensible, useful and affordable. Yes, Virginia, I'm a bit opposed to flowers and candy. And I find that booze just doesn't last very long.

When I was a kid, I was terribly disappointed if anyone gave me a gift of clothing. What a gift? I got clothing all year long. To my little mind, a necktie or a pair of glove were not what Yuletide was designed for. Even an envelope with a crisp bill inside didn't turn me on, although it was gratefully accepted, yes even down to this very day.

I was and still am, a Donder and Blitzen person, meaning that I believed in Santa Claus and had specific notions as to what was and wasn't appropriate for loading into a sleigh. Candy and money were okay for stockings hung over the fireplace. But this was merely tokenism. Basic gifts were lovingly wrapped and placed under The Tree. They didn't have to be numerous or expensive, but PLEASE no clothes.

Aunts who came to our house long after the opening of the gifts were not the problem. They invariably brought a tie, a pair of gloves, or a scarf. This category of relative could not be blamed for their insensitivity; they were born that way.

But not Mom and Dad. Curses on them if something like a *Science Fair Kit*, an *Archer Space Patrol*, or a *Realistic* radio or phonograph didn't turn up under the tinseled boughs. And when it did, the sentiment and he memory lasted for at least a year. Had the calculator been invented in my youth . . . wow, what a gift! The pain (and futility) of trying to square a root, which has scarred my entire life, would have been spared. Why, please, does anyone desire to square a root?

That Christmas has become commercial doesn't bother me a bit. For kids — all of us — It's the day of days, of glad anticipation, and fragile as a gardenia. I am absolutely positive we have the gift that won't let you down. Not wearable. Inedible. Available only at our stores. A *Radio Shack* gift proving You Really Care— isn't that what Dec. 25 is (partly) all about?

FEBRUARY 1976
"We're Fixers, Not Fakers"

NOW THAT IT'S ACTUALLY 1976 and America's bicentennial year, you'd better be prepared for an epic flood of merchandise celebrating the event. I can well remember the nation's sesquicentennial (1926) and the liberty bell postage stamp heralding our 150th birthday; it too was an occasion for commemorative products, panoply, and proclamation. I am an unabashed lover of and a believer in the United States of America. And while I also know that behind every hung flag here's a manufacturer and an incentive, I also know that making and selling is a part of our heritage, our strength, yes — our genius. How else does a flag get made to be waved?

Radio Shack did its commercial "thing" by creating our *Spirit of '76 Radio*, item #12-1776, price $19.95. It appeared on the inside front cover of our catalog, and, In January, on network television. The focal point of this attractive product is a custom casing — very solid metal — of the famous drum and fife trio. By itself, the metal group is worth more than the $19.95 if it may be compared to a recently advertised pewter version offered nationally at $125 and without a radio to sit on. Anyway I can recommend our bargain to you as a potential collector's item; the edition is limited to just 50,000 sets for a population of 220,000,000 and will never again go into production. Where, I wonder, are my once treasured sesqui-centennial cups and coins, and how much are they worth today?

Many things of interest are happening in our country today. One is the government's crackdown on advertisers who say "sale" and then don't (allergy) do everything required to back up what they say. Personally I've always taken it for granted that when a store says "sale" it only means there's a sale on certain items unless, of course, the ad says "every item in our stock." Our custom has been to specifically designate very sale item with a "regular" and "sale" price and publish an over-all termination date. I trust this hasn't fooled anyone, because foolery has no place in business.

I've often said that when we advertise a "sale" item it's our intention to sell every piece available at the sale price. However, when you're dealing with thousands of outlets, it's virtually impossible to make a perfect distribution of the affected merchandise. Managers may order too many or too few. Suppliers may goof. Trucks may get delayed. Or the Sale becomes an "overkill" because too many buyers turn up for too little goods, or the price was too deeply cut.

Please accept my apologies if you have been greeted by an empty shelf. A "sale" is not an exact science. And we are not perfect. If you ever feel "ripped off" because you got there too late and desperately want what wasn't there, write me personally and I'll search the entire country to get it for you. To quote myself, "we're fixers, not fakers," and believe me I will do everything humanly possible to satisfy you. Not only in our 200th year, but as long as I have my job!

MARCH 1976
New Ads, New Stores, New Products

AS PREVIOUSLY STATED, THIS COLUMN is written to make our rather large and far-flung company more personal and available to you. Please feel you know somebody at *Radio Shack* who may be talked to, written to, yelled at, or visited in person. I am not "Mr. Illegible" as one reader said, being unable to decipher my signature; the name is Lewis Kornfeld. Having become a grandfather for the first time on Christmas Eve, I'm in an excellent mood for détente (at the very worst) if something's bothering you.

On December 26th Paul Harvey, the famous news commentator, delivered the first of 52 weekly radio commercials for us on his early morning drive-time show heard (in Texas) at 7:30 a.m. His vehicle is the *ABC "Paul Harvey Network"* of 641 stations. As I reckon the cost to us, it's exactly $61.10 per second of our message. Hello Americans! That's what it takes to hire a super-salesman who, incidentally, writes all his copy himself without even a secretary.

Talk about bringing coals to Newcastle . . . we've just opened two new stores in Tokyo!

Talk about the Iron Curtain and the Bamboo Curtain, we've just discovered the Paper Curtain — right here in this country. The *New Yorker* magazine has rejected an ad campaign of ours. Yes: rejected! Repeated requests for a reason have been met with quote "no useful purpose would be served by pursuing the matter any further" unquote.

Our fiscal year began on July 1, 1975. I'm, pleased to report that since July, in all outlets under our control, *Radio Shack* hasn't raised its prices a single penny. Going back another 12 months before that, our prices on average have risen less than 1%, despite a variety of material and labor cost increases which were absorbed. We've never needed a "fair trade law" to trade fair — bad grammar intentional.

Watch these pages for the announcement of a new product dreamed up by Yours Truly. It's a mobile CB transceiver called *"The One Hander"* because everything you need is contained in ONE palm-sized unit you can operate with just one hand: channel-selector, on-off volume, squelch, mike, speaker! This design makes it easy to hide the whole system from light-fingered citizens.

You've wanted a loud loudspeaker from *Realistic*? Come hear our "leather-lunged" *Mach One*, designed for the disco-generation but also refined behavior when Vivaldi comes down the system. Ask our Manager to take off the grille and show you the guts. *Mach One* is just the beginning of many new *Radio-Shack* hi-fi surprises for 1976.

APRIL 1976
Hi-Fi Receivers – Calculators – Who We Are

THE MARCH ISSUE OF STEREO-REVIEW magazine has some nice things to say about our new *STA-90* hi-fi receiver, among them that it's "comparable to most receivers selling for somewhat higher prices."

Considering the quality of the competition, that particular complement is what I like to hear. We don't start on a project like the *STA-90* with the intent to price below *Pioneer, Sansui, Fisher*, et al., but that's the way it usually works out. We don't have the costs typical of 2-step or factory-rep distribution. And it could very well be that our production runs are longer, with a corresponding increase in on-line proficiency and decrease in unit cost.

Anyway, at $359.95 the STA-90 was found to perform "on a par with any under-$500 receiver we have seen." And *Stereo Revue* has seen plenty! So have we. It's not our intention to come in second. However, $359.95 is heavy money for most people. Our store system has been more comfortable in the $200-$299 range and believe me, we're not deserting those price points to gratify the whim of a few audiophiles. We do, on the other hand, aspire to become something akin to the *Leica* camera: the presold brand in audio. We've been hard at work on this image since our first *Realistic* components were born in the mid 1950s.

Some things in life seem to work out for the benefit of the consuming public. Take calculators for example. I've yet to read that a major producer has made its first nickel in this category. In their haste to lower prices before the next guy, they reduced a (1973) $130 item to a (1976) $15 football, and as a consequence produced oceans of red ink. *Radio Shack* calculators represent an incredible value because — alas for them — our suppliers couldn't calculate. The next similar product is going to be the LED or LCD watch. Any price under $90 is a sensible price. Any price over $90 will have to represent the watch's value as jewelry because accuracy and other factors are identical. I'm very glad I'm not a Swiss watchmaker!

No you're not seeing things: *Tandy* has de-conglomerated into three separate companies. *Tandy Corporation* (principally *Radio Shack*) on the New York Stock Exchange. *Tandy*crafts (principally *Tandy Leather, American Handicrafts and Color Tile*) also NYSE. And *Tandy* Brands, traded on the American exchange, and consisting of leather companies — principally *Hickok Tex Tan*. At press time *Tandy* parts were worth more to investors than *Tandy* whole.

MAY 1976
$100,000 CB Song Search – New CB Invention

IF YOU KNOW ANY BUDDING SONG WRITERS, tell them to get down to their nearest **Radio Shack** and pick up an entry blank to our *1976 $100,000 CB Song Search*. Such is the popularity of CB radio that everyone's trying to get into the act — badge designers, map makers, beer mug vendors, book writers, congressmen, radio programmers. And now, us, with our song contest.

But of course we will succeed. Because we will distribute $100,000 among 50 winners and ultimately produce an LP record and a tape of the 10 top original songs (words and music) submitted. Success is virtually guaranteed when you're giving out coin of this or any other realm.

Our book: *All About CB Radio"* is a best-seller any way you look at it. Since its publication last January, it has sold about 1,500,000 copies. Many professional publishers are working feverously on similar books but *Radio Shack* got there first with the mostest and very likely the cheapest.

After July 1, 1976, we'll make an overdue correction in our age. We'd thought he Shack was founded in 1923. Now it seems that the proper date is 1921. When the USA celebrates its 200th, we'll be 55. So popular, and hence desirable has the word *"Shack"* become in the world of electronics that our trademark lawyer glumly predicts a never-ending series of battles to protect our good name. We fight 'em all and haven't lost yet, but the copycats keep trying.

By now you may have had a chance to examine our new CB invention, the *One Hander.* It's the only radio that puts it all into the same one hand that holds the microphone — on-off, volume, squelch, channel selector, speaker, and mike. I believe our patent has just been issued. Don't know why it took us 16 years to develop a transceiver like the *One Hander*. It's that logical.

We've just gotten our third factory in the Masan Free Zone near Pusan in South Korea, giving us a total manufacturing space of 108,000 square feet in that area. Products made there include intercoms, hi-fi receivers, walkie-talkies, radios and multitesters. In Fort Worth our communications antenna factory has now been quadrupled in size. Our famous *Archer* CB antennas are made there, also *Archer* scanner antennas. You're welcome to visit if you ever come to town.

Some of our Managers have asked me again to explain to you why we ask for your name and address when you shop at *Radio Shack*. It's to keep us up to date on your whereabouts so we can mail you our flyers. Although our mailing list is computerized, neither it nor our computer is ever perfect. And our optical scanner, while it's a fabulous gadget, sometimes makes incredible boo-boos. It takes only a few seconds of your time to give our hard-working guys and gals this information. But once in a while we run into a customer who feels it is an imposition. And they run into a Manager who lives by our rules. We hope you'll appreciate that top management, not the Manager, is the source of such minor irritations. Thank you!!

JUNE 1976
Touching All the Bases – A Little of This and That

WHEN A FELLOW PHONES YOU PERSONALLY and says "I've got the only LP record album authorized by the U.S. Congress as the official bicentennial record album," you say "Hmmm," but you don't believe. Then you find out it's true. Then you buy the ALL. Then you become the only place to get it! Ask for the 2-disc album. all four American military service bands.

I hear all sorts of things just sitting on my duff in this mess that's classified as an office. For example" Muhammad Ali, the champion boxer, is an avid CBer whose handle is The Big Bopper. And then a Florida newspaper calls to report the death at 89, of one of *The Shack's* five founding brothers, none of whom has been with the company since 1963. This on the same day I had lunch with Bill Halligan, the retired founder of *Hallicrafters*, who worked for *Radio Shack* in 1924.

After leading us right up to the altar in respect to new CB channels, the FCC suddenly changed its mind (for technical reasons, not for lack of affection) and our resent 23 remain unchanged for 1976 at least. A new and faster license-processing system will be installed, however by this very diligent branch of our government of which so much is demanded by so many.

'Tis the last year for our 20 year-old *Solo-1* speaker. Born in 1956, it represented *Radio Shack*'s first venture into custom loudspeaker systems. Its place will be taken by the new *Minimus-5* weighing in at 12¼ x 9x 6½ inches and $29.95. Both systems are crafted of genuine oiled walnut veneer-wood, not plastic. We still believe in nice things and wood furniture is one of them. *Solo-1* in its two decades went through a variety of finished: mahogany, blond, teak, polished walnut, oiled walnut. See the contemporary *Minimus–5* today and be pleasantly surprised.

Our wire factory now has 90 braiders in service. These are machines which wind the shielding over the central core of CB, audio and other cables in just about the same way weaving has been done since 1895. But will we ever catch up on RG-58U? Yes, they say we will.

Get yourself an *STA-77* receiver pronto if you like good music and great value. At $149.95 it $100 off on a genuine 32-watt stereo product (16/16 RMS @ 20-20K @0.9% in FTC lingo) and, to give you a little known fact, this item is entirely manufactured by us in one of our hi-fi factories. Don't bother to compare. We're lower than anybody and prettier, too.

Just back am I from England and Spain. Rightfully (but they won't tell you) we're the envy of every society whose problems are worse than ours. And by that I mean EVERY society. Listen "I never promised you I wasn't chauvinistic!"

JULY 1976
America at 200

I HAVE DEBATED WITH MYSELF for many months on the question of what (if anything) to say in this space about the 200th birthday of this country. It should be obvious by now to any reader that this is the best and safest place in the world for working, saving, learning, medical care, bringing up families; and for thinking, saying, and publishing anything that comes to mind. There shouldn't be any need to discuss anything so obvious as the foregoing. But, alas, there is.

The memory of man is pathetically short. He forgets two centuries of progress. He doesn't see himself as a link in a never-ending chai. He has no historical sense of gratitude. He knows more about Tom Jones than Tom Paine. He hasn't the faintest idea about what keeps his society on the tracks, but it can hardly be politicians because, "they're all crooks." And as for patriotism, that's embarrassing and undignified; pornography, on the other hand, well that's a human right.

Fortunately, America is more than people. No person has lived for 200 years. But America has. America is people, too: and it is also ideas, places, things, myths and beliefs. In a world where results count, America is No.1 by a country mile.

My late old, unhappy Aunt used to say: "It will all be the same a hundred years from now." In line with those sentiments if not that meaning, I think it's about time we make plans for America's tercentenary and start celebrating just a little bit at a time from July 5th on. What could be more certain than the USA in 2076, still out front, with egg all over its shirt, ever the envy and wonder of this incredible planet.

SEPTEMBER 1976
The Catalog Issue

THAT GREAT OLD AMERICAN INSTITUTION -- the *Radio Shack* catalog-has just been published again, entirely revised, available in all our stores, and still FREE! Free to you. To us it represents an investment of over $3 million, a figure that's exactly three times *Radio Shack*'s annual sales when I came aboard (as ad manager) in 1948.

Although we have over 18 million active customers, we only print 13 million catalogs. This is what is known as an affordable shortfall. The total printing is 2,132,000,000 pages. Stretched end to end: 1,777,777,777 linear feet or 336,700 miles, or 13, 525,347 times around the world at the equator. The new 1977 edition consumed 3787.5 tons of paper and 1,222,000 pounds of ink. These statistics are revealed to discourage our competition. And to give cheer to America's postmen who don't have to deliver the catalog since none are mailed – you'll have to get your copy at one of our stores.

I want to call your attention to particular to the hi-fi section of this catalog. All but one of our stereo receivers has been replaced or updated and beautified, and if ANYONE has a better audio receiver line -- watt for watt, buck for buck, looks for looks -- then I'm a monkey's uncle. Watch out *Pioneer*!

All but three of these receivers are made in our own factories, just in case you've been thinking we're not really a do-it-yourself outfit. Our flagship model, the *STA 2000*, has 75 watts per channel by FTC measurement techniques and should really open some eyes (and ears) at $499.95. Please check it out before you fall for somebody else's pretty advertising. Anyone who needs more hear-power than 75/75 isn't thinking too carefully, in my humble opinion.

Radio Shack has reached two dizzy new plateaus: we've passed the 5,000 mark in number of worldwide retail outlets and 5 — mark in Canada. So what? I'll tell you – this enables us to build better and buy better. And the net results for the new catalog year (Detroit please copy) is that once again we have been able to hold our average price within 1% of our average 1975 prices, despite cost increases in metal, plastics, and just about everything else!

CB'er Betty Ford, the President's lady, wrote us a very nice letter after receiving a copy of our million-plus-seller book *All About CB 2-Way Radio*. She said she was "First Mama, sending all good numbers . . . along with my wishes for a good day today and a better day tomorrow." The polls say she won't be First Mama (her handle) after November, but in my opinion she's one of the most refreshing personalities we've had in Washington for a long, long time.

OCTOBER 1976
CB Radio

AS THE UNQUESTIONED LEADER IN CB SALES (my opinion, challenged by some but obvious to thinking people who are not letting their ad agencies do their talking), *Radio Shack* views on the latest FCC rulings should be of interest to all of you. Bear in mind, however, that I'm writing this in August for October publication, and things could change in the interim.

The expansion to 40 channels=legal for sale in 1977-will not really help the alleged CB crowding problem. In most places Channel 19 is used plus one or two other channels. People want to be where the action is, where there's sound and fury and somebody to talk to for certain. Until we were blessed with Ch.19, CB wasn't nearly so popular and useful.

There will be relatively few 40 channel sets available until well into 1977. First, there are still some technical "bugs" to overcome. Secondly, the FCC won't even begin to look at these radios until Sept. 10, and the FCC's type acceptance has to be earned. It's not as simple as you'd think, nor as swift.

Way back in 1958 our late great engineer, Robert H. "Bob" Lewis, said "nobody really needs more than five channels." This was before solid state and before crystal synthesis (which made 23-channel operation possible with well under half the theoretically required 46 crystals). This was a really shrewd observation. And it's still quite relevant. Adding 17 more channels doesn't make for togetherness, but togetherness (Ch. 19, 9 etc.) is what "made" CB.

Thank heaven the present day and prior CB sets are all – repeat all- useable during the rest of their natural lives and not one bit obsolete. That includes the 23 channel radios, the 12-, 6-, 3-, 2-, and 1-channel sets, the walkie-talkies, the whole shebang. People on CB -- except for businessmen -- want to congregate. The happy accident of Ch. 19 will be with us for many, many, years.

So, what's it all about? Well, Alfie, in my opinion the FCC just had to do something (anything!) and, in a very political year, they did. This will get the pols off their (the FCC's) backs and allow us to dream about getting another band someday, an FM band in addition to our present band. This will not only be good for talkers, but also manufacturers. Right now the prospect seems years away.

On another front, our love/hate relationship with Ma Bell, the phone company, goes on. Ma claimed that things like telephone answering (*Duofone*) devices were damaging her lines. Then the FCC stepped into the picture. A Wall Street Journal story (6/29/76) said that "such fear isn't justified and that the coupler is an unnecessary gimmick to thwart completion." The coupler is Ma's. The competition is us. The conclusion: Ma has been caught with HER hand in the cookie jar! Ah, there's no end to the richness of American humor. Now, Ma! Remember I'm, not only a user but also a stockholder.

NOVEMBER 1976
"All Ears"

OUR CHAIRMAN AND I HAVE LONG HELD a theory that *Radio Shack* can and should market LP records and tapes under our *Realistic* label and sell them exclusively through our North American network of 4910 stores ad dealers. Now we have put that theory into practice releasing our first effort which is called *All Ears* -- a stereo record and 8-track tape of new and original music.

The theory is that we can sell the software along with the hardware, to state it in computer terminology. But unlike the massive new releases put out by traditional record companies, ours will be on a one-at-a-time basis. Also unlike the record companies, our selling price will be well under the traditional new-release of $5.98 or $6.98 with discounts of a buck or two. *All Ears* is being offered for $3.49 -- your choice of disc or tape -- at participating *Radio Shack*s.

All Ears is great listening as well as affordably priced. Its ten songs deal with loneliness, togetherness and love, the three horsemen of popular music. And, as its title suggests, each hit has a CB theme. One of its songs, a ditty called *Hey Shirley, This is Squirrely* has already made the charts as a single. Others, including *The Night I talked to the Lord* and *Handles Hall of Fame*, are getting air play.

You can help us break into the music biz and get an unusual musical treat (at a "right" price) by buying *All Ears* at your nearest *Radio Shack*. I've told all of our Managers to play *All Ears* on all of their hi-fi systems and tape players to get your attention. We've had a press party. We've advertised heavily. We've got the inventory in place. Now, dear friend, all we need is you!

Incidentally *All Ears* is NOT the result of our famous CB Song search contest. We had about 8,000 entries and, at last look, the experts were still sorting them out to find the winners, some of whom may already have been notified by the time this column is printed.

Our Corporation has recently been distinguished by being included in *Fortune* magazine's listing of the top 50 retailers in the USA in size; and by *Financial World's* listing of the top 500 earners in American business and in another issue, the top 352 growth companies. A copy of our fiscal 1976 annual report may be obtained by writing to *Tandy* Corp. at 2727 West 7th St., Forth, Texas 76107.

No opus these days would be complete without a few words about CB. On Sept. 10, the FCC's opening date for submission of 40-channel radios for type acceptance, *Radio Shack* and contract suppliers) brought five rigs to Washington and were, we believe, first in line. In my opinion 40's will not widely available during the first quarter of 1977 thus 23's—at the current prices—are a fantastic value to the buying public. Also, and again my opinion, I don't place much stock in the idea or feasibility of remanufacturing 23S into 40s. It's un-*Realistic* to think otherwise. Pun Intended!

DECEMBER 1976
"Our 55th Noel"

CHRISTMAS IS WITH US AGAIN and even the grimmest Scrooge among us would have to admit, in his innermost person, that it's a time when the heart beats a little faster and all the sights, sounds, and odors delight the senses as perhaps never before during the entire year that is about to fall from our calendars for the twelfth and last time.

For our venerable Company, celebrating its 55th Noel with a shatter of sales records and a blaze of activity, I want to extend to every reader our very best wishes for a Joyous Season, our very deepest thanks for orders placed or contemplated. And for the privilege of serving, of earning your trust, of bringing pleasure in the humble shape of merchandise chiefly intended to entertain in a totally reliable manner.

Some vendors sell – in the proudest sense of the word meaning – education, religion, security, transportation, real estate, maintenance, duty, food, or perishable commodity of their performing art. Our destiny is to produce and market electronic parts and equipment. We have maximized this potential in the sense of growing from 9 to 5,376 to shop since April 1963, and growing, in the same period, from a few tens of employees to a number rapidly approaching 20-thousand. Additionally from a few hundred thousand customers to well above 20 million who have bought from us during 1976.

Of course it's not all peaches and cream. Or should I say tinsel and ornaments? We have let you down on occasion with a "sold out" or a "hasn't yet arrived"; and occasionally a tape head has lost it wits or a wire has decided to divorce its connections. I hasten to observe that that's what New Year's Day and turning over a new leaf are all about!

Being a peddler by occupation, I would now like to recommend some gifts for people on your list. An intercom system for parents who would like to eavesdrop on their new offspring – could be your first grandchild. A small public address system for playing carols outdoors – could be the coming together for good neighbors. A weather radio for someone with the need to know – could be for one who's in a car pool. A CB radio for your wife's car – could be for someone who's not a wife but surely for someone who "just this once" needs help on the road. A pair of stereo headphones-could be for someone who adores music and forgets you adore silence.

Give a cassette tape recorder-could be for learning a language, a part in a play, making a home movie, dictating to a diary (not for a Congressmen!). A phonograph with built-in tape and/or radio-could be for a doctor's office or a dorm or somewhere a big system is inappropriate or unaffordable. A telephone amplifier -- could be for someone who's hard of hearing or works in a noisy place or needs her hands free for other doing. A calculator -- could be for Darling who constantly makes checkbook errors or Dummy who got a low C in arithmetic. A Science Fair electronics kit -- could be for the lass or lad who wants to know how things work in an integrated (circuit) world.

Put *Radio Shack* to work on your Christmas List before the going (and the finds) get tough. And-anyway-thanks for reading this all the way through!

FEBRUARY 1977
Did You Miss Me

THE REASON THIS COLUMN WAS OMITTED last month is that I was overseas on business during October. Our printing schedule is such that being away in October means missing our January issue. Now-today-being November 26, I find I am writing for February. Don't be surprised to read a *Chat* two months after my demise.

My subject is a November "flap" over a sudden and well distributed push by the FTC to insure that consumers be aware of 40-channel CB. I first became attuned to this when I heard part of an interview with Ms. Margery Smith, Director of the Bureau of Consumer Protection of the FTC (Federal Trade Commission). This was on radio. I thought she said 23-channel radios will be "obsolete." No matter. Many newscasters thought the same, including our good friend Paul Harvey. All the media came down on us poor merchants with the caveat of all caveats, practically to the point where we were "ripping off" the public by giving away our 23's below or at or near cost.

I called Ms. Smith in Washington. A pert, undoubtedly attractive young bureaucrat of 34, she denied that in her interview with the press she used the word "obsolete." On the other hand, the Associated Press (AP) informs me that at 9:20 a.m. on Nov. 24 the word "obsolete" was "corrected at that time on all wires." In other words, the damage was done and now (ha) was to be undone. Fat chance!

Back to Ms. Smith. A graduate of Smith College and George Washington law school - Oh for a daughter with her brains, married, childless and without a CB radio, at 34 tender years of age she's the boss lady of consumer protection for all 213 million of us. A survey, she says, revealed that 40% of those who might soon buy a CB didn't know about the July expansion from 23 to 40 CB channels effective 1/1/77. Also, she says, the truckers "want to get away by moving to another channel." Which channel? 1 to 23? Or 24 to 40? No comment and no source!

Some of the FTC's points were well taken. Likewise some of a similar (similarly damaging) FCC interview. But in both cases the manufacturers and vendors of CB took a beating. Take two government agencies, add a dash of lousy journalistic interpretation and plenty of free air time-the time we dummies pay dearly for-and you have instant chaos in the glorious "free market" which we are supposed to support with jobs and taxes.

Well, dear Mrs. Smith and friends in Bureauville-on-the-Potomac, I have just taken two drams of Red Dye #2, sprayed myself all over with aerosol, and now all I need is a sharp-cornered plastic toy to hasten my departure from this increasingly gruesome world. Assuming, that is, that the X-radiation I got from sleeping last night under a color TV console doesn't do the job first.

MARCH 1977
Turning Over a Few Leaves

HAPPY NEW YEAR GREETINGS ARE IN ORDER inasmuch as I haven't yet come to grips with 1977. And with these greetings I give (gratis) a few leaves I would like to see turned over during the next few months:

JIMMY CARTER. I DON'T THINK THE JOKE THAT THEY ATE HAM FOR Thanksgiving in Georgia (because they sent the turkey to Washington) is funny or true. What you can do for us is honor your campaign pledges and be the first politician who ever did.

CYRUS VANCE. Please stay home and give some status to the State Dept. folks who have made a career out of statesmanship. But at the same time try to be as good at the job as Doctor K who, despite his numerous critics, did a hell of a job in keeping the U.S. looking (to the rest of the world) like leaders.

FTC/FCC ET AL. Kindly remember that business provides the jobs and pays the taxes, and that our "special interest" is being able to continue to do this without meddlesome provocation on a weekly basis.

CERTAIN CONGRESSMEN. It shouldn't be necessary to pad payrolls, play around with the gals, and accept large favors from unacceptable sources. But if this is your notion of representing us, how come you don't just come right out with it when you're running for office?

CERTAIN CUSTOMERS. Yes we do insist that our Managers ask for your name and address when you buy. That's so we can mail you flyers like this, complete with my *Flyer-Side Chat*. The latter is written to make our Company more personal to you and so I can promise you a rose garden, thorns and all.

THE CB INDUSTRY. This body of brave men will be better off reduced in number by those who really don't want to deliver what you (the consumer) deserve and expect" quality, value, truth in advertising, and first class service.

THE HI-FI INDUSTRY. Let's face it, lads, we need 160-watt (per channel) receivers like I need a cannon for hunting mosquitoes. Ditto a turntable with direct drive that costs double what a belt drive costs with the same specs. Ditto anything which promises undeliverable audio miracles. Totally clean sound is what we are after so please clean up your act for 1977. Make that 1978 because '77 is already put to bed (sic) sick.

RADIO SHACK MANAGERS. Do your best, gentlemen and ladies, to dress yourself and your store ina manner appropriate to receiving honored, dignified guests. Looking like Daniel Boone is not the name of the game.

MYSELF. I promise to help conduct our affairs in a way that will attract and entertain you. This includes the prompt answers of gripe mail and answering my phone when you call without making you go through four switchboards only to find that I am in Timbuktu looking for new store locations. If I don't answer just ask my Secretary (Lucille) to knock twice on the door of my office john!

APRIL 1977
Taking on the New York Times

WHEN A NEWSPAPER DECLARES ITSELF the medium whereby *all the news that's fit to print* is basic policy, what does one do if he discovers news therein that's NOT fit to print because it's untrue?

I refer to the *New York Times* issue of 12/26/76, Section F, Page 3. In the third paragraph of an article *entitled Sayonara to the C.B. Boom?* It states: "the Federal Communications Commission approved a change in the use of the air waves that will render most existing C.B. radios, or transceivers, obsolete." In ordinary usage, the word "obsolete" means no longer useful or usable. Inasmuch as 23-channel radios are neither obsolete, nor ever likely to be, this is a classically misleading statement.

Not only do I object to the mendacity, I also object to headlines which ask a question in such a manner as to imply the answer or permit the reader to assume something has gone wrong. For example, *Sayonara to the C.B. Boom?* inevitably leads one to conclude the boom is over. Equally, the question "Is Howard Hughes alive?" made for endless speculation that he wasn't. Now if, in fact, triple the number of CB sets were sold in 1976 (and will again be sold in 1977) as were sold in 1958 thru 1973 (Source" EIA release of 11/40/76), then 1977 can be looked upon not as the end of a boom but only as the end of a shortage. Further, several extremely respected poll sources predict 10-million plus set sales per year into the 1980's! And of course all these sources of data are available to the *New York Times.*

What's wrong with sources of data and semantic accuracy is, alas, they're not sufficiently titillating to make news. The media appear to require desperate and tragic situations in order to justify daily publications. Good news – the very stuff by which faith, life and hope are nourished – is thereby un-newsworthy. I have summed it up in my latest unpublished book as *The Media's Death Wish*. The wish that all things would become sufficiently sensational and catastrophic to provide the material for a journalistic story.

In case you missed it, *Radio Shack* sold the FIRST legally sold 40-channel CB radio in the USA. There's a cute catch: day breaks in the USA on the remote island of Guam! But at precisely 12:01 A.M. on Jan. 1, 1977, our enterprising Guam dealers, Chick and Dee Whitfield, sold two *Model TRC 467* radios at a New Year's Eve party at the Guam Hilton. This model, incidentally, is made by us in our Tokyo factory, not by *Cybernet* or any other source so many other look-alikes use.

We've paid $100,000 in prizes to winners of our *"Realistic 1976 CB Song Search"* contest. Nice Christmas card from Michael Kimsey, a $1,000 winner: "I was not sure where my money for spring quarter school was going to come from, but because of your contest I'll be able to finish the year. I'm a Soph at the University of Georgia majoring in Ag. Engineering. Thank you and a Very Merry Christmas and New Year to you and your Company."

Attention *New York Times*. This is OUR idea of fit-to-print news. Any time you want more please write to the undersigned.

MAY 1977
CB's Save Lives

THERE ARE TIMES WHEN THE SPIRIT moves me to do you a bit of salesmanship and at the same time do you a good turn. This is one of those times. When you read about motorists dying in their cars in Buffalo, freezing to death at home and in terrible trouble on frozen and desolate roads, if you're a thinking man it all adds up to one inevitable conclusion.

I won't keep you in suspense. Yes, if you don't put a CB radio in your vehicles the life you risk may be more than your own. The Winter of '77 can happen again, meanwhile there's a blowout on the Maine Turnpike, a 2-hour traffic jam that could be avoided, a stalled outboard motor in your future. Think it over, Sam.

As some of you may know, Maestro Arthur Fiedler has been a *Radio Shack* Audio Consultant for quite a few years. He is now joined in this category of endeavor by Peter Nero, the talented pianist/conductor. Our acquaintance began with a call from Peter who was appearing in Dallas, his interest in us stimulated by numerous purchases of *Radio Shack* equipment for personal use. What a delightful contrast to the usual celebrity-seeking indulged in by businesses desiring endorsements or other favors!

Mr. Nero asked me up to his hotel room after the concert to see his "shoe Box" hi-fi system. It consisted of one *Realistic #14-831* compact portable cassette-recorder with FM-AM radio, a 4 ½ x 8 ¼ x 2 ¼" unit we sell for $89.95. To that he'd added two of our (recently discontinued) poly-planar speakers *Scotch*-taped inside a couple of hotel side tables; a *Realistic* $59.95 stereo *SA-101* amplifier; and a tiny frequency-equalizer which wasn't ours, he said, because at that time ours hadn't come into stock. The recorder was used as the source of FM radio or tape; its output went into the equalizer, thence into the amplifier and out into the speakers. Elaborate perhaps, but super-portable 2-speaker mono and better sound than any hotel has ever provided in any guest room I've been in (and that's plenty).

While on the subject of entertainment, *Realistic* CB radios play starring roles in *Paramount's* new movie called *Citizens Band* -- in what seems to me to be an extra effort not to think of a better name. Of course they picked the name to attract the maximum audience, not to please me. I would have selected *All Ears* because I devised it for our LP. We sat in the producer's screen room in early January to see bits and pieces of the movie. I would give it a solid **five-star** rating and recommend it for the family (PG) when it hits your town. Every radio is a *Realistic*, and if that ain't a bodacious 10-4 I'll eat peanut butter in front of our Dealer Store in Plains, Georgia every day for a year!

Finally, please don't ask me if we paid Bob Hope for the (nice) joke he told about us on his recent TV spectacular. There isn't enough dough in the till to pay for that kind of publicity. Or did he know I have a Texaco credit card?

JUNE 1977
CB's in the Movies

IT'S STILL NOT TOO LATE TO SEE Paramount's motion picture entitled *Citizens Band*, a new release that deals with what are known in some circles (by squares) as interpersonal relations. The idea of the film is to show how personalities can change for better and/or worse, given a microphone and a whole host of invisible listeners. We furnished all the CB radios in the picture and some that were used to familiarize the actors with both the activity and the lingo.

When you step to the box office for tickets to *Citizens Band* you'll probably get an aluminum coin with your change. The coin was furnished by *Radio Shack*. The idea is you turn it in to any participating Shack for $1 off on any item we sell for $1 or more. Thus a $1 item is "free," in exchange for the coin. A $2 item is 50% off, and so on. The film's producer is Freddie Fields, brother of Shep Fields whose "rippling rhythm" music made the heart beat a little faster when I was in High School or maybe college.

Two giants of consumerism are deadlocked in battle, according to a *Wall Street Journal* editorial: *Consumers Union* and *Ralph Nader*. The fight's over smoke detectors, some of which use a teeny morsel of radio-active material to detect. *Nader's Raiders* say it's a danger. *Consumers' Boomers* say that even if a fellow remained 10" from a ceiling-mount unit for 2,920 hours a year the radiation would only be $1/10^{th}$ of what you'd get on a round-trip NY-LA flight. Says the *WSJ*: "The tiff illustrates that there's a right way and a wrong way to be a consumer advocate," implying the *CU* is right and *Nader* is wrong. We're happy to concur, not because we're big in detectors but because our tolerance for nit-pickers is at an all-time low. Also I was very satisfied *Corvair* owner and I feel *Nader* killed off that endangered species of Detroit iron before it had a chance to survive.

I'm delighted our customers bought so many *STA-2000* receivers in the Christmas quarter. It proves (a) that *Radio Shack* can manufacture *Cadillacs*, and (b) that *Radio Shack* can sell 'em too. We've always eschewed $500 items, frankly out of fear you'd vote NO. But then, considering the price of a good camera it's obvious a hi-fi system never goes into a closet but gets used every day. Good cameras do go into closets and don't get used every day. I've got both, and I know. Last month we (*The Shack*) were 56. We must be doing something right or you wouldn't have let us live that long. It's a privilege and an honor to make and sell a line of products that combines affordability with pleasure, utility with low energy consumption, and creates thousands of jobs at a time when jobs are a front-burner item for our country.

Of some interest, I think is the fact that our three-piece TV game is entirely made in Fort Worth, Texas in our own factory. Perhaps American industry and ingenuity aren't as dead as you'd thought? I say "perhaps" because there are times when I think we can't do much more than consumer. And complain!

Proof that history repeats itself-Jimmy Carter is fire-side chatting, blazing logs and all. But let him dare *"Flyer-Side"* chat and he'll hear from our legal department. Let me dare wear a cardigan sweater to work and I'll hear from our Chairman. It's only fair.

JULY 1977
Operation "In the Sunshine"

I'VE HAD A FEW AUDIOPHILES QUESTION my motives in saying "we need 160-watt per channel receivers like a cannon for hunting mosquitos" and at the same time producing a receiver (our fabulous *STA-2000*) with 75 watts per channel. They also complain that I knocked direct-drive turntables because we don't sell one.

While pondering my answer, the hi-fi industry came up with several 180-watt receivers (20 more expensive watts) and perhaps 50 more direct drive turntables, so I guess our competition isn't reading my column. Anyway, I don't think 75 watts are quite the same as 160 or 180 watts, but they'll do every nicely. Please consider that the average listening level is ONE watt!

Now about turntables. Charlie, let's try to recall that they're just for tuning records around and around without rumble or variation in the selected speed. Any sort of drive-puck, belt, or d-d – will do okay *IF* it's correctly made. But yes, *Realistic* will market a direct-drive this Fall. Quite aside from its drive system (which is mostly a response to the urge to compete), its other features make it the finest "unchanger" we've ever marketed. You'll be glad you waited.

A note from the *Electronics Industries Association*: "The FCC will begin operation 'in the sunshine' on March 12 1977." Hey, what' this all about? Well for heaven's sake, Martha, "the Congress has determined that public access to the decision-making (Typesetter" that's one word not two) processes honor that determination in every respect," says the FCC. What is all means is that the Carter-government is gonna let us plain folks listen in to lots of formerly closed proceedings via Government in the Sunshine Act PL 94-409.

I'm of mixed mind here because it seems to me whenever they've let the sunshine in, the legislators turn into ham actors and the audience never gets to find out whether the ending is happy or sad. And then they cancel the program-remember the Sam and Howard show?

Back to CB, Betty. It seems a maverick company from Japan is advertising more watts of output than the authorized four. And perhaps the FTC should step in because lookee here at what our resident Doctor of Engineering reports. "A 4W AM modulation CB transmitter is actually producing 6W of output power if it is 100% modulated. And 16W of peak envelope power during moments of modulation peaks. And 32W of power at the moment of modulation peak energy, and 64 watts . . . etc." So stand back and watch out for those funny claims. Again.

People who wonder if *Shack* really manufactures a lot of its own gear please ponder this: on 12/31/76 we had 4,298 manufacturing employees. Of those 2,662 are in the USA and Canadian plants, 1,636 in our Japanese and Korean factories, lodged in 1,110,003 square feet of space. Anyone who isn't impressed by these statistics is crazy as a coot. More to come, of course; *Radio Shack* is growing and growing, thanks to your appreciated patronage of our 5,483 North American stores and dealers.

AUGUST 1977
Flying the Concorde

AT THE END OF A RECENT BUSINESS TRIP, I took the supersonic Concorde from Paris to Washington. Elapsed time 3:45. And this, friend, is really stepping. What "burns" the French (and British) is our nit-picking refusal to let Concorde into New York City and places like Dallas. Two things seem obvious to me: we're flying supersonic fighters daily in the USA; and most of the world is buying our fighters and, more importantly, our subsonic commercial planes. Letting Concorde land here would, in other words, help our balance of payments. And let's face it- Concorde is marginal in comfort, unaffordable to most people, uncompetitive except where national "honor" is at stake. Remember the poet who said "I could not love thee half so much, loved I not honor more"? That's chauvinism, old buddy, but it's as integral to homo sapiens as your hypothalamus!

This is not (repeat NOT) a scare story, but the recent U.S. Customs Court "*Zenith*" ruling could mean as much as a 15% increase in your cost of goods made in Japan. At state is really whether Japan's sales tax, which is collected by the government from the manufacturer instead of the retailer, is a sales tax or a "commodity" tax. If the "commodity" ruling stands and is carried to its ultimate conclusion, then everything we import from anywhere (wine, shoes, etc.) will go up in price-'way up. Then, in turn, we'll have more inflation here because of unusual demand for domestic materials. If this is The Free Market System ten I'm a monkey's uncle. Ah so, but how far is that notion from Darwin's?

Since the above two paragraphs find me far afield from our own business, I might as well continue in these muddy waters. In July we celebrate our fifth year of manufacturing in South Korea. They have been five happy years, years during which we've seen that battered little country come a long way in providing jobs and services for its people. I cannot say that I'm an expert in their "human rights" since our business is strictly business. But when I read again and again about the state of such things in South Korea, and read nothing-nary a word-about what's happening in North Korea, I wonder.

And here's what I wonder: (1) would our reporters rather see the North take over the South in which event we'd never hear anything about human rights at all? And (2) does North Korea have a lobby of some sort which keeps up a drumbeat of bad South Korea news with the end in mind to destroy our erstwhile friends? Not to readers: please not comments. My mail gets rather full of sexist, anti-gun, pro-whale, anti-TV-violence, etc. Suffice it to say I'm for everything good, and I've never been caught saying that what's food for *Radio Shack* is good for the country. The latest true rumor is that *Radio Shack* will market a home-type computer. How, when, where and for how much? Well, our policy is to try not to sell until we have the product complete and on our shelves. It will be built in Fort Worth. By us. And well worth waiting for. In fact a breakthrough.

SEPTEMBER 1977
The *TRS 80* is Coming

WHEN OUR NEW CATALOG BECOMES AVAILABLE in our stores at the end of August, I want you to be sure to pick up your free copy. Not just because it's the 30th issue I've worked on. Not just because I'll be tickled pink if you buy something from it. But because of an innocent-looking little piece of literature bound in between the back cover and Page 162.

The leaflet describes the most important product ever offered by *Radio Shack*: The *Radio Shack TRS-80 Micro Computer*. It is also the most important product ever manufactured by *Radio Shack*. Specifically, it's being made in one of our many factories in Fort Worth, Texas.

TRS-80's importance goes far beyond the mere design, construction and sale of a fine piece of electronic merchandise. Primarily it signifies the dawn of the Micro Computer Age in respect to availability and affordability to ordinary people, schools and businesses everywhere, even for personal use and entertainment. There are plenty of cameras and TV sets that cost more! The Micro Computer Age is now, with *TRS-80*, an established fact, one of the few "facts" I consider permanent even unto the end of time.

Secondarily, *TRS-80* should convince millions of folks that *Radio Shack* is a technological company as well as a marketing company. There are too many of you who think of *Radio Shack* as a tag-line to Baseball, Apple Pie and *Chevrolet*. Okay. Nothing wrong with an opinion that has brought us close to a billion in sales. Nothing wrong! Merely an incomplete picture.

New York City, sometimes called "The Big Apple" or "Bagdad on the Subway," has just ordered list –price hi-fi advertisers to cease advertising audio products as "sale priced" when in reality the "sale" is only a discount from a list-price that seldom is anyone's regular price. And New York has won "assurance of discontinuance" from 15 prominent hi-fi concerns with 49 stores. Good for New York! I hope it spreads!

Among the CB prophets of doom in 1976 there were none so loud and haughty as those who said the forthcoming 10-year-sunspot cycle would quote destroy the service unquote. Your attention is called to *Sunspots Won't Kill CB* by the well-known Dr. T.J. Cohen, KFS-2459, who says what we've said all along: NO Way.

Our congress is to be congratulated for perceiving that South Korea is not, after all, a less desirable ally than Cuba, China and North Viet Nam. As for reparations to the latter, is there any current notion or option more ludicrous? Russia and China poured in their arms; now let them pour in their aid. A few of our friends, including the U.S. government in part, would also like to give little Taiwan the so-called shaft as a matter of diplomatic expediency. Nevertheless we have just opened our newest factory there. Not to be stubborn or romantic, but because it's the right place and the time for us.

Some of my correspondents think I'm a "right winger" because I talk about such things and occasionally wave our flag in print. In truth I'm not even entirely conservative. What I want to be is your electronics salesman. And free, at the same time, to speak my piece. At age 61, it really doesn't take much guts. At 21 I didn't have either the courage or the forum!

OCTOBER 1977
The Pay Plan

THE WAY WE PAY OUR COMPANY STORE MANAGERS is interesting and, I think very American. Aside from their base pay, they share in the pre-tax profits of their store in the same per cent as the profits of their store. Simply put: if their store makes a 10% profit pre-tax on its annual sales, the Manager gets a year-end bonus of 10% of those profits. We also have many other benefits, but the Bonus Plan is my favorite because it makes an instant capitalist out of our young people, rewards them on P&L performance, and gives them a clear and personal awareness of what business is all about.

In addition it can give them a considerable chunk of money-bigger than most employees anywhere ever see in a single check-and a chance to make an important decision on its use. I'm aware that talking about profits in front of customers is a delicate matter (in fact a no-no), but I feel many of my readers know people who need to get going in this sometimes brutal and often baffling world. And it's time again to remind you that *Radio Shack* ALWAYS has retail jobs for people who want to work, need to work, desire to learn how to be business men and women, and cherish a piece of the action. We're the place where it happens!

If you don't know what a "baud" or a "byte" is, you'd better get with it. This is computer talk and anything that isn't microprocessed by 1982 (except perhaps for tennis racquets, book matches, teething rings and sex) will certainly be microprocessed by 1983. What am I saying? Simply that not knowing about computers, particularly the micros, is going to make you virtually an idiot in the sense of understanding the basic mechanics of your real world. We'll soon be coming out with a simple book on the subject and I hope it's so cheap we can give it away. Incidentally, until this book is published and I read it, I too will have an EQ (Electronics Intelligence Quotient) of nearly zero.

We already have several products that make me feel like a zero EQ. For one, our *65-650* programmable $79.95 calculator. For another our *TRS-80 Micro Computer*. A third is *20-115*, our microprocessor programmable VHF-UHF scanner which is about a half a light year ahead of the competition. Okay: if you don't want to own one, please let our salesman show you how it works. It's so smart it's frightening. But also beautifully competent. Irresistible at $399.95?

Caught between the rules and supply-and-demand and the government (here read "FCC"), and between gumption and greed, and between good fortune and bad, most CB-related companies have cratered (here read "gone sour") in recent months. Yet CB radio continues to be a saver of lives and time, an excellent value in terms of cost, a wonderful communications medium. Don't get caught this winter without a CB system! Why The *Shack* didn't "crater" when the hula hoop turned into merely another useful wheel is really quite simple. At its peak it was just a mite over 20% of our business.

Again please: our new catalog is on our counter. Still free. None sent by mail. What's the hurry?   We print less than 14,000,000 copies. And we have over 26,000,000 customers. So 47% of you will be denied the pleasure of our Company due to the harsh realities of our ad budget!

NOVEMBER 1977
Shop Early for Christmas

IN MY LAST EDITORIAL IN THIS SPACE I told you our new catalog would have a 14-million circulation. Since then the number has been reduce to 9 million. The reason? We feel that such events as the shrink of the dollar vs. the yen, the possible increase in USA minimum wage, the continuing threat of countervailing duties and/or protectionism, all add up to a probable conclusion. To wit: we may have to raise prices on Jan. 1 1978.

Certainly we don't want to continue distributing a book with "wrong" prices. And-yes-our present low prices will remain in effect through Dec. 31, 1977. Skeptics are going to accuse me of scare talk: buy now and save. Perish the thought. Buy ANYTHING now and save! When a 7-stick pack of gum sells for 21 cents-how high is up?

I can promise you this. If you shop early for Christmas you'll be doing everyone (myself included) a real favor. If you want low prices, we've got 'em – even in comparison to 1975 and 1976. And if we can hold present prices after January, we'll do it. *Radio Shack* didn't get where it is by increasing prices a a knee-jerk reflex to every piece of bad economic news, a fact I think you know and appreciate.

During our regional meeting is August we distributed $14,511,055 in bonuses to 2,525 company store managers who, at an average age of 27 earned an average of nearly $16,000 in our fiscal year ended 6/30/77. Think back, Sir and Madam, to the sort of opportunity available to you when you were 27 and trying to get a start in life?

A naval officer writes me saying our *TRS-80* microcomputer is a "historical breakthrough" and will be remember for all the time to come. Meanwhile, we're oversold and flooded with inquiries. Orders are being filled on a first-come first-served basis. To get (or give) one for Christmas will take fast action on your part. And again, friend, this isn't a "come on."

Can you visualize a memory calculator just slightly larger than a give-away pack of book matches. Our *65-612* is just that, and I use it every day. At $29.95 it's a nifty gift, even for the man who already has three calculators. See it on Page 146 of our new catalog. And have a memorable Thanksgiving.

DECEMBER 1977
Christmas Gifts

RADIO SHACK HAS 15 COMPACT MUSIC SYSTEMS from $54.95 to $329.95 in its new *Realistic* line. I'm suggesting you give one of them for Christmas if you're in the mood to give something that plays all year instead of something that wilts, get digested or otherwise swallowed, or the third necktie that doesn't match anything he owns. Gals, too, recognize that the gift of music says more about you than a dram of *Arprege* or a pan for making crepes.

The "in" gift, quite obviously, is a *TRS-80 Radio Shack* microcomputer. If supply is tight, a gift certificate for this modern miracle of electronics will do nicely. I realize not everyone has $600 to spend. Okay. Borrow $600 or use your charge card. Pop will make it all back by using the *TRS 80* as a business tool, believe me.

Put CB radio (*Realistic*) in her car. The one time she gets stuck on the highway she'll know you're crazy about her. If you don't, well, she may go on wondering.

Anything battery-operated is a "natural" when you consider power failures, energy shortages, and the fact that the OPEC countries are lousy lovers. The list includes radios, tape recorders, weather alerts and smoke alarms. We're also the place to buy battery-driven toys at giveaway prices. And a sock full of batteries goes a lot farther than a can full of fruitcake, at least in my house.

Consider, please, that 50% of our Store Managers are 27 years of age or less. Without your Christmas business they will age rapidly. In other words, you can do a kid a good turn by shopping *The Shack* and not being a Scrooge.

Our three TV games are great for digital dexterity and inexpensive baby-sitting. And we have a fabulous calculator that's also a travel-alarm or desk clock (with 4 memories!) and a timer: all this for less than $50. What I'm trying to say is simply that *Radio Shack* wants to be your Christmas Store. And even more than that, thanks for your business, your trust, and your patience. If you've read this far, my personal "Merry Christmas" says it all for 1977.

JANUARY 1978
A Toast!

THANKS TO THE MAGAZINES for their high marks on the *Realistic* TRC-452, the $139.95 CB we reduced to $79 last September (if you can find one in any of our stores, grab it!). And thanks for the low and high marks on our *STA-90* receiver.

And thanks for the nice words, Len Feldman (prominent audio critic), on our microcomputer, even though you took one of your infamous irrelevant backhand swings at our famous trademark *Realistic*. Imagine -- he called it archaic! 'Tis almost as amusing as *Pioneer's* Bernie Mitchell's comment that if *Radio Shack* ever went into quality audio we'd be a threat to the rest of the industry. Thanks, Bernie, and thanks, too, for NOT knowing much about us; and thanks to our quality audio customers for their patronage and letters of praise.

Thanks to *Paramount Pictures* for re-releasing (soon) the movie *Citizens Band* under another title but long, long after we'd spent about $100G co-promoting it with ads, coins, books, and PR. I never did like that title. I still say thanks to producer Freddie Fields for the good ideas, the great fun. Thanks to Paramount's young-genius-chairman for scaring us off the idea of investing in the picture.

Thanks to the FCC for agreeing with us on the extension of sales of pre-40-ch walkie-talkies past the Jan.1 deadline. When I can find a government agency exhibiting good sense I say thanks with extra sincerity; this is my greatest, most ultimate form of blessing and the occasions when I use it are spaced more than four years apart. On the same subject, almost, thanks to our millions of customers over the years who set up TV, FM, CB, SW, and Scanner antennas without getting electrocuted or even sterilized. Criminey! -- can't the Potomac Pariahs find a better way to waste our money? Thanks, by inference, to the early American settlers for not complaining about the EPA rating of their wagons.

Thanks to our many people at TCE -- the sobriquet of our overseas manufacturing group. We have more stuff sold and less to fix than we had 14 years ago when *The Shack* was an all-brands house. Our lasses and lads have shipped their wares to all parts of the free (pay now, charge later) world with the kind of QC you'd like to get from your so-called "national brands"-and should.

Thanks to Hubert Humphrey and his family. They recently added the *Radio Shack* line to what they carry in their Huron, South Dakota, drug store, opened in 1902 by HHH's dad. Hubert, despite Humphrey-Hawkins and a few other gaffes, I'm proud to rate you very high on my all-time All-America Americans team, along with the likes of Jefferson, Lincoln, and Charles Tandy. Why Tandy? Well, among other things, silly, he's my Chairman and has a bit to do with my pay and perks.

Thanks, microcomputerists, for your patience in waiting for your *TRS-80* to be delivered, and to our Managers and Dealers for waiting for their floor samples, and to our factory folks who built 'em right the first time; and to our competition for not showing up at the church on time.

Thanks, finally, to our friends everywhere whose faith in *Radio Shack* has finally culminated in my getting the first brand new office in my entire 29½ year career. It's all new. Even the year 1978 to which this toast and these thanks are cheerfully dedicated!

FEBRUARY 1978
Visiting the White House

ON NOV. 10, 1977 YOUR CORRESPONDENT was invited (along with 29 other businessmen) to attend a three-hour meeting at the White House. He did! Pres. Carter spent over an hour with us. Secretaries Schlesinger, Strauss, Schultz, McIntyre, Harman and Blumenthal attended. The last member of my family to be invited to the White House was my late uncle, a personal friend for then President Calvin Coolidge. A quotable quote from Sec. Blumenthal: "We would have a $15-billion trade surplus without the energy problem.)" I pass this along to salve the consciences of those who think Japanese electronics items have done us in. In summary (and from the summit): 'taint so!

The President is now the first and only recipient of what I call our Ultimate Free Battery Card -- a lifetime model given only to American presidents still in office. If you don't already have our regular card, the one that entitles you to any one of four *Radio Shack* batteries free each month for a year, see your nearest *Shack* Manager. No cost or obligation; we just like to see our friends again and again.

Earlier in November I had to go to Washington to represent importer interests before the International Trade Commission and after sitting on my duff for 3 ½ days, I finally did. The dispute is whether imports or the FCC's new-ruling timetable are the chief cause of CB's sales problems. I was sorry to have to blame the FCC. Had they listened to folks like me on the timing of the 23- to 40-channel transition, its effect might have been minimal. Perhaps under new Chmn. Ferris the FCC will hear better? But alas for Ferris, one of his first desires -- changing FCC office hours from 8 to 9 am openings due to transcontinental time difference-was mixed by most employees. Listen, fellas, how about a split shift?

Violence-on-TV critics please note. *Radio Shack* does not sponsor ANY television shows; we just buy "spots" of time and don't know the content of the program. We have, however, told our people to try their best to avoid running an ad inside such programs. I firmly believe violence breeds violence and that stories like plane hijackings should be buried somewhere after the first news section (since the Constitution denies banning them entirely).

Watch our counters for *Supertape Gold*, our newest magnetic tape formulation. We don't think there's a better tape on the audio market at any price and will appreciate your own personal findings-negative or affirmative. *Radio Shack* tape is made in Fort Worth in one of our finest (of our 21) company-operated factories. We will NOT be out-engineered, so don't be fooled by the glamorous ads you read (just in case we're out-advertised)!

The U.S. Supreme Court, despite its knockers, occasionally does us a good turn. To quote *Consumer Electronics Daily*, it has "cleared the way for telephone equipment suppliers to sell their products without having to charge a special rate for so-called protective devices." Ma Bell is fighting back with Bell Telephone Booth stores, lots of 'em. Wow is she liberated! Anyway, we will continue to respond to this competition with our usual low prices and high quality service. Direct interconnect into the phone network is also permissible (with FCC certified gear) thanks to the Court and the FCC. It's a whole new ball game!

One little bit of amusement I picked up at the White House meeting: thanks to the ladies, it's now "person hours" instead of "man hours" when you talk labor statistics. Oh Say Can You See . . . implications, my fellow countryperson.

MARCH 1978
The Family's Bigger

RADIO SHACK'S FAMOUS TRS-80 MICROCOMPUTER is now a member of a bigger family. We've just announced two printers, a disk drive and other peripherals (the buzz word for add-ons), making *TRS-80* a truly powerful system. It's still in tight supply but we have shipped quite a few thousands systems with very few quality problems. The *TRS-80* manual is now available as a separate book at $9.95. And at least five software programs on cassettes are now in inventory.

The company capable of designing and engineering America's most popular microcomputer system is certainly capable of producing hi-fi and CB and other equipment worthy of competing with anyone in electronics, I think you'll agree. We're trying to earn your favor with technical excellence, not advertising claims. *Radio Shack* is closing in on the magic number of 7,000 stores and dealers worldwide, bringing this excellence to within a few miles of where anyone lives or works.

During a recent trip to Honolulu to visit our franchisee, Ray Chun, I had a chance to ride a "moped" motorcycle from downtown Waikiki out to the Kahala Hilton and back. Now I note the do-gooders are "concerned" with such things as helmets for mopedders. A large segment of our population must stay up nights dreaming of new things to regulate (and ways to annoy people and proliferate bureaucratic jobs). So I reprint a joke from our local newspaper for your edification. An executive, giving a report to his board, announced he had good news and bad news. "The bad news is we're broke and heavily in debt," he said. "The good news is we are in complete compliance of all existing government regulations."

Two new items worth remembering. The *Realistic STA-85* receiver, 35 watts per channel plus our three exclusive features: perfect loudness, *automagic* FM tuning, and *glidepath* volume/balance controls. Lustrous black styling and a low $299.95 price. From England, our new *Micronta* 3½ digit volt-ohm millimeter at $59.95 and a "buy" if there ever was one. I hope we've bought enough!

APRIL 1978
The Returned Battery Card

AMONG THE MANY NEW AND BEAUTIFULLY edited city magazines is one called *D Magazine*, the D standing for Dallas. Annually it publishes a list of best and worst things in our home area. Its January issue includes "Fort Worth Contribution to American Culture. Best: *Radio Shack*. Worst: John Denver." Being liked, friend, is something you take when it comes and while it last.

For those financial analysts and other pessimists who would like to see CB buried and forgotten, *Radio Shack* sold more mobile and base transceivers in its recent December quarter than in its entire fiscal year 1974. And for those moviegoers who thought *Paramount's* movie *Citizens Band* was a dead issue, they should be interested to know that after a name change to *Handle with Care*, it has received Top 10 rating from educated critics, one calling it the sleeper of the year.

The lifetime free battery-a-month card I gave to the President in November has been returned because he cannot accept anything "of significant monetary value." Assuming he might have received 12 of our 9-volt batteries during a year, the "significant value" would have been $7.08 to the penny. When seven bucks a year becomes meaningful to our government I begin to understand why the olives were so small at the White House luncheon I attended.

Radio Shack's South Korean factory chief, C.M. Park, received a very high honor from his government for the way he's conducting our affairs. The quality we've been getting from Mr. Park's place is famous throughout the Far East, especially on *Realistic* hi-fi receivers and transceivers, and *Micronta* test equipment. Our people there are really dedicated, many not having missed a single day of work in 3, 4, and 5 years. Could it be they're hungrier than we are?

An eight-year-old writes about liking one of our *Shack* toys so much the battery almost ran down, "and I tried a battery from *Target* and the slot machine kind of acted funny, and so I took it out and put in your battery again and it worked. Love, Leslie Morton." Sorry about that, *Target*, but the meek shall inherit the earth. And *Radio Shack* the battery business?

Satisfied customer from my home state (Massachusetts) writes: "I really do love my new turntable (*LAB-400*). For $199.95 it's a steal . . . my records sound new and alive. Most of my friends . . . tell me to go to *Pioneer*, to *Dual*, etc. But for the same price, yours is better in looks, in sound, in quality!" I've been telling you that all along, but when it comes unsolicited from a buyer it's that much more credible. Note: *LAB-400* did not go up in price this winter despite the shrunken dollar and fattened yen. And *Realistic* very much wants to be your turntable company.

This is one of those times when I remind you that these *Flyer-Side Chats* are intended to personalize our Company, not to enhance my notoriety or fill my incoming mail box. Corney as it may sound, we want you to feel *Radio Shack* is a people company, not just a logo on a letterhead or a division of *Tandy* Corporation. Our headquarters phone number is (817) 390-3011 in case you want to kick.

MAY 1978
Coast Guard Joins CB Radio Club

CITIZENS BAND IS GOING TO GET A REAL BOOST from the U.S. Coast Guard's decision to begin monitoring Channel 9 at 150 of its search-and-rescue stations beginning this month or next. As *Business Week* magazine pointed out on 1/30/78, the Coast Guard would prefer that boatsmen use the VHF-FM network in existence but "it reluctantly added CB because of its popularity (and) lower price tags." Great! But here's an interesting footnote: *Radio Shack* offered to supply these base stations FREE to the Coast Guard and, to make a long story short, we were turned down. Red tape prevented our government from receiving a gift worth at least $25,000 and instead the units were bought (with your money and mine). They aren't *Realistics* because we didn't get on the bid list soon enough. But yes, Jimmy, we did get on the Free Offer list in plenty of time, so I'm awaiting, please, a big 10-65.

Thanks to the Tucson *TRS-80* customer who writes: "I have been working with computers since 1960. During that time I've studied scores of assorted books and manuals relating to computers and various languages. This manual is THE BEST I've seen." Now it's available in book form (*cat. No. 62-2016*, $5.95, 232 pages) under the title *Basic Computer Language*.

By now you know *TRS-80* is a total system replete with printers, disk drives, lots of RAM options, and Level-II as well as Level-I language. Though we've only been to market for 9 months we undoubtedly shipped more personal computers than anyone in history. We've taken the mystique out of computers and their users and their prices, all without making *TRS-80* a "loss leader" in cost/sell terms. In my nearly 30 years in electronics, *TRS-80* is the biggest breakthrough I've ever been this close to. I know you're not supposed to end a sentence with a preposition, but when you're bursting with pride and gratitude you let it all hang out.

A travelling friend was surprised to see a *Radio Shack* (dealer store) in Hati. Would you believe Chile, Panama, Venezuela, Samoa and Grand Cayman Islands? Believe, believe! We do!

JUNE 1978
$1 Billion and Growing

LITTLE OLD- 57 YEAR-OLD RADIO SHACK is about to close, on June 30th, its first billion dollar sales year. Whew! When I came aboard in Sept. 1948 we were into our first million dollar sales year. The difference is merely from $2,740 per day to $2,740,000 per day. Or an improvement of 1000X. This column is my only way of telling you, as a recent customer, that your confidence in our products and service gets the real credit for our growth. It takes a lot of believers to build a billion bucks worth of credibility!

And when I'm reminded that we aren't perfect I think about the definition of a perfectionist as a guy who looks at a glass of water that 70% full and says "This glass is 30% empty." Despite that bit of whimsy, I assure you of instant, decisive and generally favorable action when you have an unsatisfactory experience with *Radio Shack*. Your glass of water must be 100% full.

It seems I'm a calculator nut: four in my desk, two at home, one in my pocket. Now comes our new *65-660,* roughly a 2 x 6 x 6½-inch desktop unit with 10 digits (not 8), full memory, and so on, but a really great key call GPM-meaning Gross Profit Margin. If you pay $51 for an item for resale and think $88.88 is a good selling price, press 5, GPM, 88.88 = 42.6192619, or by switching from a floating to a fixed 2-decimal +42.62, nicely rounding up the right-of-decimal number to 2.

Also: there's a key marked ITM; pressing it after the above, I find my answer is 1. This is handy in adding a column of figures because it tells you how many items you've entered; and you can check ITM against your list! For $29.95 (battery operated) or $35.90 with optional AC adapter! Marvelous: my eighth calculator!

If you have followed *Berkey* vs *Eastman Kodak*, there is a cause for alarm in the notion (part of the case) that innovations should be made known to competitors before they are marketed in order to give competition the chance to join or counter-attack before the battle. There are times, Jimmy, when I find "progress" disagreeable, and then there are times when I merely find it nauseating.

Warning! You're going to read a LOT of ads claiming computers at teeny prices and instant delivery this summer and autumn. Prediction: the *Radio Shack TRS-80* will do very little claiming but a LOT of delivering, and our prices will remain teeny in comparison to what anyone is either delivering or (the usual case) not delivering. Reason, "We intend to be your computer company."

During the great rush to get out of ounces, Fahrenheit and inches and into metrics, a funny thing happened. "Cycles" which everyone clearly understood turned in "Hertz" (Hz) and "centigrade" which perfectly fit the metric mold turned into "Celsius." Both Hertz and Celsius are people, meaning that the built of personality is stronger than the cult of the metric system! Although I'm dismayed, should "dollars" be changed to "Kornfelds" I will both reconsider and recant.

At press time I learned that Congressional pressure and other reliable sources of irrational judgment had combined to influence the President to raise tariffs on CB radios. Okay, one man's protection is another man's inflation. You are that other man. Note: if my info is incorrect I'll apologize promptly. I'll eat crow any time I don't have to pay more for something that I wouldn't have cost more had the government not interfered in the market place.

AUGUST 1978
The Supreme Court

BECAUSE I WAS IN THE FAR EAST on business, and America's far east (Boston) on pleasure, I was unable to fill this space in our last issue. In the interim a lot happened. *Tandy* Corp. announced a stock split. My son got his MD (cum laude) from Boston University. The President DID cave in and clobber the CB import industry with three stiff years of extra tariffs (translation: higher cost to the consumer). The Supreme Court ruled that OSHA (Occupational Safety and Health Administration) couldn't force itself into workplaces without search warrants (translation: business now has the same rights as burglars).

And the Supreme Court, on April 26, voted 5 to 4 that corporations do indeed have the right to disseminate (translation: advertise) views on matters beyond and aside from their own business; thus the First Amendment protects entities as well as individuals. I take this to mean the *Flyer-Side Chat* can legally speak out just the same as *Mobil*, albeit hopefully more entertainingly, if not more pedantically. This is a court I could learn to love. This is a court I could learn to love.

Charles Appleton, a columnist on the *Nashville Banner*, phoned to ask me why so much emphasis is placed on saying "a *Tandy* Company" in *Radio Shack*'s advertising. Well it's like this, Charlie: *Tandy* is our parent and Mr. Tandy is our Chairman. Our shares are listed on the NYSE under the name *Tandy Corp.* In brief, the reasoning is the same as that used to call you the *Nashville Banner* instead of the *Memphis Banner*. Small talk aside, *Tandy* also decides how much and when I get paid. The logic is impeccable!

If you're a devoted reader you'll recall my piece about how *New Yorker* magazine refused to accept our advertising and refused to explain its refusal. Comes now a *New York Times* (5/23/78) *New Yorker* ad to prospective advertisers saying in part: "The *New Yorker* provides. . . a quality audience. That's probably why the *New Yorker* has been first in alcoholic beverage advertising pages for just about every year since Repeal." Could it be that the *Realistic* hi-fi ads we submitted were too sobering . . . or merely too low in proof?

Now the burning question is: Will *Realistic Supertape Gold* -- our fabulous new magnetic tape formulation -- produce glass-shattering highs (*Memorex*) or be able to "record the sounds of a terrified ant" when it screams for help" (*BASF*)? Despite those not being our parameters when we set about to make the world's finest audio tape, our engineers tell me to reply thusly -- Ask and Ye Shall Receive.

A great new product you may have missed is our *Emergency Strobe Light, 61-2644.* At $10.95. Measuring a mere 6½" high by 2¼" diameter, it puts out up to 60 flashes per minute and can REALLY be seen. Great for boats, cars, driveways, and (if you insist) disco enlightenment; and (if you're into tricky pix) photography. Our June ad omitted some of these classic consumer benefits.

Another new item, our X and K Band radar detector, is available for motorists who are interested in more things around them than the scenery. If you write me concerning the ethics of selling travelers' aid equipment I promise not to reply. The price is only $99.95 and the long hot summer is upon us, as well as my 62nd birthday and 35th anniversary. Who needs letters?

SEPTEMBER 1978
No Equivocation

WELL, I'VE FINALLY GONE AND DONE IT. A letter from a Mr. Pratt of California requests his removal from our mailing list because of what I wrote about *Kodak-Berkley*. Pratt thinks I should give equal time to opposing views. No way! That's not my style! That's not the way I think my readers want it. But -- oops, I guess I just did! Seriously, most people seem to prefer a statement to equivocation, even if the statement is incorrect. And of course these *Flyer-Side Chats* are not designed to sell any idea other than that *Radio Shack* is a great place to shop for electronics equipment and parts.

Comes now an eminent professor who writes that our *TRS-80* computer's potential "rivals that of some of the great technological developments of our time . . . because (we) are not only providing an advanced technology to the public but are actually making possible the tapping of human innovation and creativity on an unprecedented scale." He is referring not to sales potential but to brain-power multiplication. This is as close to all-out praise as we've ever come, and it's music to our ears. I'm glad *TRS-80* happened in this country first, if you'll pardon my chauvinism.

Several technical guys attempted to correct my dismay at centigrade going to Celsius and cycles to Hertz. They mentioned Davenport and Watts as two of many examples of personalizing inventors. But airplanes are not Wrights, and even two Wrights would make a wrong, in my opinion. Objections overruled!

Audiophiles will welcome the second reintroduction of our *Realistic* Sound Level Meter, *#42-3019*, and at a mere $39.95 instead of the typical several centibucks for similar devices. Twice discontinued for relatively slow sales, it's back by public (no-matter-how-small) demand, and because its designer, our Mr. Gilbert, insists it's the thing for ear pollution control.

Speaking of public service, the *Realistic Pro-47* is a scanner that scans ALL four public service bands for just $169.95. Our July flyer neglected to disclaim clearly that a few areas forbid mobile scanner. Okay. *Pro-47* is primarily for 120VAC indoor use, though it's equipped for 12VDC as well. I foresee a time when advertising disclaimers will replace merchandise in ads, and our biggest headline will be "Check Your Local Rules and Regulations for Permissibility of . . . " According to George Orwell, the precise date is 1984.

They tell me department and "showroom" stores are doing a lot of audio business. I don't mind competition, but when I'm music shopping I like to get waited on, waited on intelligently; and to feel that after-sale service isn't just conversation. These are three defendable reasons to buy hi-fi at *Radio Shack*, housewares at department stores, and electric razors at showrooms. In addition to which, *Radio Shack* self-manufactures much of its hi-fi product line, meaning the egg goes directly from the hen to your table and that its parentage is beyond dispute.

Catalog time is upon us, and possibly the last of the great free 4-color electronic books will hit our stores in late August. Though it's still free for the asking, ask you must because none will be sent by mail. When I say "free" I mean "to you." Our cost for this famous enterprise is well over $3.5-milion bottom line bucks. But because it informs both our salespeople and our customers, we still find it affordable. No other catalogued consumer electronics line is so broad and well-documented as *Radio Shack's*. Right down to prices which demonstrate that "the discount came off before the price went on." Get your copy before Labor Day and find out what's really new in electronics

OCTOBER 1978
Innovation at Only 2¾ Inches

ON PAGE 14 OF OUR NEW CATALOG there's an item of which I am inordinately proud-the *Radio Shack STA-7 audio receiver*, designed and manufactured by us. Its cabinet height, not counting the feet, is just 2¾ inches. More graphically it's only ¾" higher than your American Express credit card! Since it costs only $159.95, you can easily use a card to buy it after you've verified my measurement. Note: the boys did a lousy job on this particular page of the catalog and our ad geniuses neglected to feature *STA-7's* unusual dimensions so you'll have to go to a *Shack* and see for yourself.

The reason the *STA-7* is so fabulous is that it combines beauty, elegant small size, sensible power (10 watts per channel), full frequency response (20-20,000 Hz) and low distortion (0.5% or less), and the sort of sound and mechanical quality you don't dare hope for at the price of a few steak dinners in 1978 A.D.

We've coupled *STA-7* with two *Minimus-7* die-cast aluminum speakers (each about 7" high) and created what we call *System Seven*. The system's price of $219.95 saves you $29.90 off the "each" price. Why? Don't ask me why folks who sell audio have this insane urge to discount perfectly reasonable prices. Summing it up and aside from the fact that *TA-7* and *System Seven* are available ONLY at *Radio Shack*, these are great products because they are eminently intelligent instruments of museum-quality styling. At a time when stereo has gone elephantine, *System Seven* is a pony that'll really trot. Exciting? -- yes! The bad news is we do not have them in abundance. My advice is to buy now.

There are plenty of folks who think CB is dead and gone. The government disagrees. The Secretaries of Transportation, ICC and FCC (Adams, O'Neal and Ferris, respectively) jointly proclaimed (memo dated 6/16/78) that "because CB, as an in-vehicle communications system, can offer a significant contribution to safety and service on the highways, it *is Federal policy to encourage its use to promote highway safety and service*." The italics are mine. The common sense is obvious.

No, Dear, CB is not dead and gone and our belief is that we will sell at least as many radios in 1978-79 as we did in 1977-78, a large secret number which we believe justifies my slogan that *Realistic* is "Out Front in CB by a Country Mile." With the fly-by-night drug stores out of the business, by now it may be two miles. Friend, the ONE TIME you or someone in your family gets stuck somewhere without CB in our under dash, you'll hate yourself for not having the smarts to spend $69.95 or even $169.95 on a CB.

The *TRS-80* letter of the month comes from the Senior VP of a large Pennsylvania company: "I would like to point out that I consider this investment to be one of the most significant in value to our family and to the future education of my son that we have ever seen." So when you ask me how's our famous microcomputer doing, you know I'm not kidding when I say that in my 30 years with *Radio Shack* (this coming September) I've never been near anything so gratifying in terms of filling a need which was but barely perceived when we introduced *TRS-80* on August 3, 1977. The man's son, incidentally, a 13 year older named Joseph, has "almost completed the manual and started doing some very interesting programming."

Christmas is, yes, coming. Could be that *TRS-80* is the unique, perfect gift that will have a payoff beyond your wildest dreams? Joseph, aged 13, also sent us some of his tapes, 3 games and a math test, all executed without his Dad's assistance. Verily, a child shall lead us!

NOVEMBER 1978
Free Flashlights for All

IF YOU'RE NOT A TANDY CORP. (NYSE) STOCKHOLDER, then you haven't received our Annual Report for the year which ended June 30, 1978. In it I offer my 2nd annual Electronics Industry Perspective, a great personal pleasure to write. To get your copy write to Mr. G. Asher, c/o Tandy Corp., 1800 One Tandy Center, Ft. Worth, Texas 76102. You can also read about our first billion-dollar sales year, a matter of pride for all of us who were with the Company in our first *Tandy* year (1963-64) when sales were about $12 million. Last year we were the 44th largest USA retailer. Now I suspect we're about #39.

Every so often we make a fabulous special purchase outside of our own line. Such is the case with the *RCA Studio II programmable TV game*. We bought their whole inventory. The unit has 5 built-in games or projects, and we've added 3 plug-in cartridges. *RCA's* total 1977 retail price was $199.80 for this equipment, but ours is a measly $59.95, a small cost for fun, games and ingenuity. And a magnificent gift for the upcoming season!

November is also our traditional free-flashlight month (see page 1) while the theoretically ample supply lasts. We're not peeved if you don't also buy the batteries. Just unenlightened.

About 200 stores throughout the land will by now have a vastly greater assortment of telephones (the kind you buy and sell) than our other stores. It's a great market test to see if 60 styles and colors ring up more sales than the 11 listed in our catalog. Almost every mall *Radio Shack* is a test store. Phones, too, are wonderful gift items. Or phone answerers or amplifiers. One store has a $2,500 solid silver model. Send me your order personally if your local *Shack* hasn't got it and the urge is irresistible.

Peter Nero's little traveling favorite is our sale-priced (October) AM-FM cassette recorder, a small wonder reduced from $89.95 to $59.95. If they say the sale is ended (but the memory lingers on) tell 'em "LFK" said the sale is still on for you.

A gentleman who has seen The Light recently wrote us saying that in 1969-70 he pilfered just under $300 worth of goods from us and wants to square his account even to being "ready to pay double" to save his conscience. He asked for forgiveness which, herewith, we grant. If my readers include other pilferers who wish to make good, I'm ready to accommodate any number and to donate the proceeds to whatever charity you choose.

Last winter I wrote an ad headlined "Winter? You're d-- - right you need a CB radio!!!" Several folks complained that "d -- -" was offensive. No one denied the accuracy of my warning, however, so I repeat it. "D -- -" incidentally meant either "dern" or "dead," and surely not "damn"-- a word I learned in the Marine Corps in WWII and which was innocently applied to everything and everyone in sight.

Okay. You wanted more *Realistic* watts? Our answer is the *STA 2100 stereo receiver* with 120 watts per channel at not over 0.1% distortion, designed and built by us, the finest and most powerful audio component we've ever marketed. It may give Santa a hernia and shake a few timbers, but it'll please you the rest of your days, cost you less than a fine camera, and never-ever end up in your closet. If its un*Realistic* $599.95 price goes up in 1979, don't say I didn't warn you in 1978.

DECEMBER 1978
The Gift Chat

THE WORLD MAY BE FULL OF CRUMMY NEWS, but The Holiday never fails to be good news, nice people, and an instant replay of last year's thoughtfulness. Speaking of gifts, this *Flyer-Side Chat* is one in which I get very commercial because we want to be your Christmas store and you might forget. I never fail to say that *Radio Shack* electronics make "play-all-year" presents, as opposed to candy, booze, fruitcake, plants, and some frangible/frivolous toys. The purveyors of those perishables-particularly the florists -- in turn -- never fail to say "hey, why pick on me?" The reason is that I Could Not Love Thee Half So Much, Loved I not *Radio Shack* more.

Our first in depth marketing survey came up with something interesting. Most customers like us because they like our salespeople (their attitude, knowledge, and ability to wait on them). Poor, absent or unqualified sales persons are the major complaint of department and the chainstore shoppers. In the USA we have 3,700 likeable salesfolks (plus 2,177 at our Authorized Dealers in small towns). A total of 5,877, as of 8/26/78, who positively will make your Christmas shopping a pleasure instead of a panic!

Seasonal advertising on the *TRS-80* (see elsewhere on this page) is directed at giving youngsters a gift that really says you care about bringing them INFORMED into the world of electronic data processing that is rapidly separating the Knows from the Knows-Nots. It's your first-ever chance to do this at the cost of a camera, a quality tape or video recorder, or -- suggested with a slight shudder -- a guitar. My favorite ad headline: "For your child! The most marvelous, expensive, crazy (like a fox) Christmas gift of all time. A personal computer." And to think BBD&O (Boston Branch) turned me down as an ad copywriter in 1946. And to wonder why I hate ad agencies. Well, not "hate." My favorite saying is: They're liked, but not well-liked. A line from a Broadway show.

A lovely complaint letter from a Lindenhurst, N.Y. customer had buried in it this diamond-studded accolade: "Enough brickbats. Every piece of equipment we have bought from *Radio Shack*, even going back thirty years, is not only working, but working perfectly." Merry MERRY Christmas Mister JRC!

Per Maddening News Dep. "When the White House is wired for sound this (1978) summer, it will be . . . with new component hi-fi equipment presented by members of the *Institute of High Fidelity*. A drawing was held to determine which manufacturer would contribute . . . to the installation in the President's living quarters." The value was $5,000. The gear a mix of USA/Japanese makes. No *Realistic* stuff because we're not members of IHF. This . . . THIS from the government which couldn't accept my Free Battery Card (value under $8) or our offer of free CB base stations for every Coast Guard station monitoring Channel 9. Write your Congressman. Write Jimmy. Oh, oh, OH what a travesty!

Occasionally you may find something of ours is "totally unavailable," according to your neighborhood Shack. Here's a tip that may locate it. Send your order to *Radio Shack*, att. Jack Rasmussen, 900 Terminal Road, Fort Texas 76106. Or phone (817) 624-1198. Being located at our most massive warehouse, his store is the logical "last chance to dance" source. Local Managers also please copy!

Want me to bark like a fox (or shut my mouth)? This Christmas book displays 12 *Realistic* component stereo music systems. If a piddling 1% of the 20 million customers on our mailing list buys just 1 *Realistic* system, we'll sell 200,000 systems in December. To *Pioneer* and *Technics* and *Sony* this modest proposal might sound like macho competitiveness. To me, Charlie, it sounds like a bonus.

JANUARY 1979
Charles *Tandy*

THE LEAD TIME FOR PRINTING THESE FLYERS requires submission of copy several months in advance of publication. That is why it may not come altogether as a surprise to some of our 13 million readers to learn that *Radio Shack* lost the brilliant, dedicated services of its Chairman Charles D. Tandy who passed away at age 60 on November 4th

His genius -- and no lesser adjective applies -- created the worldwide opportunities for countless thousands of people: employees, investors, suppliers, students, craftsmen, and on and on. He is perhaps the only man to simultaneously have his name attached to three companies on America's major stock exchanges: *Tandy* Corp., *Tandy*crafts, and *Tandy* Brands.

Contrary to what some would have you believe as the conventional image of a giant of industry, Mr. Tandy was neither tough nor cynical, neither selfish nor antisocial, neither greedy nor arrogant. First and last, he believed implicitly in the greatness of his country and its devotion to free enterprise.

On taking over our then ailing Company in 1963, he set its goal as becoming Number One in consumer electronics, a goal achieved in less than 15 years. His knowledge of numbers, people, quality and timing was such that in any business, including that of government, he would have been equally successful.

Charles (the way he preferred to be called), had a rare combination of brains, heart, desire, energy, and executive ability: talent that doesn't come from together in one man you could hope to meet in a long, long lifetime unless you're as fortunate as we were, who knew him

With the chances of having a really Happy New Year depending heavily upon deflating inflation, this recent clipping from TV Digest makes *Radio Shack*'s type of goods worthy of mention. The consumer price index for 1973-1977 shows that while all items rose in price by 36%, radios rose only 6% and tape equipment a mere 1.8%.

All sorts of people are surprised *Realistic* has come so far in audio expertise with our new receiver, tuner, amplifier, speaker and turntable line. Why? We think we've been at least on a par with brands such as *Pioneer* for quite some time. The answer seems to be that *Radio Shack* has developed an image for medium to low-priced stuff, and the notion that we've gone first class is surprising, particularly to audiophiles.

We're in the midst of opening 50 *Radio Shack* Computer Centers in major markets nationwide. Aside from increasing our service shops from 55 to 105, the Centers offer classes on computing, expert advice, and everything in our computer line. Open (or open soon): Fort Worth, Dallas, Atlanta, Chicago, NYC, LA, San Francisco-Oakland area, Tampa, and many more. Centers will also keep area *Radio*

Shack salespersons better informed. *TRS-80* now has more customers than any single model of ANY computer EVER!

One of the first products ever manufactured in a *Radio Shack* factory is our best-selling *Plug 'n Talk* wireless AM intercom system (two masers). You need only plug them into any AC wall jack to start talking to any other location operating on the same AC mains. For the security conscious, if you leave the remote station in its locked-on (transmit) position you can monitor the remote area from your bedroom -- great for baby tending or listening for intruders or things that go bump in the night. It's on sale in this flyer for just $27.88 a pair (20%) off. That's less expensive than this system was in our 1969 catalog-a full decade ago!

While wishing you a colossal 1979, I also reveal that I'm not going to turnover a new leaf this year. As Joe E. Lewis once remarked (when asked what he'd do if he had his life to live over)

FEBRUARY 1979
Opening the Big Apple

QUOTABLE: "CHARLES TANDY USED TO SWING through Wall Street with a warmth that set him apart from most businessmen, who like to fashion themselves in granite . . . he'd hold court with style, jaunty cigar-holder aloft, and tempt his audience with an outpouring of statistics . . . he'd draw alternative financial maneuvers for you . . . before long, you'd realize that here was one of the true marketing giants of our age."

That perceptive analysis of our late great Chairman was written for the *New York Post* on Nov. 29, 1978, by Irwin Lainoff, an investment advisor. While missing the motivational genius and good company of Mr. Tandy, *Radio Shack* will continue to be everything he desired for you and for his associates, namely: Best of Breed and getting better. But still sufficiently humble to give personal attention to complaints, to listen to ideas, to change not for the sake of change but in response to the times we live in.

From *CLOAD Magazine*. "Well, the *Radio Shack TRS-80* has now been tested to withstand earthquakes up to 5.1 on the Richter scale." During this summer's Santa Barbara quake whose epicenter was six miles from this building, "our computer was knocked off the table, bounced to the floor, and had a bottle-water stand (full of water) break over it. Drying it out and plugging it back in was all that was necessary to start it up again."

Can *Radio Shack* make a really good speaker system in its Fort Worth factory? Hirsch-Houck lab's report (*Popular Electronics* 8/78) thinks so, in reviewing our *Realistic Optimus-10, Cat. No. 40-2028*, $139.95. "The speaker system sounded just as its frequency response suggests . . . smooth and clean. It can hold its own nicely in the $150 to $200 speaker system market." The *Optimus-10* continues our tradition of genuine walnut veneer cabinetry instead of less attractive wood-grained vinyl used by many competitors. Speakers are furniture as well as music reproducers and, in our uncomplicated minds, furniture in the $100 class should BE wood, not just look like it.

Chat writers have to be able to take a little flack-right? Correspondent Hamlin from San Diego writes that my offerings are "Dumb, dumb, dumb." And my political views are "just slightly to the right of Atilla the Hun." Despite having spelled Attila incorrectly, Mr. Hamlin is no dummy because the rest of his letter indicated he is an extremely satisfied radio and computer customer. Ergo, his comments bust be taken seriously. My reply included: "that I know where the butter comes from that goes on our bread, and you -- being younger and not as dumb -- probably don't." Would it startle him to know I voted for Jimmy Carter? And did I?

Radio Shack had an absolutely stunning Grand Opening at No.9 Broadway. The Big Apple, a few weeks ago. Located a few blocks from Wall Street and within hailing distance of the Statue of Liberty, 9 Broadway is the biggest *Shack* we've opened since 195?, a majestic 7,500 square feet. Separate *TRS-80*, Safe House, Telephone Booth and audio rooms at last give New York's financial community a place to come in out of the cold. Tourists, too, are welcome. The rent is high and the veteran Manager Adelman is keenly aware he has to do a lot of selling to make his luxury affordable.

MARCH 1979
Mr. Buckley Likes Us

THE GIFTED, LOQUACIOUS, ARTICULATE and impish iconoclast intellectual William F. Buckley, who is an editor of the National Review and a TV personality, among other things, is a *TRS-80* user. His, is a complete business system including a mailing list printer. "It is too early to say whether the imposing paraphernalia we now own will transform our lives, but a least you have done your share in the bargain," writes Mr. Buckley, still full of boola-boola albeit many years out of Yale. He gives high marks to our manager, Joe Simon, of #1419 in Stamford, Conn. Having entertained us for many years-often on the other side of our position -- he's now hoping to be entertained by us. If we let him down, heaven forbid, he's certain to tell us with his famous half-smile and carefully chosen delicate epithets. Manager Simon: please monitor this situation carefully?

Borden Inc. will be allowed to keep its *ReaLemon* trademark, rules the FTC. Otherwise, says *Business Week* magazine, the order to turn over its trademark and label design to other lemon juice producers, "would have had broad implications to trademarks, if the commission had upheld it."

These are strange times, lads, when an owner has the fight the government to own his own name. They say that some names (like *Formica*) become public domain when they become so popular they're thought of as "generic" -- a word meaning "relating to or typical of an entire group or class." Rubbish is my opinion. One of *Hitachi's* top chieftains, a Mr. Naito, noted on his Christmas card to me "happiness is more than health and a poor memory." My sentiments exactly, Naito-san.

A magazine you wouldn't be apt to see, because it's trade press, is called *Consumer Electronics.* In its December issue, the ubiquitous critic Len Feldman writes about Pointless Products. Included among the latter are the *Eclaset* rack mountable products with handles for audio that's supposed to look good in a home; and mini components (tuners, amps, etc.) that nobody asked for and are in contradiction to the need for big heat sinks and convenience features. Len, if it's said that they'd be accusing me of sour grapes because *Realistic* hasn't believed in them either. I could learn to like you.

Save $310 this month by buying a fabulous audio system listed herein. Our *STA-2000D* 75W/Ch receiver with Dolby, two *Mach-One* speakers, and *LAB-200* multiplay turntable with *Shure*-built cartridge (mounted on a base) It's torrents of beautiful music for $799 and you'll thank me for the reminder.

APRIL 1979
Radio Shack Computer Centers Are Open

THE JANUARY ISSUE OF STEREO REVIEW magazine reported most pleasantly on our *Realistic SCT-3* -- stereo cassette deck, the model with three heads, double-Dolby facilities and a dual-capstan servomotor drive system. "At the price," they comment, "a three-head cassette deck with all these assets and overall quality is a rarity indeed." It sounds so much more convincing when someone else says you're beautiful!

By now about 30 of our 50 projected *Radio Shack Computer Centers* have been opened in major markets around the country. Check your local *Shack* to see if there's a Center in your area because they're offering low-cost classes in computer programming and general operation. This is in addition to system maintenance, full line display, and question answering: a very ambitious program but one which every *TRS-80* owner (or prospect) will really appreciate.

Another of many ambitious programs, our 562 overseas stores and dealers, is beginning to show signs of profitability after five years of solid, expensive spadework. If you travel abroad, remember our shops are called "*Tandy*" in those countries, but down underneath they're *Radio Shack*s to the core. Would you believe the biggest turnaround (improvement) is in England? Would you believe we're making money in France? A lot of people said it couldn't be done.

Your correspondent has finally sold a story to a magazine that's on the newsstand right now. The magazine is *Elementary Electronics*. The story is called "King of the Hobbyists" and relates how Charles Tandy earned the title. If you're in business-any business-you may learn something of value from my firsthand report of how a gifted entrepreneur thinks and acts.

Don't hold me to this, but I believe most purchases of a *TRS-80* will be found tax deductible by your accountant, even if bought for home use, so long as you use it for personal or business accounting, tax estimates, expense reports and the like. That makes our low price even lower.

Some will find this a bit of sour grapes reporting, but I'm on acquisition of a video disk system unless you just have to be the first to own one on your street. Like the TV tape recorder, there are just too many systems, too little software, too much cost for the benefits. My most colorful nightmare is a TV set with a computer, a TV game, a video tape recorder and a video disk player plugged into it. How would I feel if we were selling all those devices? Well, there is nothing like vintage Sour Grape wine to quiet your conscience!

Miscellany: because American Airlines moved offices out of New York City, Warner Communications wants its employees not to book on AA planes -- a boycott that's neither entertaining nor justifiable. From *Business Week's* 1/8 ice column -- "A CB radio is a real plus in a stranded car." *Interface Age*, during a recent threatened postal strike, told its subscribers, "In the event of a Postal Service strike, check with your nearest *Radio Shack* about picking up your issues." And an ad in the *Atlanta Journal and Constitution* tells readers that Cheetah III Lounge, exotic dancers and all, can be found on Peachtree St. "behind *Radio Shack*." So long as they're behind us, we'll (presumably) stay ahead.

JUNE 1979
The Telephone Leader

RADIO SHACK'S INCREASING INVOLVEMENT in the telephone equipment and accessory business is highlighted by our recent introduction of the *Duofone-32*, an electronic automatic dialer that we designed here in Fort Worth and manufacture locally in one of our numerous USA factories. The "32" refers to the number of different phone numbers you can store in it and recall at the push of a button. But actually a better number would be "33" because in the "Redial" position you can store a 33rd number!

I have used a 16-entry competitive product at home for several years, putting police, fire and my burglar system company in the first three positions. It's a great piece of panic button" gear and I don't need to grope for my eyeglasses to quickly communicate my panic with one touch of any finger. *Radio Shack*'s auto dialer is about 33% less costly than the competition and includes much more useful features. I've got one on my office desk-not for panic but for quick communications. Panic is for the competition when they learn about our $99.95 price tag, microcomputer technology and 100% more entry positions. Put one by your bed. Put another one on your desk.

I would like to sell 10,000 *Duofone-32* memory dialers in June and solicit your immediate support of this worthy project.

"In December," the letter reads, "a legal firm asked me to advise them about the *TRS-80* . . . to schedule and help manage lawyers' time. My recommendation was to continue looking at the *TRS-80* because it compared very favorably with the *IBM 5100* which foes for about $19.000

"Now if I had said that, Mr. Watson, who'd believed me?

Remember CB radio, the boom, the fad, the "in" thing? Well then you may remember what lit its fire-the shutdown of Arab oil. Once again we're facing potential shortages of motor fuel and/or early closings. So, once again I'm telling you: don't leave home without a CB radio in your car. *Realistic* is the best brand of CB you can buy. Our brand. The brand that's been on the road since 1959, If enough people take my advice this summer we could have a CB shortage, too, so don't be the last one, Ayatollah, to get the word!

By month's end we'll have all 25 *Radio Shack Computer Centers* in place. If your city is one of America's top 50, we're there. Any of our Managers can tell you where your nearest Center is located. You can bring them your questions, your problems, you EDP people to see the *TRS-80* systems and attend classes and purchase peripherals and supplies. Thanks, owners, for putting up with our pains in getting you what you need to occasionally on time. June is only our 23rd month in computer business and we've come a long, long, way, but not without frustrations and backlogs -- two things nobody needs in this wild and woolly world, especially when we also have a government with an endless over-supply of spokes to put in wheels of progress.

Realistic cassette recording tape in C-60 and C-90 lengths is on sale right now. One of our first USA factories makes this tape and we've sold enough of it, probably, to reach to Jupiter's newly discovered ring (unaudited estimate). Find out why it has so many confirmed addicts in every country where we have stores. Low price, Mac, isn't the only reason!

JULY 1979
Disrupting IBM

ON MAY 30, IN BAGHDAD-ON-HUDSON, we introduced our most impressive, costly and exciting self-made new product; *TRS-80 Model II*. For the record, the original *TRS-80* (now called *Model I*) remains the flagship of our computer line. But *Model II* takes over where *Model I* leaves off. And here's what's so fascinating and incredible: a *TRS-80 Model II* system at $4,600 gives you a bigger monitor and the same size memory as the *IBM 5110* at $13,800. Or to put it another way, *Radio Shack* gives you the same computer power as *IBM* but at a savings of $9,200. Or to put it still another way, you can buy THREE of our 32K 2-disk *TRS-80 Model II* microcomputers for the price of one *Model 5100 32K* by *IBM*!

Is *Radio Shack* competing with *IBM* in the small business market? Well, Sir, it may not have been our intention but it certainly seems to be our result. I realize that there will be quite a few raised eyebrows, so many in fact that I'm going to stop bragging and comparing right here. Supply will be very tight during 1979. We ARE accepting orders at our stores and Computer Centers.

Just a few of *TRS-80's* features: built-in 8" floppy disk (one-half million bytes) plus provision for three more of a total of 2-million bytes of storage; choice of 32K or 64K bytes of internal RAM; upper and lower case letters; 12" very high resolution monitor displaying 24 lines of 80 normal characters (*Model I* display 16 lines of 64 characters); twice the operating speed of *TRS-80 Model I*; and so on. Systems start at $3,450 and run to over $8,000 depending upon what you "hang on." Many of my readers will not be entertained by foregoing, having determined, perhaps, that computers are not for them. Twenty months ago, pal, I would have agreed. Today I don't.

When you make Art Buchwald's column, you've arrived. Here's how *Radio Shack* made it a few weeks ago. Art wrote an amusing column about the problems an imaginary aircraft company had in trying to collect a bill owed it by Iran, amount to $956,000,000.35. It turned that matter over to an imaginary credit collection agency which then started to its cycle of threatening letters to Ayatollah Khomeini. One letter starts out, "Dear Ayatollah, your cavalier attitude toward this obligation leaves us no choice but to inform you that unless you make partial payments on your debt . . . we will *notify Sears Roebuck, Radio Shack* and *Bloomingdale's* that you are a four-flusher and should not be permitted to buy anything on installment unless you first settle your outstanding debt for the fighter planes."

What's new? In Arizona, a hi-fi chain is sued by a consumer protection unit for allegedly incorrectly claiming the "lowest prices in town." In Mississippi, the state reading supervisor, having received our *Science Fair Store of Electronics* comic book, writes to "commend *Radio Shack* for thinking of the children in America . . .

you are helping to support the improvement of reading instruction throughout our area and it is appreciated." In court somewhere, the battle for the trademark "*Formica*" to remain a private trademark and not become -- believe it or not -- a generic term that anyone can use free of charge; and here the hope that *Formica's* attackers LOSE! In the *Wall St Journal* (4/24); "In 1955, *Sony* marketed the world's first transistor radio", but I say nix to that. In February 1955, yours truly, brought to Japan an American-made transistor radio, then being marketed by a company which I believe was the forerunner of today's *Regency Electronics*. It sold for about $50. And no one I met in Japan had ever seen such a device. So it's *Sony*-No Baloney (to quote one of their fine ads), or can you dispute my reading of radio history?

Archer's newest TV antenna has the rotator built into its totally enclosed futuristic disc-like structure (no bones or arms). Usable indoors or out, equally at home in campers, vans and boats, *Cat. No 15-1612* at $99.95 is a flying saucer that really works. And . . . it's an IFO, an Identified Flying Object you can locate at any *Radio Shack.*

AUGUST 1979
What Me, Worry?

IF EACH OF OUR 15 MILLION READERS uses the dollar coupon offered on Page 1 of this flyer, we'll have a $15,000,000 markdown on top of our customary sale (and regular low) process. As Alfred E. Newman once remarked, "What, Me worry?" Our object in giving our readers $1: you get it free, and a $2 item would be ours at half off. We want to fight inflation, not just talk about it.

What's the world coming to when the prestigious *Wall Street Journal*, in its May 14 issue, front-pages a 40½" story about one of their reports panning the *TRS-80* (and home computers in general) because he couldn't use it properly. Equivalent ad space cost: $11,578.14. Naturally, *TRS-80* is not a home computer, merely a computer that can be used at home. Our folks in Australia have, for example, a 10 year old kid named Adrian Macloud, whose dad bought him a *TRS-80 Level I* for Christmas and has become "a sheer wizard" at operating it. Well, find me a reporter who's even an opaque wizard and you'll shock me out of my socks. Did I ever tell you I was once a reporter?

To show you the generosity of my mind, I'm somewhat surprised that a group of autosound distributors was able to force *General Motors* to agree NOT to include radios as standard equipment in certain car models because of something to do with antitrust laws. Well well. Inclusion would conceivably have hurt us too. But what's next, old pal? Will *Maidenform* bras have to exclude fasteners because the fastener industry might be hurt? Meanwhile, the Japanese car come rolling in with AM radios as a standard equipment.

The founder of *Harman-Kardon*, my old friend Sidney Harman, has resigned his cabinet position as Under Secretary of Commerce. In an interview with *Electronic Industry Weekly*, Sid was quoted as observing that "contrary to the mythology that we all somehow grew up with-that oppressed people yearn for freedom-the overwhelming lesson of history is that oppressed people yearn to change places with the oppressor." I've always thought that they wanted peace, prosperity, law, order, free speech and travel, and relatively equal opportunity. An entrenched bureaucrat summarized the article by saying "Sidney Harman was no different from the rest. He was snowed under by bureaucracy." A possible moral is that, one way or another, we're all snowed under by something and that only the Eskimos will survive" the Eskimos and Ralph Nader.

Did I warn you about gas shortages in this space? And advise a CB in every car? You know I did. So get going! This isn't a sales pitch. It's horse sense.

Super-savers in this issue include a $59.95 8-track car tape player for $29.95, *#12-1802*. A great travel companion that will also entertain you while you're waiting in a gas line. And a $21.88 $21.88 TV antenna special that'll give you a clearer picture of those people waiting in that gas line should you happen to be at home watching the late late news. Our strategy of having a *Shack* nearby now proves to be just the thing to fight the energy crunch!

SEPTEMBER 1979
100,000 *TRS-80*'s Sold!

That great American institution, the FREE *Radio Shack* catalog, is again available at our stores and dealers. We do not send it by mail because postal prices do not conform to our price guidelines, as what -- except consumer electronics -- does? As I've so often said, the *Shack* catalog will show you what's really new and exclusive in our business. A prime and exciting example -- the new *Realistic STA-2200* -- it's a genuine breakthrough in all-digital microprocessor hi-fi receivers. The kind that's not all-digital (and we have one, too) has digital tuning as well as analog because the digital is for "display only." You do NOT have to be a genius to operate STA-2200. But you will have to read the operator's manual.

Some states have suits in the courts to block the sale of radar detectors. Is that what government is all about, to clobber would-be speeders? I'd have thought that gas lines, OPECers (please note the pun), trucking, SaltII, inflation, nuclear energy, etc., were more weighty. Well, er, no. The sad case of *Formica Corp's* effort to keep its 50 plus year old trademark from becoming a word any competitor can use, is still in court; the Supreme Court (on June 4) refused to block the government's attempt to take the mark away from *Formica* via proceedings begun last year by the FTC. And DC-10 grounds because of once crash. The commissars and the sheiks must think we're ridiculous, frivolous, and wasteful. Kids, that makes me sheik!

Seems my estimate of having sold enough *Radio Shack* recording tape to reach from here to Jupiter's newly discovered ring would make it 88 million miles or 5,575,680,000,000 inches, a figure derived from multiplying 5.57568 by 10 to the 12th power: You might wish to revise your estimates a bit," suggests a Dr. Snyder. Estimates, maybe. Hopes and intentions, never!

"Don't leave your CB radio" meaning you should continue to monitor Ch 9 until emergency authorities arrive. Your reports are "the most important link available until help arrives on the scene," so stay on the air, says a Mr. Sayle of Virginia. Nice thinking!.

Effective August 1, a tradition of recent years is being discontinued by *Tandy Corp.*, namely the policy of granting discounts to stock holders on periodically (personalized) issued cards. Too much handling cost and too many intercompany problems.

Elements of the press came down pretty hard on home computers over the past: The *Wall St. Journal, New York Magazine* (on us), *TV Digest* and *Ben Rosen's Electronics Letter* on TI's new entry. On the latter: "(it) proved to be anticlaimax at CES" says TV Digest; and "what a disappointment" says Mr. Rosen. Our point is that *TRS-80* is NOT a home computer, merely on that can be used at home.

Anyway, having publicly revealed we've sold over 100,000 *TRS-80*'s systems, we can't be too disappointed that (a) the press doesn't know any better after two years of being told, and (b) we don't yet perceive essential differences between so-called home computers and programmable TV games. One thing is certain: *TRS-80 Model II* is a business computer that can favorably be compared with *IBM Model 5110*. And that (Rosen report) it is substantially below (in price) any competitive product available today from the traditional computer companies." And did you know a *TRS-80 Model I* complete with Level I, 4K system is now only $499, a full C-note below its original costs?

Arthur Fiedler, old personal, family and business friend, died as I was proofing this column. And will be greatly missed.

OCTOBER 1979
No Plans for Stores in Iran

A FEW CHATS AGO I COMMENTED that *Sony's* ad claiming marketing the first transistor radio was inaccurate. Comes now a letter from Engineer James F. Regency at *Texas Instruments*. Jones puts our *TRS-80* computer alongside that radio in importance, observing, "there's a country full of kids out there that are going to learn how to think in terms of computer logic, and in terms of solving problems by programming, rather than by brute force." Please remember that when you start your Christmas list!

You're going to be very confused by claims made for digital stereo receivers, so let's try to keep it simple. First, there are analog receivers with both conventional dial scales and digital readout. A neat example is the *Realistic* 60-watt *STA -240* at $429.95. There there's something called "double-digital," where analog and digital tuning are supported by a quartz-lock system that appears to work like our *Auto-Magic* circuit. My instinct is to be wary of this sort of hybrid. Finally, there's "true digital," which to us means no analog tuning whatsoever, and total digital tuning including memory systems. The best living (affordable) example is our *STA-2200*, 60 watts, $599.95, and available NOW in most *Radio Shack*s. We hope we've got your number when it comes to digital audio.

I'm going to annoy my Persian readers, but Ayatollah Khomeini has finally turned me off with his demand for banning all music from the airwaves because "it makes your brain inactive and frivolous," he said. Music is basic to *Radio Shack's* business, so I guess we won't plan any stores or dealers in Iran. And then there's this: "I'd rather have an inactive, frivolous brain than one that sanctions death for dissidents and slavery for women."

We have annoyed a number of SSB-CBers because we wrote an opinion to the FCC stating our belief that any change in the service (such as additional and exclusive SSB channels) would add to the confusion in an already fragile marketplace. Several enthusiasts have coupled their dislike of our view with a threat to publicly boycott us. Well, the day we can be frightened out of our desire to freely voice our views -- right or wrong -- will be a sad day for this country where we have been free enough to create upwards of 20,000 jobs. Sorry lads" no white flag today.

The *New York Times* issue of 8/5 says that over half our population makes less than $15K per annum, thus placing our average store manager well above the average American in earning power. That so many have mastered the fundamentals of understanding microcomputers is also very exciting. Most are *Tandy* stockholders. The late Mr. *Tandy* couldn't understand how a person could invest his life working for a company and not have the courage to put his money where his life is. "Courage" may be the wrong word. Try "faith".

Catalogs are still available in our stores, free of charge. Missing for the first time in many years: a picture of Arthur Fiedler, our favorite Audio Consultant, who died last summer. Back for the first time in many years: a portable stereo phonograph, and an open reel hi-fi tape recorder. *Radio Shack*'s expanded and partially self-manufactured telephone line will bring this merchandise to hundreds of places it has never been before, and how tens of thousands of folks the savings in owning rather than renting phone equipment. I have come to appreciate that your need for "bread" is greater than AT&T's!

NOVEMBER 1979
Vote Wisely

GOOD NEWS FROM THE DOYLESTOWN, PA. *Daily Intelligencer* about the then 17-month-old daughter of a former *Shack* store manager. What's so special is that the youngster is learning how to read via *TRS-80 Model I*. "Now," says her proud mother, "Rachel is two years old this month, and not only does she know her alphabet, she can count to 20 and is starting to read a few words. We have found the computer an invaluable aid in her education." And the *Intelligencer* calls Rachel a "child of the computer age." This is not something I invented for Christmas selling. Phil, it's the pearly gray dawn of the 21st century.

Our Page 1 bargain is a 6-band radio made in or own factory. You can't tell by looking in our catalog which is an "our make" and which is contract manufactured because, from a qualitative standpoint, there shouldn't be any difference. But I'm always proud of our ability to stay alive in so cutthroat a market as that of the multiband radio manufacturing. Many so-called makers are really only importers. And many put a pretty case around a schlocky chassis because -- what the hell, the customer doesn't know the difference. *Radio Shack* DOES know the difference, and at no price point in our entire radio line do we gold plate a lemon. It's extremely difficult to make this point in an ad, that's why I "chat" every month with those of you who can believe that, after 31 years in this business, I can afford to tell it like it is.

Back on page 30 we show a fabulous collection of radio-control vehicles at sensible prices. The kid who won't delight in running one of these wireless toys hasn't been born. Every model has been put through our lab and, considering the complexity of R/C products, really offers a lot of reliable magic for the gift dollar. The calculator on the back cover at $10.00 is far better than the one *T-I* made for us in 1972 which, without memory, sold for $129.95. And those bucks, old friend were real USA money that brought a lot of meat and potatoes. See why I keep saying electronics are your best buys? Good calculators are now about half the price of good slide rules, but good candy bars are five times as costly as they were in 1972. Sic transit Gloria Hershey.

The first Susan B Anthony dollar I got was one I went out of my way to trade for a paper equivalent. And would believe I accidently paid for something using that ladybuck as a quarter? The same day? Andy, my *Radio Shack* calculator tells me that 12% inflation will reduce $1 to 23 cents in about 10½ years. And do I care? Yes Virginia, I care. In that scenario, our average Manager will make $60,330 a year and the free *Radio Shack* catalog will cost us $1.14 to print. A dollar gallon of gas would be $3.25. And my lifetime of estate planning would have failed in the crash of 1989. Help! Please vote wisely in 1980.

Two of many ads that have entertained me: (1) *IBM's* that says "when you start shopping seriously for a small computer, make sure you get one that's available with the little extras that can help make it work for your company. Like education. And service. And professional support." Hey, that's *TRS-80 I* and *II* country! And (2) the *3M* ad headlined "We couldn't say *Scotch* now has the world's truest sound if it weren't the absolute truth." HMMMM, I'd like to check their old ads. No . . . maybe I'd better check our *Supertape* ads. And d'ya know what "absolute truth" is in advertising, sweetie? It's relative!

DECEMBER 1979
I Love Christmas

SCROOGE HAS HAD 63 YEARS TO MAKE me hate Christmas, but I still love it. *Geritol* has given me 22,995 days in which to stop believing in Santa Claus, but I still believe. After 31 years of Yuletide retailing, I should be terrified of maybe running behind last year's sales, or fed up with green and red décor, or tired of plugging favorite items as "great gifts," but I'm not. From the first First Noel to the last sound of the final Silent Night, I have the same intimations of wonder, and my heart runneth over.

And so, to Jimmy Carter: I've used your name in an uncomplimentary manner on numerous occasions, but now 'tis the season to be jolly and what's jollier than your wonder smile? And won't somebody please give something nice from *Radio Shack* to Jane Fonda who is so fetching but so clearly needs pleasure instead of heartburn. And I fear, Mr. Iacoca, I've said many times that *Chrysler* didn't deserve a nickel of the public's already-spent money' yet at this time of year I can see a chance that some of *Chrysler's* debts-on proof that they actually were "the Devil's doing" -- should be forgiven.

And all of my favorite targets are herewith befriended for the entire month of December: *New Yorker* magazine (which would never said why they wouldn't publish our ad): the FTC (which has had most of its budget eliminated): Ralph Nader (no man born of woman can be all bad): the U.S. State Department (love that treaty with good King Wenceslas!); those SSB-CBers who think we're so big we don't need their business (negatory, good buddies, and we do appreciate your general concern for clean air around 27 MHz).

Buy your handheld electronic games early at *Radio Shack*. We've been short-shipped due to insufficient IC chips and could run out before our last ad gets printed. Don't wait until Dec. 24th to get your *STA 2200* digital *Realistic* receiver; it's one of the genuine audio breakthroughs of 1979 and our supply is limited. Check our telephone products department for gifts you've never thought to give before and prices quite consistently lower than those of phone companies and the mail order copycats.

Want to see me smile? Write for a copy of our annual report to: Tandy Corporation Shareholders Relations Dept. 1800 One *Tandy* Center, P.O. Box 17180, Fort Worth, Texas 76102. No charge. Almost excessively informative, even unto the duration of our key people (average age 48.29 years, experience 16.55 years).

Last year I authored some *TRS-80* computer system ads that raised a few hackles among parents who disliked being told that a $599 gift might be the difference between love and neglect. Of course I didn't write it that way. But now we've chopped $100 off the price of a *TRS-80 Model I* and at $499 I feel safer in warning you that the longer Junior and Cissy are isolate from computers, the closer they're coming to not being able to cope with 1984 and beyond. It's gonna be total war-mammary versus binary-and the battle lines are already forming.

Paul Harvey writes to thank us for helping his programs rate 1- 2- 3 this year, and can't you just hear him saying "among all radio programs, all networks," H-e-e----did!

A Midwest university chemistry professor writes: "I enjoyed very much your *Flyer-Side Chat* on the *Wall Street Journal* article on the *TRS-80*. My own reaction, when I received my *TRS-80*, was to buy *Tandy* stock." And elsewhere on the page he notes "there are some people who can only safely operate a pencil." Our corporate lawyers (Donder and Blitzen) tell me I am not one of those, but that if I close with THANKS, AND MERRY CHRISTMAS, THEY WILL DEFEND ME: FAITHFUL, JOYFUL, AND TRIUMPHANT.

JANUARY 1980
Biggest Computer Manufacturer

HOW THE HELL," ASKS COMPUTER BUSINESS NEWS in its Oct. 22 edition "did *Radio Shack* become one of the biggest manufacturers of computers? It is safe to say there are more programmers writing software for the *TRS-80* than any other computer in the world. We keep wondering . . . is the most important event of the decade the *TRS-80* and the bringing of computer science to the people?"

By important events, of course, the writer meant those occurring in the electronics industry. And on any scale of 1 to 10 the *TRS-80* would rate at or near the top. How we became "the biggest name in little computers" (one of my neatest trademarks, if I do say so myself) is simple. We hustled when we saw the customers coming. Just two short years after coming to market we'd dedicated 800 employees and 295,000 square feet of factory to *TRS-80* production. That's what the technical types call "ramping up quickly" and the accounting types call "putting in a lotsa bucks." And if a jealous or irritated competitor calls it "bleep luck," I tell him: you can call me Fang or you can call me Lang or you can call me Wang, but just keep your hand outta my pocket.

Newsclip excerpt offered without comment: "LOS ANGELES -- *IBM* has publicly demonstrated here its 5110 desktop computer linked to a *Radio Shack* voice synthesizer."

Lest you think *Radio Shack* is only a computer place, where else in your burg can you buy stuff like discrete silicon phototransistors, 0.3" single-digit LED readouts, and Schottky IC's? That is-right off the retail shelf? Okay. Suppose you needed a P.A. horn speaker, a code key, or an FM wireless intercom system in a hurry? (This message is given in behalf of all our wonderful people who think I only talk about hi-fi and computers and ignore their product categories.)

Compared to most of the many countries we operate in, the USA is lenient in respect to telephones and what can be added to them or sold in stores. We also have the best system. And despite what you may think from prior chats about *The Bell System*, I really love and admire it.

Hmmm. Love may be too strong a word. Yet Ma is a grand old girl, and without her we might still be communicating with smoke signals. But there is this thing about pricing: *Radio Shack* builds telephones, amplifiers, dialers and answerers that work well and sell for less. MUCH less. In short, while I'm all for the phone company and can stomach hemisemidemi monopoly, we're competing with it for your hardware business. So please sample our equipment. And if Ma "sells" you something, check her fine print to see if you're an owner or a renter.

Hunting through the headlines FCC to Deregulate Satellite Earth Stations. Metal Tape for open Reel Decks Radio Manufacturers Urge Quick FCC Decision on A<

Channel Spacing. CASA and VW moving Towards Settlement. Nothing about having a Happy New Year. Except from here!

FEBRUARY 1980
How to Survive Inflation

IN CHAT #58 I SAID OUR 12% INFLATION RATE would reduce a buck to a quarter in 10.5 years. Not quite so, says reader John Innes, enclosing two formulas which slightly improve the situation. Assuming 12% is an "effective or annual rate," the reduction occurs in 12.23 years. Assuming 12% as a "continuously compounded rate," Innes finds the shrink in buying power from $1 to $0.25 happens in 11.55 years. The reason I'm not breathing 1.73 to 1.05 years easier, old chap, is because there's nothing holy about today's 12% rate except the upcoming election year. And I feel a lot "upcoming" when I think about the February list of presidential candidates.

Most pundits won't tell you what to do about inflation. But I have five specific suggestions. (1) Make a statistical plan to eat less and drive less every year for 12 years, then sell it as a survival software program for *TRS-80* owners. (2) Learn how to be a gnome and move to Zurich. (3) Remember to write a book about the Gray (not Gay) Nineties, but publish it in the Eighties and blame it on the Seventies whose undoing was, believe me, the Sixties. (4) Retain, relish and perfect the least costly of your bad habits. (5) It may be less spiritually rewarding to aspire to become a shah than an ayatollah, but the pay is better.

On *PBS "Wall Street Week,"* Rukeyser asks Cappiello about buying retail stocks. "Lewis," says Cappiello, "the best buy of the lot is *Tandy* electronics retailer in home computers. If you had to buy one retailing stock, that's the one I would buy right now, but I've got a lot of courage." The date is Oct 19, 1979, but my clipping doesn't say who Cappiello is. Listen, kid, when your February Chat has to be written in November, you don't research Cappiellos; you tell it like it was.

Congratulations to our dapper audio Consultant. The card from his PR company reads" "In addition to touring as a pianist, composers, arranger and conductor, Peter Nero has accepted the position of Music Director and Principal Conductor of the Philly Pops." My guess is the City of Brotherly Love wants to replace the Boston Pops." My guess is the City of Brotherly Love wants to replace the Boston Pops, and that Peter, once he wraps up Gershwin (my favorite) and The Whiz (my pet peeve), can be the one who makes us forget about Arthur Fiedler (a very tall order.)

Every winter I warn you to install a CB in your car if you're planning a drive out of town. And we make it so dadblamed easy for you with our Page 1 bargain. The *TRC-421* is designed and built in a *Radio Shack* factory, so it's not somebody's lemon painted orange. The $99.95 catalog price is right down on the deck. So when you can get this mobile transceiver for $59.95 you're getting a piece right out of our collective hide. A lot of you skeptics think CB doesn't sell anymore because it has disappeared from the supermarkets Junky Acres and the drugstore's Hustle-a-Buck aisles. Wrong again, Sam. People are really smarter than they look!

What scares me about diffident or inaccurate reporting in our journals is that in this age of technical accuracy -- the kind that gets men to the moon and spacecraft to Jupiter -- it's still possible to manufacture news using defective parts. The rag that said we "began selling cheap personal computer last October" was referring to October 1978. Yah, I'm old fashioned. I think a 13-month media miss on a date is a dangerous as a 13-minute gap on a White House tape.

MARCH 1980
Remember to Write

ANNUALLY I REMIND READERS that I write this column to personalize *Radio Shack* and *Tandy*. You get a name to complain to, and it's a real one, not a Joe Doaks. And I get a chance to speak my mind, do a bit of verbal peddling, take pot shots at ayatollahs of all kinds, and give you my side of the news. Sorry my signature is a puzzle, but my checks never come back for clarification and I'm not soliciting correspondence. However, I cheerfully respond to the slightest provocation, and you'll not find me dodging such classics as lack of token racial types on our carton boxes, male chauvinism, bad taste, beefs, or roses. The address is *Radio Shack*, 1900 One Tandy Center, Ft. Worth TX 76102. I do not accept collect calls, except from Jan Fonda and Secretary (HEW) Patricia Harris.

Explanation: Jane I just like because she's a fighter. Patricia interest me because she thinks cigarette companies should discontinue ads featuring sexy guys and sexy gals (*Wall Street Journal* 12/4/79) You can look for two things. The surgeon general to issue a warning label to be worn by such deviates from the norm. And *Radio Shack* to look for uglier catalog models. Since homely folks are in the majority, isn't it about time we got recognized by Madison Avenue, and a census taken? Those in favor say Yechh.

Since we began making wire and cable in Fort Worth, our output of 3.8 million miles would wrap around the earth's equator some 152 times. We are very proud of our wire-drawing division which draws the basic copper tubing down to wire size for about 70% of our line. The division also manufactures cable harness assemblies for things like *TRS-80 Model II* disk expansion units. Find me another so-called retail chain that does these tasks and I'll find you an NFL referee who's never made a major boo-boo in the last two minutes of a game.

Come listen to the first transistor radio ever sold commercially. It's in my office, thanks to a guy from North Dakota. It's an American made *Regency*. Yes, Sunny that means it ain't a *Sony*. This radio old-timer still works, but then-so do I. The quip about *Sony* refers, sort of, to their ad people who've been on a kick about "inventing the competition." The latter claim, in respect to VCR's made by *Panasonic* (*Matsushita*) for *RCA* and others, is supposed to have been quashed by mutual consent. But my informers allege it's *Ampex* who invented the competition in video tape recording and gets the royalties. Anybody really know? Or Care?

100K-plus *TRS-80* customers have long wanted their *Model I* systems to double as word processors. "No problem," said one of our wittier engineers, and -- lo! -- 'tis an established fact. Along with our new program called *SCRIPSIT*, we're now offering an optional lower/upper case kit that makes the efforts of native softcraftsmen look amateurish. Please remember a *TRS-80 Model I* (*16K Level II*) converted to add word processing or bought originally for the purpose, is also a computer. And also-would you expect less from the Biggest Name in Little Computers? -- a hell of a lot cheaper than the competition, most of which is either equipment dedicated to word processing only, or a so-called smart typewriter. This may well be the big news in micro/personal computing for the winter of 1980.

APRIL 1980
Watch Your Claims Lucille

AMONG OUR LATEST VICTORIES (I do not discuss losses) is a Distinguished Award trophy for outstanding achievement in 1979 for effectively marketing computers, from *Sales & Marketing Management* magazine. Also, from *Stereo Review* magazine a SUPER equipment test report on our trendsetting STA 2200 digital stereo receiver (2/80 issue).

"With the *STA-2200*," says this influential audio publication, "*Radio Shack* has made it perfectly clear that the technical sophistication responsible for the overwhelming success of their *TRS-80* computer system has been applied very effectively to their high-fidelity products. (It's) a highly advanced receiver...fully worth of its place at the head of *Realistic's* 1980 audio line."

So I got a real chuckle out of *Sony's* ad in the 1/80 issue of *High Fidelity Trade News* on its digital stereo line . . . (quote) The company that virtually transistorized high fidelity has just reinvented the receiver (unquote). Makes you sort of wonder how we manufactured our *STA-2200* and brought it to market in the USA quite a few moons (or rather rising suns) before they did? Take a letter Lucille" Dear *IBM*, colon, we virtually reinvented the computer so watch your claims like a good fellow, period, Sincerely, comma, and not without affection, comma, Lewis. How's this postscript? -- on a clear day I can see Madison Avenue.

Bill Greer reminds me that *QST* magazine reminded him that *Radio Shack* opened its second store (in New Haven, Conn.) in January 1955. Since then we've opened 4,606 others -- not counting dealer and franchise stores -- or 184 stores per year on average. If you reckon it costs $75,000 to open a store, the cost of opening 4,606 of 'em works out to be $345 million, a number to make even an oil-rich Arab gasp. But wait -- at $800/oz our investment will only cost you 25.187 pounds of gold! (Wait longer and it'll be down to one pound of 24K and a 6-piece table setting of *Tiffany* sterling.)

I'm often asked why we bother to put out a tape deck like our new *TR-3000* open reel deck when cassettes are taking over. It's because there's a significant difference in sound quality and user flexibility. We won't sell 'em by the 10's of thousands. But a few thousand need (and can hear) this difference and will appreciate our offering it at a price like $499.95. Part of our so-called mystique is, I think, our willingness to invest in bringing minority audiophile projects like *TR-3000* to all corners of the land.

Manager Alan Bush of *Radio Shack* #1326 in Nashua, NH seems to agree imitation is the sincerest form of flattery, enclosing McDonald's "award winner" card, similar to our famous free-battery card, offering a hamburger, fries and a drink free once a month for a year at 8 area McD's. Well, if we-we're-the-one, that's okay. But we don't "do it all for you." Some days we work only for our lenders, and others for the IRS, because, Dolly, let's face it --- we can't all be burger kings!

MAY 1980
Thank You Japan

"WHY DONCHA SHUT UP AND GET OFF THAT EGO TRIP and just sell electronics?" asks one of my few anonymous critics. Well for one thing, old bean, I thought I was selling electronics. And for another, listen man, you don't get off an ego trip that easily. It takes time, as Messrs, Baker, Connally, Kennedy and others are discovering. About 1930 (plus or minus 3 years) there was this great song, "I Wanna Be Loved By You," about which I have this theory -- that it explains all or most of the secrets of Man's personality. And so, obscurely, we've come to the probability of a Chat #65.

There being a few people who still think Made in Japan is not a quality label, I give them this recent quote by "Pete" Estes, *General Motors'* affable president. "Thanks to the Japanese for spurring us on," said Estes, "the quality of our (*GM*) cars today is 25 per cent better than two years ago." This overdue frankness is so comforting, I won' even guess how Pete figures quality in per cents and how bad that makes the 1978 *GM* line.

Brilliant advice from the 1/80 edition of *Homestead Management*, authored by a lady from Maine" We purchased the *Radio Shack* (computer) for several reasons. It is lower priced than many; the stores provide easy service if problems arise; you can upgrade your system gradually as finances allow: and it is the largest selling home computer. For this reason," she says, "programs are readily available to buy or, if you have a program to sell, the potential market is larger."

Fascinating news from *Aviation Week and Space Technology's* 2/4/80 issue which quotes Rep. Jack Edwards (R.-Ala.) ranking minority member of the House Appropriations defense subcommittee, as saying, in a speech on the House floor, that maintenance personnel at some fighter bases are using their own money to purchase aircraft electronics parts at *Radio Shack* outlets in nearby towns "just to keep a small number of aircraft flyable." Now let's see, there, what parts could we be selling to keep our lads aloft? Couldn't be *Realistic* CB walkie-talkies -- wrong wavelength. Couldn't be wireless intercoms -- no common plane-to-plane AC mains. Gotcha! Must be those "useful knobs for any application" we catalog on Page 100. It's the kind of silly headline I fight against, but sure as shootin' military aviation is an application.

Our top merchandiser says sources for low priced transistor radios are drying up because the manufactures have turned to costlier products with better profit potentials. Any radio in The *Shack's* line, there, better be bought sooner than later. Foreign affairs being what they are (lousy with a trend to lousier), our multiband models with shortwave foreign news are selling well this Spring.

Are you waiting for a video disk? I'm not. Are you waiting for 30 more TV programs from out of space or underground? I'm not. Are you waiting for a

President of the USA who will stop playing Secretary of State, and Chief of Police of the Near/Far/Mid-East, and GET WITH domestic problems and waste? I am

A college professor writes: "I appreciate the high quality, reasonably priced, rugged apparatus which you produce. Please keep making it-well figure out ways to use it in the laboratory and classroom." This unsolicited letter will be kept on file forever. Rebuttals are not solicited.

JUNE 1980
Unfinished Stories

AS IF WE AMERICANS DON'T HAVE enough troubles, we're now told by a team of government auditors that our nation's defense computer system is a 'virtual graveyard' of tired computer hardware that breads down under stress. A highlight of the finds (NY Post 3/10/80) is that "the entire logistics system of a Midwestern army bases (is) operating on a $300 mini-computer purchased from a local *Radio Shack*." Well, it does look as if *TRS-80* has been discounted, enlarged and drafter at the age of 3. But that's life, Ronnie.

For your kids, *Radio Shack* has a new free comic book that hides a slice of computer education between two loaves of Superman. It's titled *The Computers that Save Metropolis*, Starring the "*TRS-80* Computer Whiz Kids." If not available at your nearest *Shack*, write our Ad Dept., Dept. FSC, 1300 One Tandy Center, Fort Worth, TX 76102. Did you know Superman can knock out a tornado "with a single blast of super-breath"? This is a nice to know in an election year.

One of the great unfinished journalistic tales of the entertainment industry was tersely reported in a recent issue of *Consumer Electronics Daily*: "Several companies previously indicted for pornography expected to be indicted for piracy within next few weeks." (In my heyday, a legitimate pirate knew only that X marked the spot.)

And in another unfinished story, it again seems the first transistor radio commercially marketed was undeniably the *Regency* unit that went on sale in Indianapolis on Nov. 1, 1954 at $49.95/ And not made in Japan, as a *Sony* as seemed to assert (and which provoked both myself and *Regency* into taking another look at the record.)

Since *Radio Shack*'s fiscal year ends on the upcoming 30th of June, we remind you our famous sensibly-low prices have remained intact during the entire 12-month period! Thank us by shopping soon to get the full benefit of 1979 prices in 1980, plus markdowns which resemble 1976 prices. In this issue, for example, the made-by-us *Optimus-10* speaker and *STA-100* component receiver are delightful reminders of our skill both at manufacturing and price-cutting. We'll continue to bring you bargains like these in fiscal 1981 no matter what the economic climate. That's a promise from the Hot Solderer's at *Radio Shack* (that makes our Cold Accounts shiver, even in June).

Every home and every office should have a weather radio (note when you put the words together you get *Weatheradio*, one of our favorite trademarks). You get round-the-clock NOAA weather only: no news sports, music or advertising. On Page 22, our new, improved "alert" *Weatheradio* turns itself on automatically if trouble's coming. For the warning that could save your life and property, it's very cheap insurance. And your first premium ($39.95) is your last premium. Ask for *12-154* and tell 'em "LK sent you."

Memo to our 20,000 employees and assorted friends. Grim as the choices may be, register now to vote in November. Our system needs you. If you can't think of a better reason, remember your cast vote is your permission to complain. Silence isn't golden, Robert, it's chicken!

JULY 1980
Taking On AT&T-Again

NEW TECHNOLOGY AND NEW FCC RULINGS are coming at us so quickly you'll just have to pardon the errors. For instance, those who believe the Phone Company lost out when FCC mandated a separation of phone equipment sales from phone-use sales (by 3/1/82) evidently didn't get the implication of the rest of the package. The so-called 1956 *AT&T* Consent Degree which barred Ma Bell from the computer-related communications business has been removed. *Radio Shack* picks up a welcome crumb from this table in essentially having its sales of phones, answerers and dialers blessed instead of cursed. Wanna bet how far we'll undersell Ma when she actually retails you a whole phone and quits leasing you the phone you maybe thought you'd bought.

And then there's the *Magnavox* (*Phillips*) system for AM stereo that the FCC accepted on recommended or whatever, after some of its staffers had advised simultaneous acceptance of all FIVE of the competing systems to let the marketplace determine the winner (and the customers pay for radios capable of sorting out the systems). It could only happen in America, folks, but don't bet that it HAS happened. My sources predict no AM stereo for at least two years. And I'll tell you, Charlie, I couldn't care less. Note: Charlie is Ferris, the big wheel at FCC. Pun intended. Note 2: I think we've got another problem here.

Co-inventor of the world's first electronic digital computer was the late Dr. John W Mauchly. *Datamation* magazine tells us that in his waning days "he used two *TRS-80*s and a *Nova* minicomputer" to work on his hobby of weather predicting. "He enjoyed pointing out that 'that little *TRS-80* has more power than the *ENIAC* did.'" One word from Dr. John is worth a thousand pictures!

Two dazzling quotations from *Business Week* magazine. One, in respect to their opening of a retail store -- "*Xerox* is obviously going to have a hell of a lot to learn, declares *Tandy*'s Kornfeld." And the other, in respect to products he doesn't sell ('cause he ain't on our team), is by the president of a chain of computer stores, who's said to have said "I don't think *Tandy* has done anything significant in the small business market." It's a dandy contrast in accuracy; and in all due modesty I must admit I'm a fountain of truth in comparison to some people I've never met and on the basis of excerpts from larger concepts.

Fiat-Allis, makers of earthmoving machinery, has chosen *Radio Shack* components and devices in a training program for its dealers and employees. Each package contains two *Micronta 22-201* multi-testers and five *Archer Project-Boards*. The *Fiat-Allis* release says "*Radio Shack* met requirements of both cost and near-universal availability. "The folks at F-A will be glad to know that *Shack's* going 100% universal some time after the Moscow and before the L.A. Olympics.

Come see our new telephone that looks like an intercom but actually is a pushbutton phone with a built in amplifier. Ask for *#43-295*. It's the hands-free phone you've always been able to afford -- $59.95. The discount comes off before the price goes on at *Radio Shack*!

AUGUST 1980
Changing the Retail Landscape

WITH DATA GENERAL'S RECENT ANNOUNCEMENT of a projected chain of retail computer stores, plus *Digital Equipment's* and *Xerox's* stores, and *IBM's* sort of retailish talk, *Radio Shack* may someday lay claim to having changed the way stuff like computers and copiers are sold in America. And to having affected the sales of plans of these veteran technocrat outfits more demonstrably than anyone since Carter-fone told *AT&T*. When some fall by the wayside as retailers, as they most assuredly will, *Radio Shack* would also like credit for having said so. Meanwhile, for the balance of 1980 and all of 1981, nobody but NOBODY but *Radio Shack* will have more stores and centers where computerese is spoken, the prices are lower, the assortment of goods and services more people-oriented, the advice better, and delivery quicker.

At month's end you'll be able to walk into your nearest *Shack* and pick up one of the truly last of the truly great American Freebies -- the new *Radio Shack* Catalog. For those interested in how we train our Managers, this $4 million publication is one of the ways. You thought the Catalog was designed to lure away your spare funds (a thought that, yes, had crossed our minds), but its primary value to our business lies in the book's thorough description of almost everything we intend to carry for the next 12 months, including the stock number, size and "participating stores" selling price. The cost of our 1981 issue is about 4 times the entire year's sales of *Radio Shack* when I checked in as ad manager in 1948 with positive plans for improving things as soon as I found out what they were.

In June the NYC price of the *Sunday New York Times* went from $0.85 to $1 and increase of 17.6%. While one section of my brain tells me this is well above the so-called guidelines, another reminds me the *Sunday Times* is one of America's cultural treasures and worth twice the price. That I have to import it into Texas to find out what's been going on all week, speaks of one of America's cultural voids. I don't keep my feelings secret. Recently I had a chance to tell a whole gaggle of newspaper publishers, but naturally they had come to sell us something, not to listen. Well, another Sunday has come and gone, and whaddya know -- Russia invaded Afghanistan (in The Times, sah, not in The Daily Rapist).

Now that the Olympics have been and are about gone, I'll tell you a secret if you promise me two things: (1) not to write, and (2) not to blame the Company. I'm speaking personally. My secret is I think we were wrong to boycott the games. Even Adolf Schicklgruber got to watch our superstars. You want to really shut down shop with Ivan, Jimmy, you close the UN. And one more thing: I'm also against that. But I was 64 on the 31st of last month and can claim (and prove) senility.

I hope this doesn't get Dad in trouble, but a *Boston Globe* story tells of a 14-year-old son of somebody at *Digital Equipment Corp.* who has sold more than 1,000 tape cassettes of games he worked up "in his upstairs bedroom with a *Radio Shack TRS-80* microcomputer." Dear Sir or Madam Up There, please send me a kid like Gregory next time...

Commercial tomatoes are picked green so that they will keep in transit and are aerated with ethylene gas to redden them. "They don't taste like much," says my source. Geezizz, if our animal radios needed rouge and mascara to look alive we'd still be back on Boston's Cornhill with three employees, looking for the one who was robbing us blind.

SEPTEMBER 1980
ET is Coming

FOR $0.99 YOU CAN GET A NEW Radio Shack book called TRS-80 Applications Software Sourcebook, that lists about 1,000 (that's right -- one thousand!) programs for Models I and II, subject, author, price and general description. These were solicited and collated by us on behalf of their authors; you may caveat-emptor order them directly from the author. Radio Shack has neither examined nor tested these programs and isn't liable for either the product or the programmer. An updated version is in the works and it will sell for at least $1.95, so get 26-2113 from our nearest store or dealer or Radio Shack Computer Center for $0.99 while they last. It's going to be a collector's item or my name ain't Mark Twice.

Now, folks, we jump almost 100 points to $99.95 whilst I try to peddle a new favorite item of mine, one we conceived, designed and manufactured without any advice from AT&T, GTE, ITT or Stromberg Carlson, and when they read this (or our story on the inside front cover of our new catalog-just published -- still free) they may choke on their sparkling Geritol. Obviously it's a telephone. But WHAT a telephone!

Imagine a princess-style phone with the dial in the base instead of the handset. Then imagine that when you lift off the receiver, to call or answer, there's NO WIRE between it and the base. You can ramble up to about 50 ft. from the base and talk, listen, take inventory, go back to the stove, retire to the john-well how do you know what people do when you're a grandfather? I don't even know if "princess" is a trademark, but if it is: read princox. And, Ma -- you know I love ya.

Alright, back to business. We have here a cordless phone with no visible antenna, no push-to-talk button; a phone you use just like a regular phone-pick up to talk and listen, hang up when through. But really cordless! Where the cord connecting handset to the base would emerge from the handset, there's just a red LED to tell you you've hung up properly and the system's on recharge. Tom, it is! And is there a caveat? There is, Jane, there always is. Supply will be limited at first. Shipments to stores arrive the last week of September. Please to order your Model ET-350, cat. No 43-266, today. One color only: Naturally Nicer Beige.

Well lookyhere. Pregnancy by Proxy is the title of Newsweek's 7/7/80 story about medicine. A Kentucky doc uses a computer as donor and mate selector "for matching and anonymity to avoid complications." Nice picture. Priceless, in fact. Dr. Richard Levin seated before a Radio Shack TRS 80 Model II. Ask not what we can do for the American people when we stand ready to nominate the surrogate poppa of up to every next president of the USA after the year 2008.

My scenario for a Carter re-election (1) Russia decides Jimmy is safer for them than Ronnie. (2) Russia presses Iran to release our hostages 4 to 6 weeks before the election day, by pulling out of Kabul or other over or covert means. (3) Hostages are released. (4) Public believes Carter policy of infinite patience is brilliant success. (5) Carter is elected to a second term. (6) April 1, 1981 Norman Mailer published *Leonid's Last Laugh*, which later becomes a movie with R.W. Regan playing the role of premier and Carter cast as President. It will be serialized by WGHB and win an Oscar as the best half-foreign film of the year.

Watch you public TV program listing for *Personal Computing: Adventure of the Mind*. It's a six part series produced by Johns Hopkins University, primarily funded by *Radio Shack*, and devoted to the introduction of you people to the theory and potential of microcomputers. This award-willing series will be shown in its entirety to all high schools in Massachusetts during the week of Sept. 8, just to give you a notion of the importance of this project.

OCTOBER 1980
Computers Are Expanding

RADIO SHACK'S FABULOUS LINE OF TRS-80 computers have now been expanded to five models, in case you didn't get the word. If you're thinking of a BASIC Christmas gift to make life more sensational for somebody, remember there's a genuine *TRS-80* from about $250 to about $3.500, including a new color job that makes guys like *Atari* and *T-I* look expensive by comparison, even when it's apples and apples (one of the many fruity sayings we use in business to conceal the poverty of our vocabularies). We also have a matching 13" color TV set, available with or without the computer at the tasty matching price of $399.

Please note: all prices in all *Flyer-Side Chats* past, present and future are variable at individual stores and dealers. That's a disclaimer, Ralph, like the varying from the official estimate. Why isn't one disclaimer per year per item good enough for a country that's trying to save energy?

Well, the first BASIC-language pocket computer wasn't, after all, one of those brands like *Panasonic* or *Nixdorf*. In August, we started sell it (a *TRS-80*, of course). And instead of being priced at $399 -- $499 (like we'd been hearing at the shows and neighborhood bus bars), it's a mere $249.

Speaking of low prices, *Radio Shack* has just re-invented the true digital receiver price down to a measly $429. "True digital" means no slide rule dial and perfect (8-FM and 8-AM station) memory. *STA-2250* is also slimmed down to a neat 5 1/8" high, so there's no place it won't fit, so buy one and do yourself and me a big favor. On this technology, I have to laugh at a competitor's two-page magazine ad: Left page has a true digital receiver that also has a slide rule dial (because you don't know your station number), and the right hand page has a true digital car stereo unit without a slide rule dial (because you're smarter in a car?). More about *STA-2250*: it's made by us and it's 50W per channel and its distortion is only 0.02%. Yes -- I said 0.02%, and that's lower than anyone's distortion who's running for President in 1980.

In our new, free catalog, we show FIVE new cassette tape decks for adding to any audio system! A cassette deck is the impeccable gift for music lovers, and a new deck implies state of the art. And an old deck ain't too bad, either, particularly if it's a *Realistic*. With a deck, you can prerecord your own prerecorded tapes, if you get my point (but if we sold many prerecorded tapes I'd probably keep my mouth shut, which would have a double benefit of making some people ecstatic).

Pay heed to two blockbusters in this issue. Our *14-803* tape recorder with FM and AM, reduced to $59.95 from $89.95. And our *MC-1200* speaker, reduced from $59.95 to $29.95. We only use the word "blockbuster" when it can mean very impressive savings. We use "blockhead" when our Buyer makes a mistake. Our average use of both words is 8.33 and 3.79 times per month, respectively.

The next time someone says they're going to "throw the book" at you -- laugh. A memory-capacity chart shows that the average book has a storage capacity of 1,300,000 characters versus 125,000,000,000,000 for the average human brain. To express this in "bits" you multiply by 8. To do it in "bytes" you do nothing. But you *do* note that "byte" is *not* in the 1976 edition of *The American Heritage Dictionary* you got last Christmas!

NOVEMBER 1980
VOTE!

WE SPEND A LOT OF WORTHWHILE TIME, money and energy every August by getting around to talk to and answer questions from each of our 3,900 USA store managers and 400 Canadian counterparts. One thing we told them this year that I don't mind passing along to you. VOTE! We may not have the best choice but we have by far the best system. And your vote gives you carping rights for four years, aside from helping to preserve one of the few remaining governments that's for and by the people.

While on the subject of carping rights, "guess who is the fifth largest retailer in the country?" asks *Inc. Magazine.* At about $8-billion in sales, they say, it's the U.S. Defense Department with its PX's and commissaries. Not only does it NOT thrill me. But I know for a fact that our far East PX's substantially helped wreck the U.S. audio manufacturing business by letting guys like (censored for safety) sell their wares to our overseas GI's in our PX's, thus literally building the Japanese hi-fi base that now is so dominant here. I don't blame those companies for taking advantage of a golden opportunity. I blame Uncle for being so naive. The government as a retailer, and hence an adversary, is something I don't like. Let's pay servicemen fairly and let them buy in the same bazaars as all us other taxpayers in jeans and jogging shoes.

Dear Santa: I know it's a little early, but take a tip from the September issue of *High Fidelity.* That respected monthly says not only is *Radio Shack*'s STA-2200 receiver "the best *Realistic* component we've ever tested," but also that they would be hard pressed to come up with another receiver that does as much at the price-conceivably even at twice the price."

Dean Santa: I know I just wrote you on another matter, but *Radio Shack* has a new product that needs to be given to a lot of people soon, and time's a-wasting. It's the *TRS -80 Color Computer* which, at $399 by using your present color set, but with your reputation for generosity you must go whole hog or lose face on Dec. 25th. All the best, Lew.

How could you resist a 2-LP (or cassette or 8 track album) that divides its 90 minutes of popular music time between Arthur Fiedler and Mantovani; and is exclusive at *Radio Shack* just in time for gifting? Impossible! The liner notes were written by your servant and include a shocking secret: Mantovani's first name.

We sell (and manufacture) a tiny pushbutton telephone that makes the *GTE Flip Phone* seem a bit, well, primitive. *Radio Shack*'s phone has no flip to flop off, for one thing. And its fidelity is superior. Of course, as our TV copy says: "its hang-up is a put-down." We also have memory redial for the last number dialed, and separate models for touchtone or universal dial systems. A 2¼ x 1½ x 7" sweetie that even Ma must be jealous of. Honorable gift. Will fit in small stocking. Will look good under tree. Will not cost arm and leg.

Our Buyer would bristle if I failed to mention his -- now our -- hopefully your-great assortment of electronic games. These little geniuses have made tots forget about the electric train and all that heavy stuff. Believe me, they want the blinks, beeps, burps, blips that only electronics can give. If our two dozen games and RC cars won't please Junior and Jane, please see me or Dr. Spock during visiting hours, and remember (save for future use against me) I'm cheaper.

DECEMBER 1980
Reliable and Interesting

YOU WON'T HAVE TO PLAY your musical instrument alone any more if Santa is listening. Nor will you have to play out of time, as so many of us hacker do (I'm into piano and alto recorder, and know whereof I speak). Both problems are defeated by a neat little instrument conceptually designed by me because (1) even at my age I don't like to play alone, and (2) even my largo has been known to slow down due to carelessness and (let's face it) ineptitude.

So for you and me this Christmas: the new *Realistic Concertmate* electronic rhythm accompanist and -- at the push of a button -- calibrate metronome. As an accompanist it has five rhythm keys which can be combined into eight crisp distinctive rhythms. As a metronome, it offers controllable sound level, tempo and LED indication. You can use its battery-operated internal system or play through your audio system. Not a sing-along but a sound-along that ANY music maker will appreciate. So don't be bashful, tell her to beg or borrow $79.95 and getcha a 42-2103 at The Shack, the only place in the world you can getcha one!

This may not stagger your imagination, but-holy cow!-this season you get a choice of four TV sets at emporia instead of the usual none. The 13" and two 19" models are quite deluxe color television receivers, any one of which can also be used with our new *TRS-80 Color Computer*. Naturally, you could use your present color set with it, but our Managers say they'd greatly prefer it if you would belly up to the bar and buy one of theirs. Then there's a 5" b/w set with a built in FM/AM radio that looks like a portable oscilloscope but really is an exemplary model of what we call the "semi-military" look. Buy this for him because it's on sale at $159.95, and versatile and masculine (he has quite enough aftershave, believe me).

Hey, there. Do you need more than ten clock radios to choose from? That's the number of *Realistics* we offer for Yule 1980, and personally I think it's an ideal assortment. More is confusing. Less is chintzy. None are available at competitive stores because they're customer made by (or for) us with that extra touch of reliability that's so hard to advertise in a look-alike world, but is so genuinely built in because-well for on little thing, Sah, we don't EVER want it back. The electronic digital display is so "in" this year that we've only one set left that looks like clocks looked when *Telechron* was Analog and anything else was Cuckoo.

Arrigato to *Bell Lab's* Stephen Gross for reminding us that *Ampex* "invented the competition" in video tape recording. "It was definitely *Ampex*, way back in 1956." And the video disc in 1967. And that *Bell*, not *Japan Inc.*, invented the transistor. Oh come all ye other chauvinists-it doesn't embarrass me a bit to sing our praises

Since Christmastide takes us all the way into January, it neither too late nor too early to thank you for your patronage, your sweet (and sour) letters, and your patience with our occasional lapses, by frequent needling of the Establishment. *Radio Shack* tries to be reliable but at the same time interesting. Very truly yours, etc., etc., Lewis

JANUARY 1981
Retirement is Coming

THE NEW YEAR STARTS WITH A TEST of the strength of a 70 year-old CEO to put some flutter back into the stars and stripes. My euphoric notion is that Mr. Regan has everything to gain by dressing up in an Uncle Sam suit and play his last, greatest role for the folks out front. And that he will. And that the cronyism, nepotism and vacillation that have made 'politics' a four-letter word will diminish. If it's a time for change of anything, Prez, it's time to go back to dignity and decisiveness in high office.

After a record 3 ½ year run, *TRS-80 Model I* will no longer be manufactured by *Radio Shack* in the USA. But its many owners will be satisfied, I'm sure, to know that we will continue to make and market all the peripherals and additives to keep Model I above and well for the indefinite future. Repeat: there is NO plan to discontinue total support of this epochal product.

New personal computer customers in quest of the best for the least have a choice between two excellent systems. The *TRS-80* Color Computer with an entry level of $399, or the *TRS-80 Model III* from $699. Both are expandable and backed by the industry's finest sales and service team-our over 6,000 outlets and service depots in every hill, dale and hollow of America.

Get your free copy of our annual report by writing Tandy Corp., Shareholder Relations, Dept. K 1800 One Tandy Center, Ft. Worth, TX 76102. Aside from numbers which prove that one good business plan is worth a thousand theories, it includes my annual Industry Perspective, a six-page opus laced with my usual iconoclastic bias. A Shearson broker calls it "an outstanding part of the report." A manufacturer from Massachusetts finds it "extremely interesting, and I daresay it will give many stockholders much more confidence in your organization." And a California banker really pours it on: "Congratulations on one of the finest pieces I've ever seen in an annual report. Your company obviously understands the benefit to your shareholders of your perspective, experience, and industry knowledge, and you have the ability to relate it in language that all of us outside the industry can understand."

So get the *Tandy* report and see what can be achieved in the face of over regulation, recession, inflation, discounting, falling productivity and a generation of bad mouthing business. Chats and Perspectives are designed to help you see us not as anonymous pillars of granite, brass and perks but as a team of fairly modest folks who know who to make and correct mistakes, and who aren't afraid to stand up and be counted.

Speaking of being counted, Dearly Beloved, I am in a countdown phase which began on Oct. 24, when I was made *Tandy* Vice Chairman, pending my retirement on my 65th birthday, next July 31, after just six more *Flyer-Side Chats*. We do not have a mandatory retirement age here at the Iron Works, so I invented my own. I will remain on the Board of Directors. I have just bought a *Honda* C70, an *Armstrong* flute and a *Brother* typewriter, so you can see I'm not without the makings of a program.

One of the happier developments of recent years is *Radio Shack*'s soaring ability to self-manufacture its own *Realistic* audio receivers. Nine of the 12 in our catalog are made by us. (The other three are custom made for us by someone you never heard of -- not a competitor.) When you can save $200 on an own-make powerhouse like the 120-watt *STA 2100D*, it's time to get off your duff and see what a company that builds computers can do with hi-fi components. It's on sale the whole month of January. And, by the way-we haven't raised a price since July 1, 1980, but we've lowered quite a few during our many promotions aimed at winning you over. If your other suppliers had done the same, each of your bucks would have bought you and $0.06 of fun or food. And another $0.06 from now to June 30 if Ronnie behaves!

FEBRUARY 1981
Great Contest Doing Good

THE PRIDE OF TWIN FALLS, IDAHO, must be the 21-year –old owner and operator of a small fleet of wreckers named Patrick Montgomery. He says his many *Realistic* CB's are still going as strong as the day he bought them. He says our alkaline batteries "are far superior to Eveready, Ray-O-Vac or anyone else's. "In addition, an FM radio station run by his towing association uses three *Realistic* cassette decks and several *Realistic LAB-34* turntables. In fact, he credits a lot of his success to "the dependability of *Realistic* and *Radio Shack*." As I've said: the customer is always right, particularly when he thinks WE are!

Attention all programmers and inventors. Thanks to grants from the *Radio Shack* division of *Tandy Corp*. and The National Science Foundation, an exciting competition has just been launched by Johns Hopkins University; it is nationwide in scope and will reward 100 prize winners. Entry deadline is 6/30/81.

Called "Personal Computing to Aid the Handicapped, the Johns Hopkins First National Search," it carries a $10,000 grand prize and many other awards including cash and computers. There will be 10 winners in each of 10 regions (the GSA map of America); then the top 20 of these will be invited to Washington, DC, where-at a big bash at the Smithsonian or similar place-the top 10 of these will be announced. Apart from our funding activity, *Radio Shack* is also donating the $10,000 top prize and several *TRS-80* systems, Read on and you'll see why.

It seems there are 40,000,000 handicapped persons in this country! This staggering figure came from Dr. Margaret Giannini, director of the National Institute on Handicap Research, who was a co-spokesperson at the contest involved in spreading the word. Get your contest dates and rules by writing to: Personal Computing to Aid the Handicapped, The Johns Hopkins University, P.O. Box 670, Laurel, MD 20810. No one-professional, amateur or hobbyist-is barred. In fact, you're personally invited to participate in this marvelous crusade which, thanks to our work with *TRS-80*, finds us at the head of a parade for the benefit of our disadvantaged fellow citizens.

Dear Ron: it's so nice not to have to call you Guv any more. Please, when you get time, review the government's recent decision that a certain company was guilty of a monopoly in the baseball card business. The players association, it seems, made this deal with the *Topps* Chewing Gum people in 1968. What's wrong, Ron, with guys making deals that both parties like and which seem harmless to society? Why does the government waste its time (and our dough) with such bleep? No Sir, Boss, I don't own *Topps* stock or even chew their gum, so you see I'm just one of your non-silent voters who wants to retire Uncle Sam from the nit-and-lice biz and put him back on Main Street. All the Best, Lew.

The Shack had over 900 stores overseas as of recent date. Of these, 521 are owned by us. Most are called *"Tandy"* instead of *Radio Shack* because the late Mr. Tandy outvoted me 1 - 0. I find particularly fascinating our (incomplete month) November sales gain of 58% in 142 company stores in England considering what we read about Mrs. Thatcher and unemployment. Everybody knows, too, that Belgium can't get its act together. But in 99 Belgian shops our sales in the same period were up 55%. Well, "chaos often breeds life," said Henry of the Adams Family. Care to make something of it?

MARCH 1981
Taking On the Journal

MA A.T.T. BELL IS TRYING TO BREAK OUT of her traditional role as a phone company by initiating a home/office database terminal system in 700 Austin, Texas, locations, and Texas newspaper publishers are raising hell. What they see is a "Yellow Pages Test," per a headline in *MISWeek*, a management newspaper and the newsmen don't want your eyes to do the walking in Ma's electronics pages! If I haven't said it before or recently, here I go again: the phone company's mandate is to be a Phone company, not a newspaper, a computer biz or some other kind of outfit; and that's why Ma's had a near monopoly on things since the beginning of time (it seems). What's wrong, Madam, with being a phone company, say, forever? Your fancy earnings tell me the status quo is more than adequate.

Thanks for taking my advice and giving our team another great Christmas, but O' it was so late in coming. For the car companies it never came. I even began to think of the *Wall Street Journal* (my favorite paper next to the *New York Times,* but I have to wash the ink off after reading it) as the retailers' worst friend. The scenario: 12/12 issue -- *Stereo Industry in a Quandary as Advance in Recording Nears.* 12/17 issue -- *Growth of Electronic Games Slows: Oversaturation of Market Is a Factor.* But in its 12/19 editorial, -- *Guns and Logic*, the *Journal* failed to find a logic for controlling handguns while succeeding in writing an editorial that mentioned "guns" 16 times and "handguns" not even once. Folks, that's not the way I like my chicken prepared.

The *Radio Shack* storeboard at New Year's showed we're up to 7,852 locations. Of these, 88% are in North America, 7% in England and Europe, 3% in Australia, 1% in Japan. A mere 2% of our shops are franchised, but 34% are dealer stores and 64% company operated. This month, March, is a good bet for giving birth to the 8,000[th] *Radio Shack*, so it's not a good time to beware the Ides, I guess. We're living proof that an American retailer can be successful overseas -- not a restaurant, I mean a regular retailer -- without changing the product and the business plan to meet each and everyone's notion as to what various nationals will or won't accept.

Speaking of guns (as I was in paragraph 2), you may not get a bang out of this quote. The *Journal's* 12/15 story about *Olin Corp.*, planning to sell its *Winchester Arms* business concludes with an unnamed analyst saying, "It was the right decision. Despite what's happening in the Middle East, the gun business isn't a growth market."

And this quote from *Consumer Electronics Daily's* 11/26 issue. A gent from the *Bone Fone Corp.*, which is now adding a *NeckFone*, Says, "Even lightweight headphones weigh you down after a while. When the volume is up your brains get fried." Think what a bore life might be if I didn't save these gems for you and reprint 'em in a *Chat*!

While I was feeling sorry for *Topps Gum* being hassled for allegedly monopolizing the baseball card, along comes husky *General Mills* with its additional challenge. My theory is we need a whole new court system -- for example the Lower lower court system -- to deal with issues that are not matters of life and death or our country's safety. Its judges could be applicants to Harvard Law School and appointed not on a basis of intelligence but sense of the bizarre and irrelevant.

Reader R. Salomon of Framingham, Mass., says Reader Gross (see *Chat #71*) "erred by 32 years and an ocean regarding the first videodisk." He points out that J.L. Baird of England did it in 1928 (cf. *Video Review's* July issue). And while you guys argue, the battlelines for selling them in quantity are being drawn NOW, and 1981 will see if we've picked a viable technology in the RCA system. It would be good for the country if it happens.

APRIL 1981
New Hotel in Tandy Center

OUR USA HEADQUARTERS CITY of Fort Worth is rampant and pregnant with new buildings, but the one that excites me the most opens this month: the Americana Tandy Center hotel. It's attached by a crosswalk to the atrium joining our two 19-story office buildings, and attached corporately by being on our land. Anyone who knew FW pre this hotel is in for a stunning surprise. As a teeny by-product, I'm expecting instant improvement in the local veal, fettucine and (unfrozen) seafood, etc., so that the next Catullus who visits won't be able to say "How tasteless and ill-bred it is," meaning our eatin'-out food.

Two *Radio Shack* blockbusters should really tear a hole in your budget, Maestro, if you've got the lust for audio I think you have. Our *STA-2200* true digital (60 watt) receiver cut from $599.95 to $399.95 -- hey that's MY receiver they've cut! And the greatest open-reel tape deck value in the country, our $499.95 model *TR-3000*, is slashed to $299.95. Simon sez move quickly because these are savings to make company treasurers weep and customers avid and competitors surly.

It's not good enough, sayeth a government watchdog, that no one's gotten cremated by our test lead kit *#270-332* since we started selling it just after the Uncivil War. Please to recall it due to possible danger from exposed metal touched under certain conditions. Okay. Got one? Bring it in for full refund. 'Tis the infamous Age of Recall. My one hope is Prez Ron will extend the recall to people (and make Washington small again). That done, I could stand another Sinatra gala, but only then and without Osmonds.

After some 40 years from the nest of academe, my ex, the University of Denver, honorifically rediscovered me last month by naming me its Professional of the Year. Except for the also-honored former Gov. John Love, the old familiar faces were gone' sadly the mountains west of Denver were gone, too, gone to meet the Old Smog Maker, out where the Coors begins.

Those who think of me as far right of Sen. Tower will be shocked by this. I do not NOT want to see the Corporation for Public Broadcasting dumped (cf. PBR, NPR). Anyone who's for ditching *All Things Considered*, the country's best news program, is anti-me and Susan Stamberg -- we also understand swift retaliatory action, eh Susan! Maybe it should be funded by business and education (and 100% tax on porno films, cassettes and magazines), but it's got to stay! (Fan letters in opposition will be burned in front of Jefferson's house on July 4th at 5 a.m. sharp)

People I like under many conditions: the customer who, learning this morning there really is no Betty Crocker, "still hopes I'm real . . . ". Chief tester Julian Hirsch who writes "there have been no fundamental advances in loudspeaker design in the past 25 years or more" in *Stereo Review* magazine . . . The *Philips* (read *Norelco*) executive who is opting "to create more product differentiation than now exists among the *Magnavox, Sylvania* and *Philco* brands", all owned by the same owner now . . . the boss of the Missouri outfit that calls itself *Uncle Toots Video Co* . . . and reader Cave's idea for "chocolate candy in the shape of little radios" to be called *Radio Snacks*, he says.

A gilded firmware to Boston University's Kenneth Horgan, quoted in *The Journal*: "In 10 years, everyone will have a microcomputer on his desk." And a Mr. Nevison of Concord, Mass. for predicting "eventually all executives will be computer literate." It has gotten so whenever I mention *TRS-80* to my friends, see, they think I'm trying to sell them one. Jack's wife Elsie gave me that kinda look last night. I'm sure quite sure, that's the kind of look it was.

MAY 1981
60 Years Old

JOYOUS NOTE: MY PIQUE AT THE NEW YORKER magazine (for refusing to explain their refusal to print our ad) ended with a chuckle when their Feb. 9 issue ran a cartoon in which we were whimsically celebrated. The scene: A party whose hostess tells a friend about her new robot butler. "He's an absolute treasure," she confides. "We got him for four thousand eight hundred and ninety dollars at *Radio Shack*, batteries not included." You're right, Cholly, there's something amusing about not including the batteries when you're selling expensive items that need'em. Sort of like buying a car, gas tank optional.

Wrathful note: the 2/12 *Today Show* on *NBC-TV* included an interview with their Tokyo reporter and a native spokesman implying that Japan's allegedly superior microcomputers will soon, honorable televiewer, render our fit only for (at the prompting of *NBC's* announcer) "computing our losses." 'Created' journalism from our third-ranking network (third out of three) shouldn't gram be, Freddie, but I've helped feed Little Nipper longer than you have -- see what I mean?

Warning note" last call for your innovative entry in the great search of ways to help personal computing aid the handicapped. Run with major grants from *Radio Shack* and the *National Science Foundation*, its address is "Contest," Johns Hopkins University, P.O. Box 670, Laurel, MD 20810, and the last day for submissions is June 30th. At press time, Hopkins' project boss, Paul Hazan, reports over 4,999 folks chasing our $10M first prize.

Oily note: Sheik Yamani, on another network, tells us "Saudi Arabia alone (could cause) a depression in the U.S. in which the rate of unemployment would at least double, the price of oil double again, and the inflation rate rise," by just cutting its production: "but I'm not threatening." And I'm not shaking, Sheik, out of fear, that is; I just ate too much *Jello* or something.

Prophetic note: your increases in postage play right into our hands, Sam, because the costlier it gets to put envelopes into boxes and retrieve 'em from other boxes, the sooner electronic mail (cf. *TRS-80 Videotex*) gets affordable in comparison. Aside from being faster, it eliminates stamp-licking and mailman-biting. And our cranky ones who think flyers like this are junk mail, smile when you say that about a $0.04 item that now costs about $0.16 for fewer pages. (Note to *IBM*: we're into R&D with electronic lace for the first electronic valentine; be brotherly, *Xerox*, or we'll call it a fringe benefit.)

Sexagenary note: not surprisingly, our 60th birthday means beaucoup price reductions on regular stock items, not 'brought in" closeouts. When we were born in Boston in 1921, our *TRS-80 Pocket* computer would have been impossible to find on the planet at any price, much less its catalog figure of $249. Would you believe $299 for the merry month of May? And most of us think well of a voice-actuated cassette-driven telephone answerer at $169.95, so when I tell you our *TAD-25* is being birthdayed out at $119.95-you get the picture cheap is cheaper!

Syndicated columnist Milton Moskowitz recently found we've passed *7-Eleven* and *McDonalds* in numbers of stores, observing "Today there are some pretty big companies trying to figure out what *Radio Shack* did and how they did it." Well one thing fellas, is we have a blessed event about every four weeks. If you drop by to see this one, our *Snazzy Sixty Sale*, please leave your hamburger wrappers outside. And BUY something. Okay?

JUNE 1981
A Marine Speaks

"PLATINUM COULD BE OUR BEST STRATEGIC MOVE," according to a Phoenix advertiser, but I like our 2nd generation digitally synthesized stereo receiver, the new *Realistic STA-2250*. So does *Stereo Review* magazine, recognizing us as one of the first hi-fi manufacturers to go state-of-the-art. It says the much lower-priced *STA 2250* "met or surpassed all of the performance ratings (and is) a thoroughly fine receiver at a very reasonable price." Our audio chap weighs in at 30 pounds, and, to cut back to my opening advisory, that much platinum would cost you $238,000. At $429.95 wanna rethink your best strategic move?

My March column prophetically mentioned the handgun problem, and, mercy, what a lot of flack I got! Seems hell hath no fury like citizens who think our Second Amendment is questionable, though its clear purpose was to perpetuate "a well-regulated militia," not the Saturday Night Special. In view of the events of March 30, and the First and nineth Amendments, and 'cause I've got the mike, fellas, what I say goes . . . in *Flyer-Side Chats*.

It's true, I'm not in the gun biz. It's true that if I were, I'd be less likely to bite the bullet that fed me. But true, to, our government has regulated the safety and labeling of electronic devices, changed the way caps are fitted to medicine bottles, legislated seatbelts into cars and warnings onto cigarette packages, and made many drugs "prescription only." So take another letter, Lucille. Dear Shogun: get with the scary real world and work yourself up a prescription for keeping people from aiming handguns at presidents, law officers, and each other, thanks in advance, (signed) The Rifleman, Capt. USMCR (Ret.) 02154.

While on unpopular subjects, time out in this penultimate *Chat*, to thank our Corporation for letting me speak my piece for the last seven years. Without necessarily agreeing with my views. Without editing. Without legal dept. clearance. In a world that would disclaim its own mother if somebody said that's the way to get to the next rung on the ladder, that says a lot about *Tandy Corp.* As I've often noted here, the *Chat* is a way of making us "people" instead of anonyms, and a form of advertising using words instead of pictures. Who needs another ordinary company?

Nice comment from *80 Microcomputing* magazine: "*TRS-80* is already something of a legend, and will probably be remembered as the *Univac* of personal computers -- not the first, but simply the best-known representative of its age."

Our recent news release (on a marketing and manufacturing tieup with *Tokyo Electric*) indicates how we're reorienting the rising sun: "The sales and service setup created will be the largest in the Japanese market." This amusing sequence further illuminates the excitement generated by little computers" on 1/26/81 the retailing newspaper *HFD* headlined *Kmart Said to Test Home Computers*; but a columnist for the same rag finished his 3/23/81 piece like this: "Right now, *Radio Shack*, *IBM* and *Control Data* don't have to look to their laurels (and) we'll go out on a lengthy limb and predict that men will be walking on Mars before *Kmart* is a factor in computers." What was said in fewer words by Corneille was: "Guess if you can, choose if you date." My bet is the walk on Mars comes later!

Civil lawsuits are soft of late-late events, too, in case you're thinking of one. Take these two in our industry: (1) Antitrust and dumping charges by *National Union* and *Zenith* against Japanese radio/TV makers were dismissed in March 1981 after being filed in 1970 and 1974: and (2) in *Bose vs. Consumers Union*, started in 1971, the system took 10 years to find for *Bose* on one of three complaints, but a "separate trial . . . on the issue of damages "would be needed before judgment could be entered for either party, the judge indicated. Our fiercest competitors, the Japanese, laugh up their yukata sleeves whilst we nitpick ourselves into shark-bait on a slow boat to oblivion.

Hey-want an honest USA-made bargain? Right here on this page, *Realistic C60* and *C90* cassette tapes at half our low regular price. Visit our tape factory if your summerfest takes you to Fort Worth. Tell 'em "LK said to treat you like a customer." (Real nice.)

JULY 1981
Signing Off and Still Teaching

AS I'VE SAID RIGHT ALONG FOR SEVEN chatty years, this column's purpose is to sell *Radio Shack* as a human, warts-and-all place to buy reliable electronics at sensible prices. In this last opus as a *Shack/Tandy* employee, I'm again reminding you that our merchandise can't be found in the me-too shops because nearly half of it is made by our people in our 26 factories, and the rest contract-made by others to our specs. So, like don't look for us in *Sears* or *The Audio Nightmare*.

Conventional wisdom says it's impossible for a manufacturer to succeed as a retailer, and for a retailer to succeed by selling only his own brand. *Radio Shack* has proved the exception to both of these nutty notions, and, in doing so, created 25.000 new jobs. That, in my book, is our proudest achievement. It's what makes America's P&L System work, particularly when you know that none of these jobs means working for the government.

Kids, there's nothing wrong with working for Uncle. It just results in too much bureaucracy and not enough buckracy (my way of saying Capital Formation). I like Reagan's crowd for not being embarrassed to seek out waste in any activity, regardless of its alleged untouchability. And take this last letter, Lucille: Dear Ron, we'll be glad to interview surplus -- or, as the British say, redundant -- government employees. Our experience with retired military types, for example, has been first rate. Yours for a clean sweep, Lewis.

Look Ma, No Betadisc

One of my retirement programs, aside from remaining on the *Tandy* board as a Director, is to write a book about advertising. One of its sections will be about adversary advertising -- ads that knock the competition. One of its paragraphs might mention the recent *Sony* "attack on videodisc in 20 major markets," to quote *Consumer Electronics Daily*. *Sony's* two-page ad praises their *Betamax* video recorder and says, to paraphrase: Who needs a video player that doesn't also record? (The answer's easy if you don't market a disc player like *RCA, Magnavox*, and – soon -- *The Shack*!) I'll say adversary advertising is a tough way to make friends and customers, and I'll guarantee you can't stop progress with *Sony*/No Baloney Money when progress is spelled videodisc. I see v-tapes and v-discs coexisting into the 21st century, regardless of whose technology wins The Battle of Boobtube.

Several readers complained about my *On No, Ma (AT&T)* commentary, mentioning that on nearby flyer pages we advertise competitive products. I wonder if you know how cleverly Ma Bell fought to keep our sort of challenge from happening, and for how long? The AT&T Company has made it big as a phone enterprise with its de facto monopoly and protected gross margins, two things you and I will never see, Babe, and ditto for the late *W. T. Grant* and the maybe-too-late *Chrysler Corp.* With $6,079,000,000 in 1980 profits (profits Charlie not sales) *Bell's* lust for the computer business, electronic advertising, cellular radio domination and similar new conquests, does seem a bit indecent, to give you my personal opinion, and not necessarily *Tandy*'s, and my last disclaimer of 1981.

Okay, will the meeting come to order? Are there any seconds to my motion that *AT&T* remain exclusively the world's best phone company? Motion carried. Now, any seconds to my motion that *AT&T* profits be partly used (along with *Exxon's*) to bail out both *Chrysler* and *Ford*, and really help the country?

There's a Doctor in the House!

My greatest-ever award came last May when Boston University gave me an honorary degree for what it called my "exceptional role in the development of a great corporation that has had a profound and beneficial influence on American life." Without fine employees to build and sell, without you to believe in us, without *Tandy*'s investors and lenders to do their thing, I'd surely have been Mister instead of Doctor to the end of time. (It's Dr. of Humane Letters.)

Speaking of The Hub, my oldest friend there putters in puns and wordplay. Ray Goodman comes up with these squibs on the silly sexual situation that sees us substitute salesperson for salesman. A man with a rupture has a *himnia*, not a hernia. A dangerous lady driver isn't a menace, she's a *feninace*. That many recluse isn't a hermit, he's a *himit*. (And soon mail -- and *femailgrams*, so I'm taking this talk about unisex more seriously.)

When a liberal US congressman takes on a business-oriented job, what happens? First, New York City's Mayor Koch one-lines it by saying "Mayor Culpa, they called me." But then he gives us this gem: "So now I'm an executive, I look at what has to be done and I say to myself" how could I have voted for all those dumb programs?" And then there's columnist Jack Anderson with this footnote on 'guvamint' red tape: Unfortunately for the taxpayers, the Marines couldn't just send a supply sergeant out with some loose change to buy a diode at the *Radio Shack* in Havelock, N.C. They had to go through proper procurement channels." Sometimes the simper makes you sic!

Is Tandy's Torment, IBM's Fury?

Will the Japanese try to take over personal computers the way they took over audio? Will *IBM* just sit there and let *Shack* run the microshow? Query #1 will soon have a partial response in that *NEC* (N is for Nippon, not for Nothing as one wag put it) is supposed to be ready to take orders. The second is addressed by Barron's fierce pundit, Alan Abelson, who punds-it like this: "One increasingly evident change wrought by Mr. Reagan is that anti-trust ain't what it used to be. And as a result, we expect *IBM* to boldly vent its competitive fury on rivals * big and small including . . . *Tandy*.

The asterisk (*) is because right there, no fooling, the letter R popped off my *IBM Selectric II* and fell to the floor. As for *IBM*, shame on you if your venting on little shots like us is more fun than going after *NEC*, *Fujitsu*, and *Matsu-somebody*. The Armonk Monster Versus Japan Inc. is a battle I'd love to blow-by-blow for *ABC*, Howard.

Fair trade, free market, and all that schmoose notwithstanding, I never thought we should roll over and play clown for the Japanese auto industry. Remember, Alice, a car's not just a car. It's five tires, windows, steel, a battery, carpeting, sparkplugs, antifreeze, yards of textiles, bundles of wires, beau-coup de plastic and paint. You impact almost every domestic industry when you turn your back on Detroit Iron by labeling an import "just an automobile." Wanna know why I was especially mad, Eddie? It's because Brother Ishihara told the press that suggestions they hold down car exports to the U.S. market are "out of the question." Sez you, Brother, is what we sezzed when I wore knickers.

Sounding Off, Signing Off

More on motorcars, please. "Now that your customers are driving up in the newest, smallest cars, demanding the biggest sound on wheels, what are you going to do? Since you're an *Alpine* dealer," observes *Alpine's* autosound ad, "you can blow their doors off." But not to worry, old friend, 'cause I' not an *Alpine* dealer and my *Realistic* car stereos will leave your doors where I think you like 'em -- anywhere but off.

Something old: the original cube *Weatheradio*, zillions sold at $17.95, yours for $12.95 in July. *Something new*: TAD-112 dual-cassette plus remote telephone answerer, just introduced at $159.95 (compare!) quality-built in a *Radio Shack* factory. *Something borrowed*: we want to be your 19" remote color TV set source, so all month take $100 off our $579 catalog price: and if you can buy a better one for less than $479.95 I'll be a monkey's uncle (which Darwin and some of you think I am, anyway). *Something blue*: Lewis Kornfeld (so now you know how it's spelled) signing off.